MEDIATION

MEDIATION
WHY PEOPLE FIGHT AND HOW TO HELP THEM TO STOP

MICHAEL WILLIAMS

POOLBEG

Published 1998
by Poolbeg Press Ltd
123 Baldoyle Industrial Estate
Dublin 13, Ireland

© Michael Williams 1998

The moral right of the author has been asserted.

A catalogue record for this book is available from the British Library.

ISBN 1 85371 731 2

Cover design by Poolbeg Group Services Ltd
Set by Poolbeg Group Services Ltd in Times 11/14
Printed by The Guernsey Press Ltd,
Vale, Guernsey, Channel Islands.

THANKS

I want to thank the people who encouraged me to think I could write this book, and those who shaped the experience from which it comes.

Of the first, Conor Cruise O'Brien told me, over lunch, with confidence based on his own experience as a writer, and good red wine, that I had inside me an interesting book based on my work.

Kate Cruise O'Brien encouraged me to believe what Conor had said, gave me just the advice I needed about how to design and plan the book, and encouragement in its early stages.

Mary Maher read every word of each draft, including a first much longer than the present book, and showed me how to identify the shape it should take, and how to rescue it from the detritus with which I had covered it. Like a superb mediator, she did not tell me what to do, but ensured that I saw the options and the arguments each way, and that my choices were informed.

Of those who shaped the experience from which this book comes, I want to thank first my father Barney Williams, who during the first twenty-three years of my life – which turned out to be the last twenty-three of his – taught me more than anyone else about what it means to be a human being, and how one can live so as to be both loved and respected by others.

For the past thirty-five years, Jane Williams has been carrying on the education process my father started.

I have been extraordinarily lucky in my friends and teachers – categories with a lot of overlap – some of whom are named in this book, and all of whom have shown so much tolerance and acceptance of me, and taught me so many and such valuable lessons.

Alexis FitzGerald, especially in the first few years of a relationship that was at times stormy but always respectful on both sides, taught me what it means to be a professional in client-service.

John Haynes first inspired, then encouraged, later trained and always supported me in my journey towards being a mediator, and showed me how to use Alexis's lessons in a different but at least equally demanding profession. Over the years we have moved from a master-disciple relationship to one closer to equality, without disturbing our friendship.

Three other friends and teachers, in related arts, enriched my understanding of mediation: the late Dennis Noble, and Lorcan Gogan and Brendan Dowling.

Colleagues in the Academy of Family Mediators, some mentioned in this book, have taught me and inspired me with their dedication to excellence. I cannot name them all, but am especially grateful to Dorothy Della Noce for agreeing to be my consultant, for shedding the clear light of her intelligence on my problems, and inspiring me with her gentleness, kindness, perceptiveness and acceptance.

Everybody who has asked me to be their mediator or to train them in mediation has honoured and educated me, and I am grateful.

If I did not always give all of them what they wanted, it was not because I did not try.

For Jane

CONTENTS

INTRODUCTION

Learned books have been written, and some have even been published, about mediation, for mediators. This is not a learned book, and it is not intended to be read by mediators. Or, at least, not only by mediators. It is written for people who have heard about mediation, are interested in the idea, and want to know more about it, and how it works.

You will not find footnotes, references, or "authorities" in this book. Nor will it discuss theory. You will not find quotations from books on mediation. This is not because I have rejected most of what I have read, but because I have assimilated material I have read about mediation that I agreed with, and built it into my way of working and it has become part of my way of doing things and thinking about my work. I no longer remember who I learnt it from. This is an illustration of a process of "internalising", and I will talk about it in more depth in Chapter Four. I do not promise you a final and authoritative description of mediation. If it were possible to write something all mediators would agree with, it would be a great deal longer than this book, or, more probably, a great deal shorter.

Nor will I include a list of other books about mediation. As you will gather from this book, I see mediation as a skill, and do not think it can be learnt from books. If you are interested in developing the skills, your next step will be to look for someone to train you. Your trainer's reading list, not mine, is the one you should follow. You will get a lot more from your reading after a training that gives you a real sense of how mediation works than you would from pursuing further reading, without exposure to the process.

I imagine the first thing a reader who does not work in the field, and has never needed to consult a mediator will ask is: "What is mediation?" One of the things mediators constantly do is to repeat a question, but in different words, so that it can be answered more readily. We call this "reframing", and this, too I will discuss in more detail when we come to look at techniques, in Chapter Seven.

So, instead of answering the question "What is mediation?" I will give an example of a "reframe" by pretending I was asked: "What is a mediator, and what does he do?"

But before answering, I should explain why I have just referred to the mediator as "he". I know more women mediators than men, but I have been a man all my life and have spent the last twelve years or so trying to be a mediator, so my reflex is to think of a mediator as "he" rather than "she". When I started to write this book I thought I might avoid "sexing the mediator" by talking about mediators in the plural instead of a mediator in the singular, and referring to mediators as "they". But the parties in conflict have to be "they" which means the mediator must be "he", "she", "he/she" or "I". I have made a choice, and hope nobody will feel excluded if I refer to mediators as "I" or "he", or that anybody who does will understand the reasons for it, and accept them.

The question as reframed was "What is a mediator, and what does he do?" My answer is: a mediator is a person who manages other people's conflicts, neutrally, with a view to helping the disputants to resolve them. And, of course, mediation is what that person does. So, by answering a question that was not exactly what I was asked, I hope I have given an answer to the one I was asked. Reframing works!

The mediator is a neutral outsider

I want you to focus on the words "other people's conflicts". The mediator is an outsider, is not a party to the conflict, and is involved with it only because the people in conflict invite him to help them to resolve it. (Please note: "help them to resolve it", not "solve it for them".) If the mediator takes sides he ceases to be an outsider. He becomes a party to the conflict, and is no longer a mediator.

How far does the concept of neutrality go? I think a good mediator is neutral not only as between the parties, taking sides with neither: he is neutral about whether they will reach an agreement at all. And, if they do, he is neutral about what it will be. He may grow to like and respect the parties as he works with them, and to hope that they will reach an agreement, because he thinks they will be happier if they do. He will hope, as someone who has come to care for them, that any agreement they may reach will be a good one, that will last. But he does not care about these things in his role as a mediator, and he does not allow his hopes for his clients to come between him and his professional duties. Nor does he assume he knows better than they do what is good for them.

It must seem strange that people consult a mediator if their objective is to make an agreement, and their chosen mediator brings into his work an attitude of not caring if they agree or not. We don't consult a doctor who doesn't care if we live or die, or a lawyer who emulates Kipling's ideal by treating Triumph and Disaster just the same. But I think this apparent indifference is an essential part of a mediator's equipment. If he is to serve his clients well, he must let them work out for themselves what they need.

I came across an illustration of this in an Italian railway carriage when I was on holiday recently. A safety message appeared in four languages:

"E pericoloso sporgersi."

"Ne pas se penser au dehors."

"Nicht hinauslehnen."

"It is dangerous to lean out."

French and German speakers were instructed not to lean out. Italian and English speakers were given information, and left to make up their own minds. These different ways of communicating illustrate an essential aspect of mediation. Mediators work in the English and Italian mode, not the Franco-Prussian one. We aim to ensure our clients are informed, and we leave decision-making to them. If they decide to lean out it is not our job to stop them. Nor do we have a right to. The heads they risk are their own.

Most of my mediation work is with couples who have married, or at least have lived together, and have had children together, and most of the examples in this book are about family conflicts, based on my work as a family mediator. I have not reproduced actual situations. Respecting client confidence is a core value for a mediator. If I quote the words of a client, the quote is a compositeor I have changed the circumstances to hide identities, or I have permission to quote.

Labels

I use the word "clients" as often in this book as the phrase "the people I am working with". I avoid it in my work as a mediator though it is a word I am used to, having been a lawyer for years, and it does carry the connotation "someone

4

who retains me, and whose interests I strive to advance". My friend Michael Lang, a mediator and teacher in the US, from whom I have learnt much, used the phrase "the people with whom we have the privilege of working" instead of the word "clients", at a seminar he gave recently. I was happy with the language, and inspired – not for the first time, in his company – by the thought that it a privilege to do this work. I like the phrase, and find thinking of my clients in this way helps me to do my work, but it is too long for regular use.

Talking about the word "client" reminds us that labels matter. A mediator should recognise that every word he uses is a label, that the labelling process is inherent in the use of language, and that he should be sensitive to what labels he uses. I will talk more about labelling in Chapter Three.

The mediation process

How does the process work? When I describe it throughout this book it will have to be from the mediator's viewpoint, because I know no other, and because each client experiences the process, and the mediator, in his or her own way. All I can do is tell you how I work, and leave you to imagine how you would react if you were in a client's chair.

There is a school of thought that holds that a mediator should keep tight control over the clients and the process. I do not belong to that school, and do not aim to prevent my clients from saying what they feel, when they feel it. I may suppress discussion of a topic at a particular time, but only for what I think is a good reason. I may take up one topic and, just when the parties are getting comfortable with it and feel they are making progress, may switch topics, or introduce something that seems irrelevant.

In much the same way, you will find that some topics re-appear in different parts of this book, in different contexts.

5

This is a reflection of how things are, in two ways. When people are in serious conflict their disagreement will spread from its original subject to anything else that they can fightabout. A normal marital row between people who will live out their lives together contentedly, may start about who is to blame for not switching off an electric heater, but as it gathers momentum, the field of battle will widen to include things like each other's families, and their unacceptable behaviour at the couple's wedding. People who know each other well know exactly where to stick the knife in. Spouses trust each other with embarrassing secrets. So there is always plenty of ammunition.

Moreover, in marital mediation topics are inter-dependent. If, after a separation, one of the spouses (let's say the husband, to avoid he/she) is going to buy a new home, he will need a lump sum as a deposit, and that will affect how they divide any capital assets. The more capital he can raise to buy his new home, the less he will need to borrow. The amount he borrows determines the level of repayments, which will affect the amount of support he can pay for his wife and children. Or, depending on his priorities, the amount of support he feels bound to pay will affect the amount of the mortgage he feels he can support. Either way, where his new home will be, and how big it will be, will affect plans for children to spend time in each parent's home. So, as separating spouses decide on any one of these issues – capital division, income sharing, "parenting" – the decisions they make on each will affect their decisions on other topics, and may require them to review decisions already made.

If there is no obvious orderly sequence, the mediation process might sound disorganised to anyone listening in. So long as I think a disorganised-seeming approach helps my clients, that is what they will get. And if this book sometimes seems to imitate the apparently random pattern of a mediation

6

session. It will be for much the same reason: to get through the work as easily and pleasantly as we can.

I read somewhere that if Napoleon Bonaparte was asked to approve the promotion of a soldier, he would ask: "Is he lucky?" I think this apparently simple question was short-hand for a series of more complex questions: Does he produce good results? Does he know when to stick to a pre-determined plan, when to modify it, and when to abandon it? Does he have a mixture of rational judgement and instinct that will lead him to act wisely in a crisis? If he is in a difficult situation, will he emerge well from it, looking as though he did so by luck?"

Mediators, like French army officers, need luck. A good mediator is one who makes his clients lucky.

CHAPTER ONE

WHAT MEDIATION IS – AND ISN'T

The idea of mediation as a professional skill is new to us, and some of its enthusiasts have claimed more for it than I think is justified, and built it up as a wonder-drug that can cure a wide range of ailments. I believe mediation is wonderful in what it can do for people who are locked into conflict, and it may be wonderful, too, in how the work can transform the lives and personalities of those who do it. But it is not a cure for all conflicts. Perfectly adequate machinery exists for dealing with most disputes without recourse to this new-fangled idea. If a motorist knocks me down and my arm is broken, my claim for damages against the car-owner's insurers will be best handled on both sides by lawyers trained to establish the facts and apply legal principles to them.

Similarly, if I buy a refrigerator, or a car, and later claim it is defective, lawyers are usually the people best qualified to advise on whether I am entitled to return the defective machine and get my money back, and if not what compensation I should get for being lumbered with faulty goods. Usually, the answer is a sum of money. The only thing buyer and seller probably have in common is a hope not to have to see each other again. Luckily, this shared wish can usually be met.

Who needs mediation?

But what if my job is to sell motor cars or refrigerators? If I am a distributor for the manufacturer who I claim has supplied me with defective goods? And those goods represent a large part of my business? The danger is that if our dispute escalates it can lead to our terminating a commercial relationship that may be beneficial to both, and that each would prefer to continue.

If a dispute between parties in constant contact has been addressed but not resolved to the satisfaction of both parties, it is likely to emerge again. Co-operation between the protagonists dwindles. Thousands of other problems develop. If the parties continue to have dealings with each other, the hostility which their dispute engendered, and which has not been dealt with, will emerge somewhere else in their continuing relationship. The danger is that it will poison it.

A decision by an outsider – for example, a judge – can determine a dispute, but cannot resolve it. People who have a conflict within a continuing relationship do not merely need to have their dispute *determined*: they need it to be *resolved*. *Determining* the dispute – that is, answering the question: "what compensation should the supplier pay to the consumer?" does not help them to put the dispute behind them, and get on with their relationship.

Mediation, then, as I see it, is valuable to parties who need to maintain a continuing relationship. It can help them to resolve their dispute in a way that meets their need to restore harmony. That is the reason for the emergence of mediation in recent years as a new professional service. It can be useful in commercial and neighbourhood disputes, but the most common relationship, fraught with dispute, that often needs resolution not determination, is that between a man and a woman who have together brought children into the world, and who will no longer live together.

9

People who have passed through the process of disengaging from a previously loved partner have told us about the feelings of confusion, anger, grief and bitterness that they went through. Feelings about the ex-partner often come in contrasting waves, of profound love and sympathy alternating with complete aversion. As separating spouses, on an emotional roller-coaster, they may be overwhelmed by the tasks that face them, at perhaps the most sensitive and vulnerable stage in their lives. While disengaging from an emotional, intimate relationship, they also have to deal with the ownership and occupation of what used to be a shared home, how to share income, and divide jointly owned property.

Finally, and most importantly, they have to decide how they are going to rear their children after they cease to share a home. And, of course, at the time of the parents' separation, their children still need them, need to be reassured of their continuing love, and need them to co-operate as parents. Not only do children of separating spouses need from their parents all the things that children seek from their parents throughout their childhood (and sometimes beyond), but their needs are probably more intense than they have ever been or will ever be again. Children's needs often peak just at the time when their parents are most taken up with their own pain and anger, and are least capable of meeting them.

Probably for this reason, mediation has been used most often, and has seemed to be most useful, in disputes arising from marital collapse. Most of the examples in this book will come from that area.

Mediation and therapy

This may be a good place to clarify the distinction between marital mediation and counselling, or therapy. These are words I will use interchangeably at this point because I do not

10

need to discuss the distinction. I know therapists who resent being called counsellors, and counsellors who resist being called therapists, and I hope both will bear with me. (For the sake of clarity, when I talk about therapists in this book I will use "she" and "her", while I speak of a mediator as "he" or "him".)

The skills of a counsellor will be useful to a mediator, and the processes of mediation and counselling may look alike but they differ in their objectives, in their methods, and in their boundaries. The best description I ever heard of the difference between the objectives of mediation and counselling was at a workshop given by Joan Kelly, co-author of *Surviving the Break-up*. I cannot quote her exact words, but their effect was:

> "The objective of therapy is to ease pain, to heal, or to cure. The objective of mediation is an agreement that can be put on paper.
>
> "Mediation may be therapeutic in its effects. For example, if a husband and wife reach agreement on parenting, they may feel better, or the agreement may help them to come to terms with the end of their relationship. But the therapeutic result, if it happens, is a side-effect, not the purpose of the process. A mediator should always have in his mind the objective of a written agreement, and should not allow himself to practise therapy with a couple, whether he is qualified as a therapist or not, if they have contracted with him for mediation, not therapy."

I understand a marital therapist, working with a couple whose marriage is in trouble, will often approach their problem by looking at it in a logical timeframe, something like this:

> "What patterns in your relationship cause problems?
>
> "Having identified the patterns, can we go back into your past lives, and try to see where those patterns

11

come from: what are the roots in the past that cause one of you to behave in a certain way, or that makes that pattern of behaviour so unacceptable to the other? Can we get a better understanding of the patterns by looking at their roots?

"Finally, if we understand the historical reasons for the problems, does this help you to eliminate them, control them or reduce them?"

A mediator does not work like this. When spouses decide to separate and want to reach a workable agreement on how to handle the consequences of that decision, the issue is how they and their children will live for the future. Past patterns are no longer relevant.

Often, people I work with want to tell me about some past crime of the other. I usually want to hear it: I enjoy gossip, and – more respectably – it is interesting to know why and how a relationship foundered. But I am being paid to do something different, something that was defined with clarity and precision by Joan Kelly, as described above. I should not spend my time and my clients' money listening to stories that will not help me to help them with their task. Indeed, if I encourage them to go back into the past, I may be not just wasting their money and my time, but actually damaging their prospects of agreement. The past is where their fights are located. They probably each have a huge storeroom full of grievances and guilt. The more time they spend rooting around there, the more likely it is that they will remember or discover something they can use to start the fight again. Their visit to the past is likely to leave them further away from agreement, not closer to it. It is my job to get them out of their storeroom, into the open air.

People who have trained as therapists and extended their range into working as mediators need to be aware of a subtle temptation. In the course of discussion, or perhaps of recrimination, one party may say something that interests the therapist/mediator. She begins to see a pattern in their relationship. Perhaps she sees a possibility that, if the pattern were identified and understood, they might reverse their decision to separate. She feels she should explore this because, if her hypothesis is valid, it may lead to a marriage being saved from dissolution.

In my view she has no right to pursue this without first clarifying with the couple what she is doing, and getting their consent. Otherwise, she is selling one type of service to people who have come to her for another. They are vulnerable, feel helpless, and recognise that she is a professional, skilled in an area where they have never been before. They are dependent on her expertise. Can she ethically take advantage of their helplessness, and the likelihood that they will not realise what she is doing, to foist on them a service which they have not contracted for? In my view, there can only be one answer to this question.

However, it does not necessarily follow that a mediator with therapy qualification must ignore signs she has seen, which indicate to her that a therapeutic approach may help the couple, provided she is open with them about what she is doing. She may say something like:

"When you, Mary, said AB, it interested me very much because it made me think of XY. I wonder would you, or would both of you, like to take a few minutes out from what we are doing, to explore that?

"I am a therapist as well as a mediator, and, wearing that hat I felt this was worth exploring further. And that it might be helpful for you (or both of you) to look at that issue with a therapist.

"If so, I think you have choices. We could take time out from what we are talking about to explore it, with me working as a therapist, helping you to look at it, not

13

as a mediator helping you to negotiate your separation agreement. If that didn't lead anywhere, we could stop, and resume the task we started on.

"If you thought there was something worth looking at further, you could take it to another therapist. In which case, you could either suspend the mediation process with me, or continue it.

"Of course, if you are not interested in looking at this with a therapist or without, we can get on with the mediation process.

"The choice is yours. What would you like to do?"

Extent of control

A mediation session takes the form of a conversation between the parties and their mediator. If a mediator exercises too much control over the flow of that conversation, the sense that people are saying what is on their minds, talking through their problems, and being listened to, is likely to be lost. It is the free flow of opinions, hopes, needs and ideas, and the fact that they are listened to and understood, that makes mediation worthwhile, and gives clients a model for handling disputes in the future. Informality and lack of apparent structure are an important part of the way I choose to work as a mediator. That choice is dictated by my wish to give my clients the best service I am capable of, and by my wish to treat them with respect. (I say more about respect in Chapter Twelve.)

If the couple have growing children, new disputes will arise. They may have agreed on how to fund two households when children are still in primary school, but the kids will need a lot more financial support when they go on to secondary, and more again if they advance to third level education. The needs of the household where they live will change, and the demands on the non-resident parent will increase. An agreement reached about their daughter going to children's parties on Saturday afternoon will not be relevant when she wants to go to a disco that ends at three in the morning, and sleep over in her boyfriend's house. Couples have come to me after rearing their children successfully, at a complete impasse about how to handle a graduation or a wedding. My aim is to make myself redundant. I want them not to need to come back to me, because they can handle disputes without my help.

Of course, if the mediator doesn't manage the process, it may get out of hand, and, again, the prospect of the people making a bargain may recede. The mediator's frame of mind is crucial. If I am in control of myself and of the process (the two go together), I can be a calming influence. I will feel quite relaxed about the clients squabbling when they need to let off a little steam, if I am confident that I can stop the squabbling before it gets out of hand. My confidence will be conveyed to the clients in some subtle way that I do not fully understand. If I do not intervene immediately to stop their fight, they will stop it if I ask them to, later. If I am tense, I will not be able to bring into the room this easy, relaxed control over the process. I cannot help my clients to relax.

If certain clients always make me feel tense – which has happened – it will be my duty to ask myself whether I can serve them, and if not whether I should continue to work with them. Because, of course, any couple coming to a mediator, especially for the first time, feel enormous stress and nervousness. There are two things I can do about this, even before we sit down together. The first is that I never make a first appointment with people who come to me for marital mediation at a time that will require them to travel by car or bus through rush-hour traffic. The second, which may also seem odd, is to dress casually. How I dress is partly a reaction to my former work as a lawyer. I noticed how little is done to calm people who face the ordeal of giving evidence in court, and how insensitive as a group lawyers are to the fears of clients and witnesses. I decided when I started this work that so far as I could avoid it I was not going to present an intimidating appearance to my clients. Dressing casually is part of how I implement that decision, but, of course, what I wear is less important than how I behave. I aim to keep the conversation as informal as I can, and to avoid using my lawyer vocabulary. Indeed, I like to think I have more or less shed it over the years.

I also avoid taking notes during a session. If I need to record anything, such as date of marriage, dates of births of children, telephone numbers, and so on, I take up a pad and pen, write down the necessary information, and then put the pen and pad away. The message of laying the pad down is, "we talk off the record; nothing is recorded."

The "balancing trick"

A mediator is a conflict-manager, and he does not sit above the conflict, detached from the parties, and watching them negotiate. While avoiding becoming a party to the conflict, he will aim to control it – for example, to reframe issues in a way that may help his clients to resolve them. (You will come across reframing further on, especially in Chapter Seven.) The point I want to make now about the process is that the mediator's job may require him to seem at one moment to be helping one party, at another, helping the other; now putting one under pressure, next, pressurising the other, and, at another time, sitting back and doing nothing.

If he switches between being helpful to one party, then to the other, next to both and then to neither, he is going to find it hard to hold on to the idea that he should always be balanced between the two. If he is seen by one party to side with the other he may lose the confidence of the one who sees him as biased on the other parties's side. (It is wrong, but usually less serious, to be seen by one party to be biased in his favour.) So, if he spends time in one person's chair, he will balance by visiting the other's too. It is like riding a bike. In order to keep our balance, we need to lean over sometimes, especially in a tight corner. But the normal balanced posture for a bike and cyclist is vertical, leaning neither to right nor left, and we go back to normal as soon as we round the bend.

Appearing to switch from side to side in this way may seem strange, but I think it is an essential ingredient in the process. My shorthand for identifying with one client is "sitting in his chair", or even "getting into his skin". Equally important is the concept of balance. It is essential for a mediator to sit in both chairs, and to be seen by both parties to do so. Indeed, it may be especially important for him to sit in the one he is less comfortable in, and to be seen to do so.

There is another balancing-act for mediators. I said earlier that I believe a mediator should not care whether his clients make an agreement at all, or, if they do, what it may contain. He helps them to evolve it, and to "reality-test" it (Chapter Eight) for weaknesses that might emerge when they put it into practice, and then stands back. If they are happy with their bargain, he has done his job. If he thinks it is a foolish bargain, he does not say so, because it is their bargain, not his.

It can be hard to watch people we have come to like and respect make what we think is a foolish bargain. But if we respect them, we must also respect their right to make their own decisions. (The problems a mediator has with himself here are not the same as those where he sees a bad bargain emerging from unequal bargaining ability or intimidation, each of which we will look at later on.)

17

Trench warfare

I mentioned that a core part of how I work lies in "joining" people who need help to move on. We try to help people to become mobile by sitting with them, or even by trying to get inside their skulls, to help them to change their patterns. Very often, when people come to mediation, they have dug themselves into positions which they find it hard to abandon. I sometimes compare them in my mind to the two armies in Northern France in the 1914-18 war, who found themselves confronting an enemy army, and reacted by taking out spades and digging themselves into trenches. Being in a trench gives us short-term, partial safety from people with guns in the other army, but once we are in the trench it is hard to get out. We fear that as soon as we pop our heads over the edge the enemy will take a pot-shot at us. A trench has the drawback that the view is extremely limited. Part of a mediator's job, as I see it, is to help "entrenched" people to move away from the illusory safety of the trench.

If I am trying to help one of my clients out of his trench, I find it is usually not enough for me to stand on the edge, looking down, telling him he will be better off out beside me than in the stinking hole where he is crouching. Like the person in the water telling the reluctant shiverer on the edge that it's "lovely when you're in", it doesn't work. What the person in the trench usually needs in order to climb out is positive help beside him, not wise exhortations from above. He needs me to get down into the trench with him to give him the courage to climb out of it. So, a large part of a mediator's work lies in getting into the trench where his clients live in discomfort and fear, and helping them to climb out so that they can see the terrain.

If I get down into one trench, how am I seen from the other side? In 1914-18 terms, how will the German army view me if

18

they see me clambering down into a French or British trench? The answer is clear: they will see me as an ally of the enemy. The balancing-act is between seeming to be neutral, and actually being so. A mediator must – sometimes, and temporarily – take sides, not by advocating one party's position, in debate with the other, but by imaginatively projecting himself into one party's skin – or trench.

Having done so, a mediator needs to remember that what he was doing may have been interpreted by the other party as taking the first person's side. Accordingly, I will usually not embark on that kind of "visit" until I have created a rapport with both parties, and feel they have some trust in me. And I will remember, when I emerge from one trench, that the person who is peering through the barbed wire at what is happening on the other side will expect me to visit his or her trench, too.

"Representing" a client

It is one thing to visit each party's encampment, and quite another to negotiate on behalf of one party. If we accept the position of "representative" of one party, late in the process, we are acknowledging that the process has failed to equip them to negotiate on their own behalf for the future, and has been, to that extent, a failure. If we do so at the beginning of the process, we may throw away an opportunity to educate the passive party in the skills of negotiation. If the passivity is a ploy, designed to ensure that others will do for the "helpless" party what he does not want to do for himself, then the mediator has been trapped, and the client, not the mediator, is now in control of the process.

I think a mediator may represent one party in negotiation with the other if two conditions are met. One is that the client is handling the negotiation incompetently, and the other is that a demonstration of how to do it may educate either party or both.

For example, people who have an unanswerable argument on a particular issue will often start the discussion by stating their position, and adding that there is no room for argument on it. "There is nothing to discuss. The children have to stay in their present home. That's all there is about it!" is an example.

Refusing to discuss the issue ignores the fact that that is exactly what they have come to me to do. More seriously, from the speaker's viewpoint, he or she fails to recognise that if the facts are unarguably in your favour, you will emerge from a rational discussion with what you need. So if a mediator demonstrates that the result of the discussion will favour one party and that therefore she loses nothing by engaging in rational discussion, he may give them both a useful lesson in how to negotiate calmly and rationally. And if the result on that issue was inevitable, he will not have affected the outcome.

Two final comments on this. A mediator who becomes a negotiator should be uncomfortable in that role and stay in it for the shortest possible time. Before a competent mediator decides to enter the debate with support for one party, he will have looked at the issue and decided whether it would be more effective to reframe it (Chapter Seven), and has not seen any reframe he could usefully offer.

How deep should a mediator dig?

My answer is that he should dig as deep as he feels he needs to, *provided he digs only for mediation purposes.* I worked with a couple recently who were so pleasant and understanding to each other at our first two sessions that I wondered would they later regret separating. (Note: I did not ask myself "are they wise to separate?" That would have meant second-guessing their decision.) The wife was clear that she wanted a separation. That was why she had come to me, and what she wanted from me was help in working out its terms. I did not feel I had the right, even if I had the skills or qualification, to investigate the reasons for her decision, or to explore whether it was as firm as it seemed.

However, when we had worked through the main issues and were not completing the process, I thought I was justified in encouraging them (allowing them, might be more accurate) to discuss what had gone wrong in their relationship, and ventilate their feelings. I thought it was right because their emotions about each other, in which very strong negative feelings only marginally outweighed powerful positive ones, were blocking them from reaching an agreement about their separation, which was what they needed, and was why they had come to me. Once they had expressed their feelings to each other in a "safe" environment, they were able to go ahead and complete their negotiation. I think both of them needed to talk to their former lover about their life together which they were leaving, and how they had experienced it. Once they had talked, and each had more understanding, they could move on into their next phase.

I was on the borders between mediation and therapy here, but I think just to the right side of the border.

Mediation and law

I want to say something here about the relationship between law and mediation. (I will have more to say in Chapters Five and Six where I compare how bargains are negotiated, depending on how close to the legal process the negotiations take place.) I want my clients to recognise that while I am there for them, I am not on either party's side. They pay me to be balanced, and I will do my best not to let them down. If they need the advice of someone who is on their side, and only on their side, they should talk to their lawyers. (There are probably other people around who are also exclusively on their side, but the value of their advice is more doubtful. I will discuss this in Chapter Ten where I talk about the "Absent Warrior".) I want my clients to talk to their lawyers, preferably during the mediation process, not when it is over. Otherwise, the danger is that the lawyer looks at a mediated bargain, believes he serves the interests of his client by pulling it to pieces, and in the process destroys whatever willingness to co-operate the parties may have built up with the mediator's help.

If I seem to criticise lawyers in this book more often than I praise them, I hope they will forgive me. Mediators become aware of what lawyers are doing only when problems arise. Nine times out of ten, I find that a bargain my clients have negotiated, and that I have recorded in a "Note of Understanding", is translated by their lawyers into a legally binding separation agreement. The tenth time, when one of the lawyers dislikes his client's bargain, mediators tend to get annoyed: "Why is the lawyer interfering and trying to prevent his client from making up her own mind?" is a question mediators ask. The answer usually is: "Because he thinks that is his duty. And he is the only person in the world entitled to answer the question: what is my duty?"

When the tenth case out of ten arises, the lawyer is likely to be critical of the mediator, too. He may ask: "How could a competent mediator allow my client to make such a rotten bargain?" And if the mediator were to say: "Your client had the right to make up her own mind", the reply from the lawyer might be: "Were you so blind, or so indifferent, that you failed to see she was terrified of her husband?"

And, unfortunately, the cases that lodge in the memories of both the lawyer and the mediator are not the nine that went through smoothly, but the tenth, where they each felt critical of the other, and impatient with the profession that the other personified.

I was a lawyer for thirty years before I became a mediator and know something of the pressures and problems of the life, and the impatience any professional feels when his area of expertise is invaded by amateurs. And, a thousand times worse, amateurs who think they are experts. If mediators want to be accepted by lawyers – as they should – then they need to show the lawyers that they are professionals too, by acting like professionals. A mediator who goes about his work in a less than professional way helps to delay the acceptance of mediation as a profession.

I ask my former colleagues if you think your ex-colleague is too harsh with you in this book to understand the frustrations you have caused him, once in ten cases, and that he shares your tendency to forget the other nine.

Roles of mediator

Although a mediator is first and always a conflict-manager, he is other things, too. He is a catalyst. That is, he combines with both parties to help them to change, in much the same way as yeast combines with sugar, to help the sugar to change into alcohol. Their change is from being people who are unable to agree with each other, to being people who not merely can but do. They not only agree on paper, but can give effect to that agreement, day to day.

Indeed, we usually have a higher ambition for change in our clients. I understand that robot machines are now designed to correct themselves if they go wrong. I know that after my clients leave me with their agreement worked out and recorded on paper, they will hit snags. Things will go wrong from time to time. They will need to re-negotiate some aspects of their bargain over the years to come, for example, as children grow older and their needs change. I hope the process of mediation, and what they have learnt about listening to each other and trying to find common ground, will give my clients an ability to correct or repair their bargain as needed, without my help. To that extent, I see myself as an educator of my clients. I want them to learn how to listen, how to accept, and how to agree.

The mediator also tries to be a role-model. This may seem conceited, but one of the things he does is to demonstrate an approach to conflict that he hopes his clients will carry out of the process. The constant message and example are: "Here is how I listen to each of you. Here is how I respond. If you can follow my example, life may be easier and pleasanter for both of you and for your children."

He hopes they will continue after they say goodbye to him to use the model he offers of effective communication and principled negotiation that he has tried to give them.

He also hopes the fact that he is less competent at handling conflict in his own life than they are, does not affect his usefulness as a role-model.

CHAPTER TWO

DIFFERENT APPROACHES TO MEDIATION

Hardly a week goes by without somebody being invited to act as a "mediator" in a public dispute. When a major industry is threatened with closure because of industrial relationship problems a prominent local person – such as a lord mayor, or bishop of the diocese – is invited, or offers, to act as "mediator". We also often see people described as "mediators" in conflicts between states, though, on analysis, the mediator is usually nominated by another state which has a patron-client relationship with one of the disputants or some other interest in a speedy resolution of their conflict.

These "mediators" usually have things in common. They have an interest in the dispute being settled. As discussions develop, and they feel increasing pressure to produce a result, they will probably begin to side with whichever they think is the more reasonable party. And, of course, siding with one means ceasing to be an outsider to the dispute, and becoming a party to it.

Secondly, more often than not, their perceived qualification for acting as mediator lies in their position in the community (lord mayor, bishop, international envoy, ruler of interested country or whatever) and not in professional training and skill. They may not have access to the "box of tricks" that a mediator – in the sense in which I use that word – develops over his years of practice.

Thirdly, because their focus is on being able to announce an end to the dispute, they will be tempted to work, single-mindedly, towards that result. Paradoxically, this can cause another problem. Negotiation enables people to prolong their conflict, because conflict continues until they reach resolution. A mediator who will not give up and walk away from the conflict enables the protagonists to continue it. If they know their mediator has so much invested in the conflict that he will not stand up and say "I am going home. You can go to – wherever" then, in effect, they have a licence from their mediator to prolong the conflict indefinitely. "Combatants are locked in conflict, and a third party facilitates them in not resolving it" is a fair summary.

The fourth thing what I call "amateur mediators" often – not always – have in common is a reluctance to help the parties to explore the roots of the conflict so as to find a true resolution. Especially if that exploration is likely to prolong the process and therefore delay an announcement that hostilities are over.

I do not criticise people who do this work. Indeed, I admire them. Their work is done under huge stress and pressure, often including physical danger. It may save jobs, or lives, or avert civic strife. I salute them. The only problem I have with them (apart from envy) is when they are called, usually by other people, "mediators". And as I use the word "mediator" it refers only to peace-makers who have no involvement in the conflict, and no stake in its resolution.

As I say in the Introduction, a mediator is neutral, not just in the sense that he does not take sides in his clients' conflict, but also about whether they will reach an agreement at all. If they do, he is neutral about what it will be. People who say they want an agreement often mean, "I want the other party

26

to bring the conflict to an end, by accepting my position." The parallel for the family therapist is the wife who says the marriage would be fine but for her husband's attitude, or the husband whose message to the therapist is "fix her!"

What I hope for is that my clients may come to view their conflict in a different light, and have a better understanding of it. I recognise that there are some conflicts where the wishes and needs of both parties cannot be reconciled. If there are two people in the water, and only one life-jacket, then one must drown. A mediator cannot help people in this predicament to reach an agreement. (Luckily, he is unlikely to be asked to.) The most he can do is to help them to realise that both will drown if they continue to struggle for the life-jacket.

In what I call "true mediation" it is the clients who decide whether the distance between their respective aspirations is too wide to be bridged by an agreement. If their mediator wants them to agree, and wants it badly enough, it is likely that they will leave his room with an "agreement". It is also likely that it will represent the mediator's ambition for his clients, not necessarily a bargain that they both find acceptable. If so, it will not work in practice.

I do not say a short-term solution is never helpful. For example, I sometimes work with spouses whose conflict is so raw, and their feelings so powerful, that they have no immediate prospect of being able to reach a sensible long-term agreement, and a short-term one is the best they can hope for. It may take the form of an agreement to separate, and live apart for a while, in the hope that the comparative peace created by their no longer being trapped under the same roof may help them to negotiate a lasting peace. (A parallel would be with a war that is first suspended by a truce, with the truce later being replaced by a peace treaty.)

The essential difference between the two situations is that

in one the parties agree to a short-term truce, knowing that they are postponing the long-term negotiations, and in the other, the short-term bargain is seen as the end of the negotiations. Too often, the second type of "agreement" is based on a shared decision, conscious or not, to ignore the roots of the conflict. A truce that is mis-described as a peace-treaty will probably unravel, and, if it does, its collapse will seem to be a greater disaster than it might have been if it had been properly labelled when it was announced.

A true mediator aims at helping to enlighten the parties to the dispute. That is, literally, to bring light to their conflict, and to enable them to see the conflict in that light. If that is achieved, it may lead to the dispute being resolved genuinely and effectively, and in a way that has prospects of being permanent. However, when the parties are "enlightened", and see their dispute in a clearer way, they may decide that it is not capable of being resolved, and may decide to continue it or even to escalate it. We may all be tempted to paper over the cracks, but someone who serves other interests, not just those of the disputants, may find the temptation irresistible. What I call a true mediator, serving only his clients, may feel attracted to a short-term illusory solution, but, because of his training and background, is more likely to recognise the nature of the temptation, and to resist it.

That is why I disagree with marital mediators who see it as part of their function to act as "advocates for the children". I see it as my job to manage my clients' conflict, not to usurp their role as parents. Nor do I think I am entitled to bring into my work as a conflict manager another agenda, hidden from my clients, of ensuring that their children are looked after in accordance with my standards. (As my wise colleague and friend Lisa Parkinson said, when she was asked should mediators not act as "advocates for the children", "who appointed us?") The furthest I will go in that direction is that sometimes I say to parents, "So the three of us are working for the five of you. Right?" And they are entitled to say, "Wrong!"

Shuttle mediation

I do not practise "shuttle mediation" which usually works something like this. The parties meet the mediator in one room, and exchange positions and arguments. They then withdraw into separate rooms, and the mediator shuttles between them, persuading each to grant some concession, until mutual concession-making results in agreement. That is achieved by a combination of two things. One is concessions made by each party to the other's demands, and the other is the way a skilful shuttle mediator uses the process, and the fact that he has complete control over communication, to whittle down demands on each side.

This is often an effective way of handling negotiations. In one way at least it resembles the "distinguished outsider" described above with a separate agenda: it can produce results.

But if the parties resolve their current dispute without communicating directly with each other, and talk only through their mediator, the mediator may become indispensable to their future communication. Having had their wish to avoid speaking to each other indulged, and having reached agreement without having to be civil to each other, it may actually become harder for them to talk civilly to each other later, on future issues of conflict. I know this kind of process usually ends with the mediator bringing the parties together to record their agreement and exchange uneasy handshakes, but I doubt if that cures the damage done by keeping them apart while the real work is being done.

Next, shuttle mediation will often involve the mediator not telling either party everything that the other has said. If he does, he makes himself redundant, because people do not need a translator if they sit in the same room and talk the same language. The way he works necessarily leads to the distinction between truth and half-truth being blurred. And "half-truths" is a euphemism for lies.

Merits of face-to-face mediation

What influences me most in not using shuttle mediation is the conviction I have formed about the educational power of face-to-face mediation for parties in a dispute who need to maintain a continuing relationship.

People who are entrenched in a fight will rarely listen to the other party. They will perhaps listen to their arguments, but if they do, it will be in order to be able to produce refuting arguments in order to prove the justice of their cause. Disputants do not listen with a mindset of: "I want to hear what you have to say, in order to understand how you feel and what you want, so that we can then see what can be done to give you what you reasonably want, without depriving me of what I feel I need. And I hope that, if I listen to you in that spirit, you will listen to me." People who listen to each other with that mindset are not disputants, even if they want different things, and people who are willing and able to listen to each other in that way have a good prospect of not becoming disputants in the future, even if they do want different things.

In "open mediation" as opposed to "shuttle" everybody is in the room and hears what everybody else says. Feelings of fear and pressure are inherent in any dispute, but instead of increasing them to put pressure on the parties to settle, the mediator will try to diminish them. For example, if I am working with separating spouses who show more than average tension, I might say: "I get the sense that you are both very tense. Tom, will you tell me what it is that worries you most? What is the worst possible thing that could result from this process?" In marital mediation what Tom usually fears most is that he will lose contact with his children. I will then ask the same question of his wife, Anne. Often, her answer, will be that she is afraid of having to cope with bringing up the children on her own, in poverty. I will then say something like: "Tom, you have heard Anne say that what she most fears is that you will not contribute enough to the household for her to keep her head above water, and stay out of debt. Can you reassure her that you will not let this happen?" Invariably, his answer is "Yes, of course. I wouldn't let the children go without."

When Anne has absorbed this answer, I may ask her: "Anne, Tom has said that he is afraid of losing his place as a father in the children's lives, as they grow up in the home you make for them. Can you reassure him that you will not let that happen?" It is now in her interests to be on good terms with Tom, and to say "Yes. The children need their father." When both parties have named their greatest fear, and have been reassured by the other that it will not happen, the atmosphere is transformed.

This is the reverse of the process of intimidating both parties into a truce for fear of the alternative. The difference in approach results from a fundamental difference in objective: I am concerned with increased understanding between the parties, because I believe it is likely to lead to a genuine, lasting peace. And that is one reason why, as I said before, I am pretty well indifferent to the specific terms they may agree.

There is a practical reason for not being too worried about the content of their bargain. This is that if the mediation process works well for the disputants, it will enable (or "empower") them to renegotiate, if their initial bargain doesn't seem to work. In marital separation, for example, it can be very hard to assess how much money two households,

31

one completely new, and the other changed, are going to need. Spouses who are about to separate will often agree to work on a "best guess" for the first six months or so, and then review income sharing in the light of experience. Of course, people who decide to make a short-term bargain rather than negotiate a long-term arrangement initially are postponing what may be the hardest topic of negotiation. Some of you may feel that a mediator who encourages them to do this is letting them off the hook, or not completing his work with them. Maybe so, but there are other ways of looking at this. One is that it is a mistake to make a decision until all the relevant facts are known – and in relation to income-sharing the amount it will cost someone to live is a very relevant fact (especially to that someone) which can usually only be guessed at, not known, before both households have experience of the money they need.

Also, so long as there are children living in the home of one of their parents, their needs will change constantly. (They usually increase consistently until the first child ceases to be dependent, and then gradually diminish.) If the parents are going to have to renegotiate in the light of their children's changing needs, the sooner they learn to do so the better for their children.

Some mediators who do not practise "shuttle mediation" do something called "caucussing". I see caucussing as a modified form of shuttling, though many who caucus might not agree. Mediation with caucussing is a mixed process that includes face-to-face meetings with all parties – mediator and disputants – interspersed with separate meetings between the mediator and each party, separately. Such separate meetings are commonly called caucuses. A number of mediators I know and respect use caucussing routinely. My reservations about it are related to a core concept of mediation, loosely called "empowerment". Let me explain.

Clients versus "colonists"

A decision to separate is not a stand-alone decision. It requires the spouses to make further decisions: financial, social, familial, emotional. Before they make any of these decisions, or even start to look at their options, a separating couple may usefully start to look at a prior question, which is fundamental but is often not addressed, and is, therefore, answered by default. It is: who is going to make those decisions?

This may seem a silly question. Who should make them but the people involved? However, life is not so simple. When a couple separate, outsiders often enter their lives, in a way they would not have presumed to had the couple stayed together, and take over decision-making, or influence decisions about how the pair should live their lives and bring up their children after they have ceased to be a couple. John Haynes calls this process "colonisation", by analogy with a process by which people from an economically or militarily strong country invade a weaker, and therefore vulnerable, country and either start to govern it or exercise significant control over how it is governed.

In the seventeenth to nineteenth centuries, European countries were major colonisers. In the first half of the twentieth, especially in the 30s, colonisation, such as German annexation of adjoining territory, Italian occupation of parts of North Africa, and (after the war that these led to) Russian extension of "sphere of influence" to Eastern European countries was, justly, seen as aggression. US activity in Central and Southern American countries and in South-East Asia has been seen by some but not all commentators as a form of colonisation.

Features common to international colonisations include:
◆ the colonised country is weak, either temporarily or permanently;
◆ in colonising the weaker territory the coloniser pursues its own interests;

- the coloniser will, almost always, proclaim that it occupies the colonised territory for the good of its inhabitants;
- usually, though not always, the coloniser can point to a group of people in the colonised territory who have asked the coloniser to intervene. The weaker and more fragmented the colonised territory is, the easier it is to identify or create a disaffected group to issue the invitation. If no such group exists it is often not hard to bring one into existence or to invent one.

Much the same is true of the colonisation of failed marriages, by which outsiders take over decision-making about how the spouses and their children should live their lives, "for their own good". In each case, the motives of the coloniser are, at best, suspect.

The analogy with territorial or political colonisation is relevant in another way also: the colonised party seldom benefits from being occupied.

Separating spouses are extremely vulnerable to being colonised. Often, one or both will welcome the colonist. Colonists in this sense may include: family, close friends, less close friends, therapists, social workers, legal advisers, and, ultimately, judges. All of these are self-explanatory, except the "less close friends", and I talk about them in Chapter Ten.

During the years I worked as a lawyer I used to think that when a family collapsed, wisdom about what its members should do next was to be found among outsiders, because they could observe the family calmly and take a detached view. My attitude has changed since I stopped lawyering and started mediating. I now believe the reverse. Even in the chaos of separating, I believe a normal family, perhaps with a little help, can look after themselves better than outsiders can live their lives for them, and that outsiders will usually serve them best by staying on the outside. If they do not, they run the risk of becoming intruders rather than helpers.

When couples separate, the walls (also known as "privacy") that a family builds between itself and the outside world collapse. Outsiders come rushing in to take over the decision-making functions that in an intact family are exercised by the couple alone. It is like losing your skin, the membrane that protects your body, and separates what is "you" from what is "not-you".

Having been a besieger for years, I am now on the side of the besieged. The enemy is outside, not inside. I now believe with the fervour of a convert that the duty and responsibility of making decisions, about their own lives and how to rear their children, belong to the parents, and, unless there is convincing evidence that they cannot take those decisions, and that their children are in danger of being injured by their inability to take them, nobody else should interfere.

There are situations where it will be right – indeed, it may even be a duty – for an outsider to become involved in the affairs of a separating family, without being invited to. But I think that too often, when outsiders become involved, they become intruders rather than helpers, and their involvement is an interference, not an intervention.

I go further and argue that second-rate decisions by parents are better than decisions by outsiders, that in theory might seem more "appropriate".

One of the objectives of mediation and, I believe, one of the great benefits it can bestow on people who use it, is that the process of making decisions is vested, or re-vested, in the people who will carry those decisions into effect. In marital mediation, these people are the couple, as people and as parents.

The process of ensuring that decisions are taken by the people who will have to carry them into effect in their daily lives and live with their consequences, is often called – not quite accurately – "empowerment". "Empowerment" aims to

35

restore to spouses the power to make decisions about their lives and their children's lives, which the "system" tends to take over when they decide to separate.

Caucussing, which involves the mediator talking to one party in the absence of the other, seems to me the reverse of empowering. When I am tempted to caucus, I think of the tension, the helplessness, the inability to influence events, that the absent party must feel while I talk to his or her spouse behind closed doors. When I balance this against the prospective gain, it rarely seems worth it. Of course, having talked to one party, the mediator will then talk to the other, but I do not believe this cures the damage done to the confidence of the people who are successively excluded from discussions that will affect their future lives.

As well as helplessness, each absent party must suffer from ignorance and fear. Let us put ourselves in the shoes of somebody whose ex-spouse is in a separate, private, meeting with their mediator. Most of us think of ourselves as honest people, who speak our minds, put our cards face up on the table, and certainly do not keep any up our sleeves. If we caucus with our mediator, we expect to behave honourably. If we say something to him that we do not want him to tell the other, it will be for good reason. Perhaps, for the good of that person, because we are protecting him or her from knowing things that would be upsetting.

On the other hand, when the mediator meets our ex-spouse in our absence we can be sure that he or she is doing two things: first, telling the mediator things it is vital we should know, but which are to be hidden from us; second, presenting us, and all our married life, in an unattractive light, so that the mediator will take the ex-spouse's side. We assume that when the mediator caucuses with our ex-spouse he or she will aim to "triangulate" him (see below).

Also, the fact that caucussing has taken place carries its own message: that things have been said between the mediator and one party that are to be kept from the other. That is: secrets. I believe one of the objectives of mediation is to build trust, and help people to co-operate in future. I see this as one part of the "empowerment" that mediation offers, and I see caucussing as designed to increase suspicion, kill trust, cast a shadow over the parties' ability to co-operate in the future, and as the reverse of "empowering".

Language – "appropriate"

I used the word "appropriate" above, and put it between inverted commas to draw attention to the dangers that lurk behind it, and to introduce the fact that the language we use is central in a mediator's work. "Appropriate" and "inappropriate" are words that have been used increasingly in recent years, in a way that gives them a sinister power. If I do something which you describe as "wrong", you accuse me openly, and if I reject your accusation you will have to justify it or withdraw it. If you describe what I have done as "inappropriate" you are really saying the same thing, but you are more likely to get away with it because you have used a word that does not seem to be an accusation. Because I am not accused, I do not have the right to defend myself. Even more helpful to you, if you want me to change my ways without either putting me under pressure, or allowing me to justify them, would be to say: "Michael, I am not saying what you did was wrong, but I think it would have been more appropriate to have done . . . "

An example of this in sexual harassment complaints is: "I am not saying that Joe's behaviour constituted sexual harassment. But I am saying it was inappropriate in the circumstances." Translated, that means "Joe harassed Cathy and got away with it."

These words will sometimes be used validly and usefully by an outside "expert" to educate an uninformed "client"

37

without seeming to admonish him. But the danger is that these apparently harmless words may become a means by which the person who uses them simultaneously does two things: the first is make a judgement, and the second is conceal the fact that he has done so. And a concealed judgement, hiding itself behind those words, is like a mediator unconsciously influencing the decision-making of his clients. It is wrong, and it is insidious in a way that an obviously judgemental approach is not.

So, if I am tempted to describe something as "appropriate" I believe I should ask myself: "Is that an appropriate word for me to use?" And before I use the word "inappropriate" I should first ask myself would it be inappropriate for me to do so.

"Triangulation" and caucussing

"Triangulation" is the name for what happens when a mediator takes sides with one party, or is thought by the other to have done so. Each party in mediation wants to gain the approval of the mediator, both because most of us want to be approved of – or at least not disapproved of – and because people in mediation will see their mediator as an influential person in their lives for as long as the process lasts. A mediator should not blame either party for trying to get him on their side, but he should not join the "triangulator".

An attempt by either party to triangulate the mediator – say, a wife, with a male mediator – threatens the process in two ways. The first, of course, is that she will succeed, and get the mediator to join her in opposition to her husband. We need to be on the watch for this, and to be aware that triangulation can creep up on us without our noticing it. The second is that the husband will believe the mediator has taken his wife's side. It may make no difference that the mediator has recognised what was happening, and avoided being caught. If the husband

38

believes the mediator has sided with his wife, he will lose confidence in the process and probably bring it to an end.

Triangulation is to mediation what blight is to potatoes: something that, if we do not guard against it, can ruin the entire harvest.

If you wanted to create opportunities for parties to triangulate their mediator, and for each of them to suspect that the other has succeeded in triangulating him, it would be hard to improve on a set-up in which each party, in turn, has a meeting with the mediator from which the other is excluded.

The problems with caucusing are such that I do not exclude it, but use it only as a last resort when all other approaches have been tried and have failed.

Mediation-arbitration

Mediation-arbitration, often shortened to "med-arb", is less fashionable than it used to be, but I do not want to ignore it, especially as talking about it will help to introduce themes that will run through this book. As it first emerged, the concept was that parties to a dispute asked someone to act as their mediator, but agreed that if they failed to reach an agreement with his help then he would issue a decision or recommendation which they agreed in advance would bind them. A different form has emerged since, which I will describe below.

I think people who seek "med-arb" as a means of solving their dispute hope to compress two systems into one space and get the best from each, and I see advantages in it for the protagonists. But I decided, for my own sake and the sake of my clients, that I do not want to play that game. I think it is important in the mediation process that all parties feel free to say what is in their minds, and to make offers or proposals off the record – on what lawyers call a "without prejudice" basis. I value this freedom, not because it makes my life as a mediator easier – though it does. I value it because I believe my clients need it if they are to negotiate a good bargain. If they know their discussions are "off the record" they may feel free to say what they think and feel, and to make offers, in a way they might not if they feared that whatever they said might later be quoted against them. I see this as "empowering".

I do not see how a discussion can be "off the record" if it takes place in the presence of someone who may turn into an arbitrator. If I act as a mediator, I cannot wipe what has been said from my mind, if I have to take off the mediator's hat and put on an arbitrator's. Even if I were foolish enough to think that my mind was a blackboard, and anything written on it could be cleared off with a damp sponge, who else would believe me?

Secondly, what distinguishes mediation from other methods of dealing with conflict is the fact that I avoid exercising influence over the decision-making of my clients. Among other things, a person who excludes himself from decision-making is free to ask silly questions, and make silly suggestions. I often do both in the hope that it will encourage the parties to come forward with their own ideas, and in the certainty that they will be willing to ignore what I have said.

If an arbitrator (including someone who, under the med-arb system, might become an arbitrator) were to ask silly questions or make silly suggestions, the parties (if they did not seek to have him removed as an obvious incompetent) would certainly be afraid to risk antagonising him by telling him he was talking through his ear-hole. It is easy to envisage their panic at the thought of being stuck with an arbitrator who could say such stupid things, and their attempts to conciliate the idiot they are stuck with, in the hope that his daft decision will at least be daft in their favour. This brings us back to a recurring theme: that mediators should have no power over the decisions their clients make.

A med-arb model has emerged more recently under which, if the mediation process does not lead to an agreement, the mediator withdraws from the process altogether and is replaced by someone else from within the same organisation, who will then act as arbitrator without having heard the "off the record" discussions. If the mediation and arbitration processes are conducted by separate people, that would meet the objections I have made above. However, I prefer to work under a system by which clients who try to resolve their issues with my help as mediator without success are "empowered" to choose their arbitrator for the next stage, without pressure to appoint someone I recommend.

Process-control versus content-control

I say the mediator should control the process, and the clients should determine the outcome, with no influence from the mediator. In theory, the distinction between controlling the process and influencing the content is clear, but it may be harder to see in practice, and I hope an illustration will bring this out.

Like many other married couples, Peter and Anne have a conflict about whether the family home should be sold, and, if so, when. Peter is the principal provider. Anne is to continue to provide the main home for their children. Peter argues that the family home should be sold, the children should be moved to a less expensive one, and cash released. He says "trading down" along these lines offers him the only chance he will ever have to finance a new home for himself. When they look more closely at their children's needs and how the children would be affected by moving from their home, they agree that the sale should be postponed. This raises a problem for Peter: where is he going to live? He doesn't see himself living in a bed-sit, where the children couldn't stay with him, for the rest of his life. Let us look at

41

how a mediator's intervention, directed at keeping the negotiations moving, might also influence its outcome:

> *Peter:* "I would go mad if I had to live in a crummy bed-sit for the rest of my life!"
>
> *Anne:* "I can see your problem, but I don't see what we can do about it, since the house is not to be sold until Jacinta is grown up."
>
> *Peter:* "Well, if I have to choose between a bed-sit, a mental hospital and selling the house, maybe we will just have to sell the house!"
>
> *Mediator:* "But you have agreed the house should not be sold, so there is no point in going over that again."

This intervention by the mediator looks like a process-control one; he is preventing the parties from wasting time by reopening something already agreed. But it is more than that. He has made an assumption that the parties are not free to change their minds on any issue when once they have agreed. His words are intended to veto any such change of mind. But this is an assumption he has no right to make. The entire process is a search for a bargain that will suit both parties (or at least be acceptable to both), and it is not within the rights of anyone except the parties themselves to declare that that search is at an end. The effect of the mediator's intervention may be to influence the outcome, if it prevents the parties from looking at all options.

So when Peter wants to reopen the decision about not selling the house what should the mediator do? The first question he might ask himself is: "Do I say anything?" Unless there are convincing reasons for opening his mouth, a mediator may best serve his clients at some stages in the process by keeping it closed. (This is a lesson I have found hard to learn, and still put into effect with some difficulty.) If there is good reason to speak, what he says should be designed to move the process forward, not to stall it, but, at the same time, not to prohibit any change of mind. He might say:

"I think you have agreed that, *if at all possible*, the house should not be sold, as it would disrupt the children. In particular, you don't want them to have to move just now, in the aftermath of your separation, because you feel they are at their most upset and vulnerable.

"On the other hand, Peter wants to have a home where the children can stay with him, including staying overnight. I think Anne sees that as a benefit to her, too. If the children are with their father, this will give her time to herself.

"So do you want to see if you can find a way for Peter to have an acceptable place of his own, without Anne and the children having to give up their home? If we can't manage that, you may have to look at other options. And they may include a sale. But maybe we can find a way of using available resources to meet Peter's need for a home of his own, without disrupting Anne and the children. Would you like to explore that possibility, on the understanding that no option is closed?"

I think an intervention of that kind from a mediator would facilitate further discussion of the problem without making Peter feel trapped. It reminds Anne that if Peter solves his problem she and the children will not have to move, and she has an interest in co-operating with him. It is an example of a "reframe", a concept that we will look at in Chapter Seven. And it puts the mediator and his clients back where they should be, with the mediator exercising control over the process of negotiation, while the clients determine its outcome. I repeat: this concept is central to the work of conscientious mediators.

But no matter how careful we may be not to intervene consciously to shape the content of the bargain we may be unable to avoid influencing it, because in hundreds of subtle ways our values will permeate the process. For example, if

Anne says she does not want Peter to be around her children because he has shown himself to be irresponsible to her, I might reverse (or reframe) this, and talk about the children seeing their father, or not being allowed to see him. Shifting the focus from father to children will lead their mother to see things differently, so the reframe will affect the outcome.

What should a mediator say if the clients ask, as they often do: "What do you think we should do?" My answer is that we avoid answering that question, because it is the wrong one. The aim of the process is not to discover what the mediator thinks they should do, but what they themselves think. If the mediator gives his opinion, his answer both parties may see it as "the right answer" which they must accept. They will not have reached their own agreement, but accepted arbitration. And they did not hire an arbitrator.

One of the best answers I ever heard to that question was given by my friend and colleague Larry Fong, of Calgary, in a role-play. He was asked: "What do you think we should do about Jim?" At first he ignored the question. (We do not have to respond to everything said in the process, and it is often better to risk annoying a client by ignoring his question than to annoy him three times as much by an answer.) When the question was repeated, Larry looked the questioner full in the face and replied: "He's not my kid." His ability to help his notional clients to solve their problem was enormously enhanced by his refusal to solve it for them, or to contribute to solving it. Conversely, if he had given his opinion, either he would have pleased one client and become aligned to that client, and, inevitably, against the other, or he would have pleased neither. (It can be a good move to please neither, but only when we judge they are unlikely to make a joint decision to leave the process.)

Mediators need constantly to remind themselves that there is no objective answer to the question "what is the best solution?" The best solution to a problem in mediation is the one the parties decide suits them best.

CHAPTER THREE

THE LANGUAGE OF MEDIATION

Dysfunctional communication between clients is one of the things that keeps mediators busy and justifies our existence. An extreme example, not as rare as one might hope, is hearing the word "not" when the other party has not used it, or vice-versa, completely reversing what has been said. The logical explanation (to the extent that logic has anything to do with it) may be that each partner expects the other to say something bad, and alters what is actually said to fit expectations.

There are three things to understand about dysfunctional communication. The first, and most important, is that it is the root cause of most of the conflicts I talk about in this book. When people in continuing relationships fight instead of talking through their problems, the most common single reason is that each of them starts to tell the other what should be done to solve the problem. If the other seems not to accept the solution, their reaction is to repeat it, louder. Both wind up talking at the top of their voices, get hoarse (metaphorically, and often physically) and annoyed. Their irritation is all the greater because someone who up to now has seemed to be a reasonable person has suddenly changed his aspect, and becomes obstinate and unreasonable. Each winds up shouting his views, and neither listens to what the other says. Probably most people who read this book have experienced this, in their personal relationships, or in work, or both.

If a third party, like a mediator, can join the disputants, and get them to talk quietly and listen to each other, there is a good chance that in the changed environment they will resolve their problem. I do not want to say this is the core of mediation, because that would over-simplify a complex process, and I'm not sure there is a single core to a mediator's work, but if there is, then that is what it is.

The second thing to remember is that dysfunctional communication rarely results from a failure to articulate clearly what is in the speaker's mind. Most people say clearly what they feel, think and want, and in mediation say it all too clearly – and often too frequently. The ability to listen and understand what other people feel, think and want is rarer. It is even rarer when one ex-partner expresses his or her feelings, thoughts, and desires to the other ex-partner at a time when their mutual hostility is at its highest. Failure in communication is usually in the receiving system, not the broadcasting one.

The third thing that mediators need to remember about dysfunctional listening is that the clients are so full of pent-up feelings that the mediator's words, as well as the other party's, are liable to be distorted. A husband was explaining to me, during a first session, how difficult he found it to leave the family home, because he had worked hard to make it comfortable, and to improve it. Offering feedback (Chapter Seven) I said: "So, Peter, you feel you have put a lot of work into the house, and got it to the point where you find it very hard to leave it. Right?" Before he could agree, the wife broke out in a storm of angry tears: "You are saying I did nothing in the house. That is so unfair." Of course, I had said nothing of the sort, but she was convinced I had. We finished

46

the session, and they left with an appointment for a second one, but he phoned later to say that she was not willing to come back, because she thought I was biased.

My immediate reaction was to blame myself. Thinking about it rationally, later, I cannot see that I really was to blame, but I do have a sense that, if I had been more sensitive to her reaction, I might have saved the process.

Another experience, which still shakes me when I think of it, was at a second session with a couple, when I was told by the husband that I had accused him at the first session of being an absentee father. I was appalled by what it seemed I had said, and apologised abjectly. At the same time, in the back of my mind, a small voice, representing whatever common sense I possess, was asking: "Could I really have said that? Am I quite so incompetent?" When the couple had left, I examined my notes, which confirmed what common sense had suspected. I had been mis-heard.

The wife – Petria – did not work outside the home, and was proud of her dedication as a mother. She had said to me that she felt her daughter, June, would not miss her father too much after the separation because she rarely saw him. I had offered feedback, omitting the hostile element in her message, and saying something like: "You have been there for June when she comes home from school, and you want her to feel you are still there for her. If you and Henry separate, you are the parent she would expect to be around, and might miss more. Right?"

This was a fair summary of what Petria had said, and she clearly felt it strongly. She had probably often accused Henry of being an absentee father. When she spoke to me, what Henry "heard" was not what she said, but an accusation she had often thrown at him in the past. Next, hearing me feed back what Petria had said he took me to be repeating and adopting her accusation.

47

That was interesting, and instructive, in itself. Equally interesting, if not more so, was that Petria agreed with him that I had accused him of being an absentee father, and I was in a minority in my belief about what I had really said.

Why did she agree? I can see two possible explanations. One is that when he complained about me, after the session, she felt she should support him. Perhaps she felt intimidated by him, or wanted to "soften him up" for future negotiations. The other, which I think is more likely with that couple, is that what she said to me during a mediation session was intended to carry the accusation he "heard". She "heard" my feedback as carrying the coded message she had intended to convey.

So any of you who want to put the concepts discussed in this book into practice in your daily lives should remember that it is not only what one disputant says that is open to being mis-heard by the other. The mediator is not immune. We can reduce the risk of being misunderstood by very careful use of language, including body language, but we can never eliminate it. Nor can we completely eliminate a danger of ourselves misunderstanding what our clients say.

I take three lessons from this. First, I must never relax my vigilance in trying to ensure that my words are not open to misinterpretation. Secondly, I must accept that however hard I try, people who want to misunderstand me will. Finally, I should remind myself that when I offer feedback I am more limited than my clients, who express their feelings, not only in their words, but in inflection, tone of voice, and body language. (If a husband said: "Of course, *she* is a *model wife and mother. Nothing* that goes wrong is ever her fault!" and I fed this back as: "You are saying that Mary is a very good mother and wife, and has no responsibility for your present problems" I would lose at least one of my clients on the spot.) Clients can express their negative feelings in all sorts of

48

ways, but the mediator should never offer feedback that relies on intonation, irony, gesture, or sarcasm. This is because his way of speaking must offer his clients a model of clear, neutral communication. Any attempt to reproduce sarcasm or irony is out. His body language must always be calm and non-threatening, and if he offers feedback he does so with words, and only with words, excluding emphasis, inflection or gesture. If he feels he needs to feedback something he thinks underlies the words, and is expressed only through body language, or tone of voice, he must do so by careful use of words, not by reproducing non-verbal communication.

So you may ask how would I feedback heavy sarcasm? I wouldn't. If I hear a negative message that is not going to contribute to developing an agreement, why should I give it weight and legitimacy by repeating it?

This brings us to what I say later, in Chapter Five, about earning the trust of the parties. If they trust their mediator, they are less likely to misunderstand him. If he blunders, and says something ambiguous, they are more likely to give him the benefit of the doubt, or ask him to clarify what he meant. However, we often have to offer feedback at an early stage in the process, when trust has not yet been established. Indeed, feedback is part of the process of building trust, because it is a way of telling the speaker that you have listened to him, and understood and absorbed this message.

The Button Factory War

The person whose statement is being fed back needs to know that the mediator has listened, and understood what he or she said, but the other person will need to know that the mediator has not bought into the first party's views. Let us take another example, this time, for variety, not drawn from family mediation. One of the most fruitful tensions in commerce is between the sales staff and the production staff of a manufacturing enterprise. Let us assume that this tension has boiled over into outright confrontation, and that I have been asked by Owen, the managing director of a button factory, to mediate a dispute between a sales manager, Peter, and a production manager, Tom, after they have had a blazing row, which ended with Tom taking a swing at Peter.

If I know these facts before I meet them, I will probably ask Tom, the person who delivered the punch, to speak first and describe the problem as he sees it. I will expect him to offer a combination of narrative of events and diatribe against Peter. Let us assume he accuses Peter, as the best way he can see of excusing himself for hitting him, because he knows he is in the wrong on this, whatever about other issues. When he finishes, I might say:

"So, Tom, as you see it, Peter seems to you to be booking orders for more buttons than you can produce. Orders get delayed. Customers complain, and blame you. Owen blames you. Nobody blames Peter. He gets praised for his selling record. You feel you are being blamed in the wrong. And as you see it, the problem goes back to the fact that Peter has agreed to sell more buttons than you can produce.

"You are also worried about quality. If you are forced to produce too many buttons, too fast, you think one of two things must happen. Either you will not be able to produce what is demanded, or you will not be able to keep up the quality that your customers expect. And quality is also important to your job satisfaction. You want to produce only good quality stuff that you can stand over.

"Since this pattern started, about six months ago, you have been finding your job stressful, where you used to enjoy it.

"Last Thursday, after Owen had given out to you about

50

customer complaints, Peter and you got into a discussion that turned into a row, and you hit him.

"You say you shouldn't have hit him, but at the time you felt at the end of your tether.

"Is that a fair summary?"

Let us look at that piece of feedback, and identify a few points about it. First is that it addresses only Tom's perspective. He has spoken from his point of view, and if I feed back to him something he has not said, or offer a different point of view, he will reject it.

Second is that although Tom has accused Peter, I do not join in the accusation. I did not say: "Peter is booking orders for more buttons than you can produce". I said "*As you see it*, Peter seems to you to be booking orders for more buttons than you can produce". As well as not accusing Peter, I am not saying anything he can deny. I don't think he will say, "you are quite wrong, Michael. I am not booking orders for more buttons than the plant can produce", because he, too, has been listening closely to my words. If he does, I can reply, "I hope I didn't say you were. If I did, I shouldn't have. What I meant to say was that this was how it seemed to Tom. He may be right or wrong, but what I was trying to do was to understand how he sees things. I also want to get a sense of how you see things. So, let me ask you about that."

In my feedback to Tom I have laid the ground for him to apologise to Peter for hitting him. It happens that I think provocation may partly *excuse* Tom, but nothing can *justify* him in hitting Peter, but my view is irrelevant here and I should not allow it to intrude. What is relevant is that already I am forming three hypotheses about this conflict. First is that their dispute will not be *resolved* unless Tom apologises to Peter; second is that Tom knows he has put himself in the wrong, and that he will feel a lot better if he apologises; third is that if he does, Peter will accept the apology.

When I talk about a hypothesis I do not mean something that I will hold on to indefinitely. A hypothesis is like binoculars. I use it to look at something a long way away, to get a clearer sense of what it would look like close up, but I will discard it when I no longer need it. Or, if you prefer, like a bus that I might see passing by, and jump on board. I will stay on the bus as long as it seems to me to be going in the right direction and travelling faster than I can walk. If it starts going somewhere I don't want to go, or gets stuck in traffic I will hop off. During a session, I might hop on board five or six different buses, and leave them all until I found one that was going in the right direction, and avoiding traffic jams.

My reason for asking Tom to speak first is an example of how hypothesising works in mediation. I often try to make space for someone who is seen by himself or others to be a "wrong-doer" to apologise, and for the "wronged" person to accept the apology. So, knowing Tom has hit Peter, I start with a hypothesis – which I am ready to abandon, but I must start somewhere – that the dispute is most likely to be resolved if Tom apologises, and Peter accepts his apology. If that is my hypothesis, then the party who is likely to have to make the apology is the person I will ask to speak first. In a legal trial the aggrieved party should first be given the floor to explain his grievance, but this is not a trial. I am not a judge, but a mediator, trying to manage and resolve a conflict. If I were to invite Peter to speak first, he would start by accusing Tom, this would put Tom on the defensive and the prospect of an apology offered and accepted would recede, and with it one path out of the conflict. And if I create an atmosphere in which it is hard for the "wrong-doer" not to make an apology, it is also one in which it is hard for the "wronged" party not to accept it.

The language in the above feedback is simple. The sentences are short. The words are everyday. I aim for simplicity – Orwell's "prose like a window pane" – because I recognise that all communication is a minefield, full of potentially explosive opportunities for misunderstanding. (I do not work in the field of conflict-resolution, but in the minefield of conflict-resolution.)

Whether the Tom/Peter conflict is going to be resolved will depend on their temperaments and my skill. If it is resolved, it may happen quite simply. The steps might be like this: Tom gets a chance of explaining the frustrations that led him to hit Peter. I then turn to Peter, and say something like:

"Peter, I would like you to respond to some of what Tom said. Please, if you don't mind, don't dwell on the fact that Tom hit you. I know it happened, and I know it upset you and you are angry about it. Tom hasn't tried to justify it. He has said that there are problems in the way you two work together, and I would like you to concentrate on that issue, for the moment. Of course I will come back to the punch, but for now I'd like to understand from you the frustration on your side that led to the big row with Tom, so that we can see what can be done to eliminate it for the future."

If Peter does what I have asked him to, we will probably move into a constructive discussion. (If he does not, I will quite likely continue to make the same request to him, perhaps in different ways, until he does.) However, I hope you will notice that the form of request I made to him allows him to ventilate as well. It would be wrong to allow Tom to complain about Peter, and not allow Peter a similar opportunity. At some stage, when discussion is moving positively, I will probably come back to Tom and put him under as much pressure as is needed to apologise to Peter, for example:

"Tom, you've said to me that you were out of line in hitting Peter. Am I the person to say that to?"

or:

"Am I the only person to say it to?"

53

If Tom responds – or, better, if he apologises without needing to be pressurised – and Peter accepts, we can start looking to the future, and re-stating the problem as: "What system can Peter and Tom put into place that will enable them to avoid rows for the future?"

At this point, assuming Peter and Tom are on the way towards a resolution, let's think for a moment about Owen, the managing director of the company, how he handled the conflict, and with what result. He was faced with a crisis where he could lose a valued member of his team. If he condoned his production manager striking a colleague, he would create a precedent that would cause problems in the future, and he would probably lose a good sales manager. He might also face a claim for damages for "constructive dismissal" by Peter, which might cost more money, and would certainly create more hassle and ill-will. Instead of facing the conflict head-on and taking a decision which would probably lead to the loss of one of his key management team, Owen decided to push Peter and Tom towards mediation. If they came back on good terms, that would be a triumph for him. If the mediation did not produce results, he had lost nothing, and perhaps bought time. And, if Owen, instead of being managing director of a button-maker in the late twentieth century, had been a French army officer in the early nineteenth, his emperor would have been likely to diagnose him as "lucky", and approve his promotion. (See Introduction.)

Language – "wrong-doer"

I used the words "wrong-doer" and "wronged" above and put them in quotes to remind you that it is not part of the mediator's job to apply those labels, or any other label, to his clients. Calling one party a "wrong-doer", even to myself, involves making a judgement, which a mediator should not do in his working life. It also involves attaching a label to a fellow human being, who is a person, not a thing.

Body language

Even more important than what is said, though impossible to convey effectively on paper, is the mediator's body language. I aim to go into a mediation session feeling calm, in control, keen to do a good job, fairly confident that I can, wanting to help the clients and sensitive to their distress. If I feel this way, I can give that impression. I will seem relaxed, because I feel relaxed. I will appear alert, and in control, because I am. I will seem sympathetic, because, if my clients are in pain, I feel sympathy.

I even hope that, although I have a face that makes me think, when I glimpse it unexpectedly, "I wouldn't buy a used car from him", I may even seem worthy of trust.

The more relaxed I am the more readily and effectively I will deal with my tasks, and respond to the unexpected. A tense person's listening is not as good as it should be: his tension distracts him from what others are saying, or their body language. If something happens that is not part of his plan, he may not be able to respond to it readily and smoothly. Instead, he may react to it. One of the big differences between good mediation and the other kind is reflected in the words: respond and react, and in their related adjectives: responsible and responsive; and reactionary. I want to be responsive to my clients needs, and to the changing situation. I do not want to limit myself to reacting, which often means holding on to certainties and inhibiting change.

Recently when I was talking to a couple, I noticed that the easy, relaxed gestures of my hands were changing to tense, jerky movements. While we went on with our work, I also asked myself "What is wrong? Why have I tensed up?" As soon as I asked the question, I was able to identify the problem. It was a simple, physical one: I needed to take a toilet break and was wondering could I hold out for the remainder of our time, or would I have to have it before the session ended and risk leaving a volatile couple on their own. As soon as I recognised that this was why I was no longer relaxed, and no longer gave the impression of being in control, I solved the problem by telling the couple that, being twice their age, I only had half their bladder control, and needed a break. They were smiling when I left, still smiling when I came back, and smiled even more when I started again by saying: "You are lucky, because I am an exceptionally clever chap who can pee and think at the same time, and what I have been thinking is . . . "

It's interesting – especially to people who may have the same problem – that when I came under that physical pressure the location of control over the process had changed radically. I had lost it. What would happen inside the room was controlled by what was happening inside my body. My rule now is: go before they arrive – and don't drink coffee!

The mediator's ability to represent calm is important too in our aim to train our clients to resolve future disputes without outside help. A mediator can be a role-model for the disputants, and his message of calmness and alert interest in their dispute may be more important than anything he says. In this, too, body language is essential. I want my body language to give the impression that I am a mediator: that my attitude is suitable to my task and that I am calm and relaxed but alert and sympathetic. All of which are positive.

I do not want to seem smug when I talk about the educational aspect of mediation, or to give the impression that it is a one-way process. It is not. The mediation process works best if the parties learn from their mediator, and the mediator learns from them. If I go into a mediation session hoping to learn from my clients, there is a good prospect that I will, and that it will be a two-way street. If I lose that hope, the time has come to stop mediating.

Intimidation

It is clear from this that a mediator needs to listen to all that his clients say, and that his concentration is more intense than in normal conversation. He listens to their words, but needs to pay equal attention – or even more attention – to their tone of voice and to their body language.

Their words may give the impression that they are prepared to make a bargain along lines they have been negotiating. But if one of them gives a reverse message by his or her body language or tone of voice, that message, not the verbal one, is reliable. Even if the parties were to write down their oral agreement and to sign it, they will not carry it through successfully if one of them has said no to it by tone of voice or body language. We know the truth of this from experience, but reason might tell us, too, that while we can control our words, and choose them carefully – whether to convey our thoughts or to conceal them – we cannot control our unconscious responses.

The message a mediator reads in this kind of contradiction in a client, is: "I cannot express in words why I do not like this bargain, but I know I do not like it." A responsible mediator will bring this ambivalence to the surface, but only after he has explored another possibility, and satisfied himself that he will not do more damage by doing so. (See below.) If he fails to find a more subtle approach – and in the middle of a session it can be hard to be subtle – he might say:

> "Peggy, you are saying yes to this plan, but I am getting a sense from you that you don't really like it. Am I right?"

And, if he gets a "yes" to this:

"Tell me what is bothering you?"

A responsible mediator who spots a difference between what one party says and what she conveys with tone of voice, or body language will ask himself another question: "if this person is agreeing orally to something she does not find acceptable, is this a sign that she feels intimidated and is afraid to say the no that she feels?" If the answer to that question is "yes" or "maybe", a mediator should ask himself, "Is she afraid of me? or of the process? or of her husband?"

In a perfectly conducted mediation, where the mediator has worked to establish rapport with both parties and they have accepted the concept that they, and only they, control the outcome, neither party should be in awe of the mediator or reluctant to tell him he is talking nonsense. But no mediator does his work perfectly, and even those who do it pretty well, most of the time (a high score!) have bad days. So it is right for the mediator to ask himself whether a wife who gives mixed messages is afraid of the mediator, or of the process.

Unfortunately, she may be afraid of her husband. Quite a few women are. (Men can be afraid of their wives, too, but let's stick with the more common situation where it is the wife who feels intimidated.) If we form that hypothesis we will need to test it with great care and very thoroughly, and be sure it is correct, before we act on it. The consequences are serious, as described in Chapter Ten.

One way of checking it may be to look for differences in the way the wife talks to the two other people in the room. If she never argues with her husband, that is one sign, especially if she sometimes "talks back" to the mediator. It can also be a sign of intimidation if she never "talks back" to either. If the mediator notices that when he asks a question, the wife never answers it first, but waits for her husband to respond, that may be another sign. The mediator should be alert for this

58

kind of sign, and fails in his duty if he does not notice it. This can be tested out further by asking questions in an area where she, not her husband, is the expert. If she defers to him in the area of her own expertise, that is a strong indicator of a pattern of intimidation. Yet another test is for a mediator to suggest something that he knows the wife will not like. If she seems reluctant to say no to something he knows she hates, that is a powerful sign of intimidation. But her body language, which she does not consciously control, as she does her words, is the biggest giveaway.

If one party's will overwhelms or dominates the other's the result cannot be a real agreement. It follows that if this emerges during the mediation process the mediator is bound to terminate the process. How he will do so is the only question, and there is no single universal answer to it. He can only hope to find a way that respects the integrity of the process, honours his duty to be truthful and of course does not expose the vulnerable party to any new danger. (We will have more to say about intimidation in Chapter Ten.)

Language

When I started to train aspirant mediators and thought about how to describe the language of mediation, I coined the mnemonic "The three Cs". A mediator's language should be: Clear, Colourless, and Congruent.

Being clear means two things: simplicity and precision. The words used should be as simple as they can be, so that their meaning is not hidden. A mediator should not use words that are not part of ordinary, everyday speech. As the words are simple, so should his sentence structure be. When I was a lawyer, it seemed natural to me to write: "Peter will ensure that, if he is called away from Dublin unexpectedly, he will so inform Nora, at the earliest possible moment, and notify her of an address and/or phone number where, in the event of a crisis, she can contact him." It has taken years for me to unlearn that type of language, and for it to become more natural for me to write: "If Peter has to leave Dublin at short notice, he will let Nora know as soon as he can, and give her a phone number where she can reach him if she needs to." Similarly, "In no circumstances shall either of the spouses do any of the following:" has, at last, become "Neither of us will."

Clarity includes precision. When talking to his clients, the mediator avoids saying anything that is open to misunderstanding, and his record of their bargain should be easily understood and unambiguous. Before he gives it to his clients, the mediator needs to read it carefully, in draft form, and ask himself "could I express this more simply?", and "could anybody misinterpret what I have written? Or somehow twist the words to seem to mean something I do not intend?" Having a colleague read our draft notes critically can be a great help, especially in our early days, when we are inexperienced.

A conscientious mediator will not release a draft note to his clients until he is satisfied that the wording is as good as he is capable of producing. He will put hours of time and effort into preparing the first notes he produces, knowing that time spent in developing skill with the written word will not be wasted. Finally, he will remember what Joan Kelly said, as quoted in Chapter One, that his written record of his clients' agreement is the object of the process, what his clients sought from him, what they will take from the process, and what will be examined by their lawyers. His work as mediator, and the profession of mediation, will be judged more on the quality of his record of their bargain than on anything else.

The second "C", is Colourless, which means we exclude judgemental language. Up to now, I have tried to offer

60

examples from my own work, but I am not going to offer an example of the use of judgemental or prejudicial language from my mediation work or my notes of understanding. There is a limit on how far I am willing to go in humiliating myself in public. Rather, let me quote from the language of the new Catholic catechism, quoted by a clerical correspondent in the letters section of *The Irish Times*. It apparently says legal divorce is "immoral also, because it introduces disorder into the family and into society. This disorder brings grave harm to the deserted spouse, to children traumatised by the separation of their parents, and often torn between them, and because of its contagious effect, which makes it truly a plague on society."

The words I want you to focus on are "deserted" and "contagious". I offer the text, without further comment, as an example of coloured language.

The third "C", Congruent, includes avoiding jargon, and not allowing either your prejudice or your vocabulary to show. For example, I will not tell my clients I think their "communication" is "dysfunctional". I may say: "It seems to me, listening to you both, that your feelings about each other sometimes get in the way when you talk, and you are liable to have misunderstandings. What we have just seen is an example . . . "

The words "custody" and "access" are part of lawyers' vocabulary. To me, custody means imprisonment, and access is what a defending lawyer has when he needs to talk to a client in custody. When my clients read a note I have prepared to record what they have agreed, they will not see the word "custody". They may read: "Important decisions affecting Angela will be made jointly, not by either of us alone, except in emergency. We aim to be equally involved in all decision-making affecting her." They will not see the word "access" but may see: "Angela will live mostly with her Mum, and spend time with her Dad as follows: . . . "

I believe the first of these covers what lawyers call "custody", and the second covers "access" and they do so in language which is more congruent (or less incongruous) with how parents see their children, and aim to look after them.

My last comment on language is that a competent mediator will find out early in the process what the children call their parents, and he will use their language, not his own. For example, if he called his mother: "Mum", and his father "Dad", but his clients' children call their parents "Daddy" and "Mammy", then those are the words he will use, both in talking about the children and in his written record of their parents' bargain.

CHAPTER FOUR

THE BASIC SKILLS OF MEDIATION

Skills and attitude are what make a mediator. Knowledge is secondary. Most people might assume that the knowledge a mediator requires will vary, depending on the area in which he works – that a family mediator needs to know a lot about families, family theory, systemic thinking, and the legal, taxation and fiscal issues affecting families; a mediator who works with partnership and boardroom rows needs to know all about partnership and company law and taxation, and one who works in the construction industry needs to be expert in load-bearing walls and rolled steel joists.

Not so. A mediator is a conflict manager. What he needs to know about is conflict, how it manifests itself, how it affects our behaviour, and how it can be controlled, redirected and resolved. Indeed, he needs more than simply to know about conflict: he needs to understand. Any moderately intelligent person, with access to suitable textbooks, could absorb the required knowledge in less than a week's not too taxing work. But he would then spend years converting his knowledge into understanding, and internalising his skills before he could be justified in saying: "I am a mediator!"

If he is going to work in a specialised area he needs to have a sense of how the law and any other limiting factors operate, so that he can anticipate problems and develop a sense of whether one party is trying to pull the wool over the other's eyes, but he does not need to be expert in any area of knowledge relevant to how the parties live or work. Indeed, there are good reasons why he should not be. The first is that a mediator has no prospect of having the same level of expertise on his clients' business as they do, so that, in any discussions about the detail of it, he will be the most ignorant person present. Secondly, the more he concentrates on such matters, the more his attention is likely to be distracted from his area of expertise, which is what the parties pay him for: namely his ability to understand, manage and resolve conflict.

The range of skills a mediator needs – or, rather, that parties in conflict need from him – are a little less primitive than his knowledge-base, but they are simply stated. They consist of:

Client-related skills

These cover how we communicate with our clients, both in words and otherwise. Communication is a two-way process: it is at least as important that the mediator listens to and understands what his clients say as that they hear and understand what he says. What we say will not be worth listening to if it does not come from a good understanding. We gain that understanding by close attention to their words and their body language.

Client-related skills include:
- deciding what to say, and what not to say;
- receiving the clients' verbal and non-verbal messages;
- communicating messages that suit their circumstances;
- establishing rapport; earning the trust of our clients;
- listening attentively, which includes "listening" to our clients' body language;

- applying a range of simple "techniques" some of which I describe in Chapters Seven and Eight;
- remaining impartial and non-judgemental;
- being in touch with our own prejudices and sensitive to other people's values, so as to remain impartial;
- "empowering" our clients;
- not allowing them to transfer power back to us;

Process-related skills

These are the skills a mediator needs to maintain control of the process, make it as comfortable as possible for his clients, and keep them focussed on their task. The skills needed include recognising triangulation and learning how to deal with it; and understanding our own feelings and prejudices, and attitude to conflict. They also include exercising judgement on how rigidly the mediator should keep control over what happens in the process.

Topic-related skills

These include: identifying genuine issues; distinguishing issues from non-issues, and eliminating the latter; separating interests from positions, and eliminating add-ons; establishing criteria for examining issues; listing options and placing them in the clients' order of preference; helping to approach intractable problems imaginatively.

Finally what I call **"literary skills"**

These consist of recording on paper what the clients have agreed, in suitable language. What I say in Chapter Three about the language of mediation applies equally to the language a mediator uses to record what his clients have agreed. The language needs to follow "the three "Cs" – *clear*, *colourless*, and *congruent*. And when I come to work on the note I will prepare of what they have agreed, I include a "fourth C" – *colloquial* – to remind me that when I record their bargain I should not write it as though I were still working as a lawyer.

These are all simple skills, easy to understand, and not hard to apply. A professional mediator is someone who understands a range of simple skills and knows how to apply them, but he should be a lot more than that. To have acquired and *internalised* a range of skills, so that he can apply them instinctively to the resolution of his clients' conflicts, and an attitude of mind towards conflict and its resolution that will enable those skills to be productive, is the objective of a mediator's training and practice, and the essence of his work.

While the skills may be applied instinctively, the work must be done self-critically. We need to go over what happened during each session, and examine what we did, and ask how, when, and why? Sometimes we will say it went well, and feel entitled to credit for that. At other times we will say: the way I handled that session was disastrous, and I must seriously ask myself whether someone who can make such foolish blunders should continue as a mediator. Is it fair to my clients?

On the "should I give up" feeling, let me say two things. First, of all the times in a mediator's life when he needs a mentor, this is the time he needs one most. A good mentor will either encourage us to persevere and learn from our mistakes, or support us in a decision to give up the work, if that is our decision. Secondly, if we often ask ourselves the question: "should someone as incompetent as I am stay on in this line of work?" there is a good chance that the right answer will be "yes". A mediator who does not ask himself that question often, sincerely and painfully, has fallen into complacency. He offers a service without constant self-criticism and mental strife – that is, without striving to produce his best. And he fails to treat his clients with respect.

Internalising

I mentioned "internalising" earlier. For the purpose of this chapter, I would put it this way: a good basic training in mediation should equip each trainee with a tool-box full of ways of dealing constructively with other people's conflicts, an understanding of what the process is about, and a reduced risk of making major blunders. That is about all that any training can offer.

A mediator who has taken a basic training, and starts with his first clients, will very soon ask himself what my guru John Haynes, described as the constantly recurring question in a mediator's work: "What the **** do I do now?" The training is his standby. He can open the box, peer inside, and select whatever tool seems to be most likely to help at that moment. Later, with more experience and confidence, he will know his way around the toolbox without having to look inside. If, at a given moment, he decides he needs a spanner to separate a particularly tightly locked couple, he will be able to put his hand into the box, and find the spanner, by feel, without breaking eye-contact with the clients.

Later again, with further experience, he may find that when he needs a spanner, he no longer has to put his hand into the toolbox to find one. When a spanner is needed, his hand has become a spanner, without any thought or conscious decision on his part. At that stage, he may not even realise that he has used a spanner, any more than an experienced driver has noticed that he changed gear as he approached a sharp curve. He did not do it: his hand and foot operated without needing to be told to by his conscious mind.

The story told by the mediator's notes may be very different at his stage from what they would have told in his earlier days. They will no longer say: "I decided to reality-test the parenting arrangements, and asked: What will happen if Peter has to work late at short notice?" They will more likely say: "They clarified that if Peter had to work late at short notice it would be up to him to contact Nora; that a message on her answering machine would not be enough, as she might not get it; and that unless she had agreed to vary the plan it would be up to him to ensure the children were collected. They recognised that if Nora was un-cooperative, it could put Peter in a spot, and she will co-operate as far as possible. If they hit snags on this, they will come back to me."

He does not mention reality-testing because he is no longer conscious that it is what he did. The technique is now part of him. He applies it without thinking of it.

This is fine, and, indeed, it is the sign of a mature, fully self-trained mediator, but it is only fine during the session with clients, and only so long as things go well. In the unceasing self-examination that the mediator will continue to conduct after each session, he will regularly "de-construct" what happened, and when he does this he will recall clearly what happened. He may not remember what techniques he used, but he will be vividly aware of those he might have used and did not.

"Internalising", then, is a name for the process by which we continue to use the techniques we have learnt, but cease to apply them consciously. (See also the beginning of Chapter Seven.)

Attitude

Having talked about techniques, let me say something about attitude. An outsider might assume that an attitude of wanting to help to resolve conflict was what was required of a

68

mediator. It is not as simple as that. Indeed we sometimes show indifference to our clients' wish to resolve their conflict, if that seems the right approach at a given moment.

From what I have observed in myself and other mediators, we share an attitude towards conflict. What we feel, when we see conflict approaching, is terror. Most mediators hate disputes, and when they cannot avoid becoming personally involved as disputants, handle them badly – probably worse than the average. In one way, you might say that mediators are like cowards who when war breaks out are the first to enlist, so as not to be found out. But I think it may be more accurate to say that many of us become involved in trying to resolve other people's conflicts, because we are afraid to face conflicts in our own lives, where we are parties, not outsiders. Being mediators allows us to look at what we most fear, but from a safe distance. A bit like going to horror films.

We do not start with a constructive attitude to conflict; we have to develop it, and the process takes longer than you might think. Looking back, I think I have passed through a number of stages. And some of them have a familiar look, which makes me think I may have met them more than once.

Different people will take different paths, but I suspect most of us pass similar staging points, not necessarily in the same order. One of the first, for most of us, is panic: what will I do if they start to scream at each other? When we find we can handle high conflict, panic is often followed by a sense of liberation, and even exhilaration: I can ride the storm and survive.

The next phase may be: not only do I want to survive the storm, but I want to learn to control it. I don't want to spend the rest of my life as a cork, bobbing on the waters, even though it is nice to know I won't sink. I want to be like a sailing boat that uses the winds, even at storm force, to bring me in the direction I have chosen. If the wind blows in the right direction, I will ride it. If it blows the wrong way, I don't mind tacking, and going on a devious journey, because I know I can guide myself to the destination I seek. The sense of being able not just to ride the storm but to control it, and even to use the winds to generate electric power (to change the metaphor) is hugely exciting. This is a stage that some of us stay in, and most of us re-visit.

Oddly enough, there is another phase, quite like that of being satisfied to survive, but subtly different. It involves not just being pleased to have got through a session, but actually enjoying the storm. There is a sense of pleasure, indeed, of harmony, in being a cork on stormy waters. I don't mind it when huge breakers crash over me, because I know that, being made of cork, I am lighter than water, and it doesn't matter how many waves break over me, or how huge they are: I will always come back to the surface. When I am there, I will look around, and describe what I see, but I will not try to move in any direction.

However, not all a mediator's time is taken up with surviving storms. Often we help people to navigate in fairly calm waters. Here again, our attitudes may change. A mediator starting out with his first couple will feel very tense. (If he doesn't, he should be in a different line of work.) If the first clients who come to him leave without agreeing, his gut will tell him this is his failure, even if his mind says it is not. If his clients agree, he will feel validated. "I brought them to agreement!"

Not all his clients will reach agreement. (If they do, I do not know what he is doing, but it is not mediation.) He may become more relaxed about the outcome. The quality of his work improves strikingly. He will then start to evolve in a different direction, and say, to himself, if not to his clients: "I do not mind what they decide, provided I am satisfied that I have done my job adequately. That I have created calm, as far

70

as possible, and that they understood the issues, their options, and the likely consequences of each option." Later again, he may pass through a phase of taking an even more detached approach, but he will not maintain detachment for long. Or he may come to feel that, while it is important that the clients understand their options, and choose the one best suited to their needs, leading to "satisfaction", it is even more important that they develop and refine a different approach to the business of making choices. This has been called "transformation", but I prefer to describe it as "converting the clients into a machine that can fix itself if it goes wrong".

Let me say just one final thing about a mediator's attitude. It should not be fixed. I think about my work as a mediator today quite differently from how I thought about it last year. I have not rejected last year's ideas, but have moved on, and am excited about new ones. Last year, my pet notion was that our task is to take our clients out of the trench, and help them to view the landscape. This year, I am enthused about the sense of being seen by each party to share in their experience. Next year, if I should still be working in this field, I should be very excited about another approach, or I should have rediscovered something that I knew already, but now see in a different light. Our understanding about what we are doing changes as we continue to work, and discover new challenges in the work. If our sense about it becomes static, instead of changing, we have problems. Our clients have problems. And we exist as mediators only to serve our clients.

What I see as the unchanging core of our attitude seems to have been summed up by Samuel Beckett, though I have not yet traced the source: "No matter. Try again. Fail again. Fail better."

CHAPTER FIVE

HOW MEDIATORS WORK

Couples who decide to separate have four ways of implementing that decision, each of which will produce a different answer to the question: who is going to make the decisions that have to be made in consequence of our separating?

1) They can go to court, where the decision-making function will be exercised by a stranger – a judge.

In court, the strengths of the arguments the parties' lawyers can advance, often based largely on accusations of past misconduct, will determine the outcome. What has happened in the past determines what will happen in the future.

2) They can both retain legal representatives, and have their separation agreement negotiated for them by their lawyers.

When lawyers negotiate, the outcome will in theory reflect two things, and in practice will usually reflect three. First of course is the instructions the lawyer has received from his client. (For the purpose of this book, lawyers, like mediators and unlike therapists, are male.) The lawyer will try to negotiate the deal the client wants.

Second, it will reflect the views each lawyer forms of the strengths and weaknesses of his client's case, and the case the opposition could advance if they fought out their marital discord in court. It has been said that the outcome of lawyers' negotiation is often the same as that of a court hearing, but without the judge, and that this validates the performance of both lawyers. They hope to produce a result no worse for their clients than if the case had been dealt with in court, on the basis that past events determine "liability", and, hence, future actions. Their negotiations will produce a result that will differ from a likely court decision only to the extent that one lawyer is more skilled in negotiation than the other, or that one client has instructed his or her lawyer to make a concession he would otherwise have refused.

Of course, if the client has fallen into a colonised relationship with his lawyer (Chapter Two) it is unlikely the lawyer will have received specific instructions contrary to his advice. It is hard for a colonised party to issue dictation to its colonial governor.

The third ingredient that has a major – though often unconscious – influence on the flavour of a dish prepared by lawyer negotiation is the lawyers' value systems.

These value systems may be based on professional experience, and be worthy of respect, or they may come from *assumptions* the lawyer has drawn from his own life experience. More often than lawyers themselves recognise, they may be dictated by a "hidden agenda" related to the lawyer's own life. As an example of life-experience colouring the lawyer's attitude, let's assume a lawyer, a married man whose wife does not work outside the home, but works full-time caring for their children. Assume he works very long hours, and, in consequence, spends little time with his children. He may approach negotiating a separation agreement with an assumption that his way of life is "normal", and how things should be. He may not be sensitive to a client wife's wish to return to a career she interrupted, or a client husband's craving not to be isolated from his children.

The hidden agenda may flavour the eventual dish in

different way. What if the lawyer feels guilty about working such long hours, and fears he is a neglectful father? What if his relationship with his own wife is in crisis, and the relationship between his client and his or her spouse has echoes of his own deteriorating marriage? We cannot foretell how much these additional ingredients will affect the separation agreement he collaborates in negotiating. The only thing we can be sure of is that they will affect it.

3) The couple can negotiate their separation without outside help.

It can be done, but I think only exceptional people can do it really well. A couple seeking to negotiate their separation one-to-one may try to look at the interests of all involved, but they are starting their negotiations at a time when, probably more strongly and vividly than any other in their lives, they are dominated by their emotions, including guilt, shame, resentment, anger, depression and fear. It is not easy to be rational with all of these seething inside you. It is even harder when you have to negotiate and discuss with the person who, more than anyone else, you regard as the cause of your misery, and who excites these powerful emotions within you. The danger is that these feelings will push them into confrontation rooted in their relationship as spouses in the past, and away from co-operation as parents in the future.

If these feelings intrude in mediation – as anyone can imagine they must, and mediators know from experience they do – we can assume that couples who do not use mediation confront the same problem with even greater intensity.

4) Finally, they can negotiate it with help of a mediator.

The process

A family mediator does not need much equipment: a room where he will not be interrupted, three chairs and a box of tissues. That is all. He arranges the three chairs in a triangle,

74

all about three feet apart, facing into the centre of the triangle, and places the box of tissues near the chair he is going to occupy, so that he can hand it to either client as needed. He is now in business. All he needs is clients. When they arrive, he tells them to sit in two of the chairs, he sits in the third, and the process starts.

The first and most important thing a mediator's clients need to do is to trust their mediator. His first duty is to earn their trust. Let me emphasise the word "earn". We gain the trust of our clients by showing ourselves to be worthy of it. We keep it by continuing to show ourselves to be trustworthy. We aim to earn our clients' trust in a number of different ways, but the essential one is by being scrupulously truthful. I discuss this in more detail in Chapter Twelve, where I talk about a mediator's ethical duties.

My last word, for the moment, about the clients' trust in their mediator is that earning it is a continuing process. We set out to gain their confidence, and aim to ensure we do not to lose it during the process. And always by giving them the same, truthful, message: "You can trust me, because I am trustworthy."

In theory, the steps in the mediation process are defined, and occur in an orderly sequence. We explain the process and get the clients' agreement to it, and to the ground rules within which we will work. Then we assemble the agenda, that is, establish the areas where the parties need help in reaching agreement. Next we ask whether further information is needed in order that each agenda item can be discussed. If information has to be collected we identify who will collect it. ("Okay. Peter will find out about rights under his pension scheme. Joan will check how much is outstanding on the mortgage, and how long it has to run, and find out if Miriam is going to need orthodontistry. She will also talk to Miriam's teacher about her behaviour in class, and let us know what

75

the teacher said, next time we meet.") When relevant information has been identified, gathered and shared, options are developed and negotiation takes place. Finally, if it has been successful, the mediator records the agreement, and amends his record as the clients direct. This brings the process to an end.

Postponing negotiation

The mediator must be aware of the logic of the ordered sequence, but he should be responsive to his clients' needs, and not arbitrarily refuse to discuss topics they feel are pressing. More often than not, a couple will want to plunge into negotiation at once on the one item that most bothers them. This is when the mediator has his first panic attack. He asks himself: "Do I cut this discussion short now? If I do, I am establishing my control over the process, and that may be good. On the other hand, if they are really keen to discuss it, and I don't let them, I may alienate them. Is there any reason not to let them talk about it?" Will I lose control over the process if I try to stop a negotiation, and fail? If I lose control temporarily, will I be able to regain it?" In my experience, if you lose control, it is very hard to regain it, but if you *relinquish* control temporarily, it is easy to reassert it.

There is no universal answer. Mediation is not a science. It is a performance art. If the mediator thinks that by working on that problem now, when they want to, they will lessen the prospect of reaching an over-all agreement, he should exercise his process control and not allow discussion of that issue at that time. He may assess with one set of clients that their prospects of working out a bargain will be better if he has done a reframe (Chapter Seven) on this topic, before they start to negotiate on it. With different clients he may decide: "they want to talk about the topic so badly that if I decide to postpone, they won't concentrate on anything else, and we will make no progress until it has been aired". Later he may decide "this topic is getting them so excited and upset that we are in danger of moving backwards. They need to be better prepared for this topic, so I will switch from it".

Whatever decision he makes, he should be open to reverse it at any moment. If he relinquishes the power to move from topic to topic he has substantially lost control over the process.

Few good mediators are consistent in how they treat the agenda. Nor should they be: an unpredictable mediator is worth more to his clients than a predictable one.

Surely, you may be thinking, a mediator should aim to be consistent? Yes, I reply, with deliberate inconsistency, and no. We should be consistent, in the sense that our clients should feel they can rely on us. There should never be a question mark in our clients' minds about our honesty, truthfulness and ethical standards. But if we are predictable in other ways, our usefulness may be curtailed. If a mediator aims to transform his clients from people stuck in conflictual communication into joint problem-solvers, he sets himself up as an agent of change. Modelling flexibility in what he does may be a good way of helping them to become more flexible.

However, there are two situations where I will not allow negotiation. The first is where the rules under which the process is to run have not been agreed between the parties and the mediator. If I allow negotiation to start before they have agreed that any discussions will be off the record, I may find myself caught in the middle in a dispute about whether, even if that concept is agreed later, it applies to the discussions that took place before it was agreed.

The other is where I diagnose that negotiation would be "premature". I do not want to discuss that concept in depth in this book, so let me just say that I think of negotiation as premature if the parties need more information or understanding about an issue (either in itself or in relation to other issues) in order to negotiate on it rationally. An example from marital mediation would be discussing income support at a time when one party is unemployed, expecting a job offer, but does not know if it will materialise, or if it does what the starting salary will be.

I am not talking here about identifying the topics to be discussed, but about serious negotiation on a topic. A mediator can say at any time: "I can see that this issue is important to you both, and we are going to have to spend time on it, to be sure we get it right. But tell me are there other issues on which you need to agree?" Or, if there is a pause, he can readily steer the conversation away from the doubtful topic by asking something like: "For example, have you agreed where Peter should go to school next September?"

If an issue needs to be reframed (Chapter Seven), the reframe is needed before they start to negotiate on it. I may use my process-control to prevent serious negotiation on an issue until I have reframed it, or decided a re frame is not needed.

I aim to prevent serious negotiation on any one topic until I am confident that the couple have given me a complete list of all the topics on which they need to agree. This is because apparently unrelated topics may be linked in a way that is not obvious.

Finally on this, if one party seems to need more time than the other to reach decisions or take advice, it can be helpful to suggest they take time out to allow second thoughts to develop, or to decide if they are happy with what has emerged to date.

Mediator control

If we are too fixated on remaining in control we can lose touch with how the process is moving. I remember a couple I worked with in my early days as a mediator. For two sessions, neither would listen to what the other said. They each made speeches to me, which I fed back to the other. I then carefully fed back to the first speaker the response of the second, not to the first speaker's oration, but to my re-statement of it.

I felt secure. I was sanitising their communication, and was in complete control of the process. No communication took place, except through me. I was like a telephone switch-board operator: all phone calls passed through my machine. If I pulled the plug, there would be silence. The problem was that I could not see how to move them out of this mode of non-communication. It was good training in the technique of feedback (Chapter Seven) for an inexperienced mediator, but not much else.

They both chain-smoked – this was before I made a no-smoking rule – each from his or her own packet. At the beginning of the third session, the husband produced his packet of poison, hesitated, and then, grudgingly, with his hand held only halfway, offered the packet to his wife. She hesitated and then took one. Early in that session, the husband first addressed a remark to his wife instead of to me. She replied, and they began to talk directly. I panicked. I had become redundant. What should I do? Luckily, I remembered some good advice: if you don't know what to do, do nothing. After a few minutes of silence on my part, I realised that what was happening – the two of them communicating directly with each other – had been what I had been working for throughout the previous two sessions. And I allowed myself a moment of self-congratulation.

Nowadays, I would not allow non-communication to continue for anything like two sessions. I might start with feedback, but if the parties did not talk to each other, I would find a way to break down their silence. Perhaps by falling silent myself.

A mediator's assumptions

A mediator starts with two assumptions which he will be reluctant to abandon. One is that the needs of the people affected by the separation are more important than their legal rights. He will hold to that assumption, perhaps even against resistance from the couple, unless it becomes clear they are not willing to negotiate on that basis. (He may then have to decide whether he should continue the process.)

In his mind, if not always with his mouth, he will be asking questions that focus on the phases of their lives they are entering, not the phases they are leaving:

(To the wife) What do you need to get on with your life to best advantage, following separation from your husband?

(To the husband) What do you need to get on with your life to best advantage, following your separation from your wife?

(To both of them) What do your children need to get on with their lives to best advantage, following their parents' separation?

The last question is one question only, if the couple have only one child. If not, it is as many different questions as there are children. What does Joe need? What does Samantha need? The answers from each parent to each of these questions about each child, may be different. Children may each need their parents to accept and accommodate that difference.

The mediator's second assumption is that human beings are born with the ability to make rational decisions, and live their lives on the basis of those decisions. He believes that a way of life from which reason and logic are excluded is less likely to be fulfilling for those who live it than one in which the use of the reasoning faculty has had an influence. (Of course he recognises that a life based on pure reason, with emotional factors excluded, is sterile, but he also recognises that if reason is excluded, and decisions are based only on emotions, this too may lead to disaster.)

He also believes that the ability to be logical and reasonable as well as loving and tender is important in bringing up children. He believes in bringing up children so that they can engage in tender, loving relationships with others, and, perhaps, bring into the world children of their own whom they may bring up in the same way.

He is a mediator because he wants to help people in crisis. He recognises that the values he brings to his work leave him open to becoming a colonist, and he is determined not to let that happen.

"Transformation"

I say in Chapter One that mediation, which aims to resolve conflict, not just to determine it, is most useful for people who are in conflict and cannot avoid each other altogether for the future. Mediators want their clients to develop an ability to negotiate one to one, and not to need to come back to mediation, later. I call this helping my clients to become a "machine that fixes itself".

Most parents who separate recognise – and those who do not, find out – that the arrangements they make for each of them to share in their children's lives will need to be revised as the children grow up. A baby can be picked up, moved, and put down. A six-year-old may resist being picked up, but if she is told she is going to be with Dad next weekend, she may trot off with him, obediently and happily. A sixteen-year-old will decide where she is going to stay next weekend, and her decision will probably be made on the basis of where her friends are going to be, more than on her parents' hopes or feelings. If staying with Dad does not fit in with her plans, she will say so, and very likely refuse to go. Parenting arrangements put in place when a daughter was six years old, will no longer function effectively ten years later. They will need to be modified, probably several times, during that ten years.

Parents are also likely to need to agree revised arrangements for financial support for their children, as the children grow older. Anyone who has brought up children will agree that they grow more expensive every year. If arrangements for financial support are not adjusted or are adjusted only in light of changes in the cost of living, the standard of living in the children's home will decline.

So ideally, our clients will need to be able to renegotiate their bargain without outside help. That is, to transform themselves into a machine that can fix itself if it goes wrong. This is a huge change. It is from being people who only express their own viewpoint, and if it is contradicted, repeat it, louder, into people who listen to the other's viewpoint, and try to understand it.

Who decides that this is what the clients want? When I start working with clients, as soon as we have gone through the preliminaries, I usually ask what are the areas where they are in conflict and need to reach agreement? These will almost always include matters with two recurring characteristics: they will need to be renegotiated in the future; and they cannot be resolved effectively unless each party gains some understanding of the other party's needs. When each recognises that the other has legitimate needs, and that the needs of all the family will change, they usually recognise that they need to become "a machine that can repair itself". Even if they have not been expressly asked if this is what they want and said yes, it will often be clear that it is.

The timing of asking that question – or not asking it – is

important. Suppose a couple come to me, and I ask them in the first ten minutes: "Do you want me to help you to work out an agreement, now, full stop? Or would you like me to help you to change your relationship in such a way that you will be able to work out future problems and not have to come back to me?" Most people would probably say: "Don't be absurd." The fact is that this is not an absurd ambition for most separating couples. Not easy, but not impossible either. Mark Twain was once asked whether he believed in baptism, and replied: "I don't have to believe in it. I have seen it done."

As the process changes from one of confrontation to one of mutual recognition of shared problems, and mutual efforts to resolve them, the question I did not ask begins to seem realistic. At that point, I may ask it. But more often than not I won't, because the answer is clear, and by asking I may disturb a delicate balance within the process.

The tempo of the process

I find a musical analogy helpful here. Music becomes monotonous if the performer keeps the same steady tempo throughout. A good performer will sometimes slow the tempo, and sometimes accelerate. In Harry Plunket Greene's book *Interpretation in Song* which I mention throughout this book because I have found it so useful to me in my work, he says, "practically every song has at least one point, if not more than one, in which it pays to spread out the phrase, and hold up the rhythm, and it is not that holding up which pays in itself, but *the resumption of the 'tempo primo'*." (His emphasis.) He also makes the point that "rubato" – slowing down fractionally, "stealing" a few fractions of a second from what strict tempo requires – works only if the performer has the strict tempo in his pulse, and later repays what he has stolen. I am happy to allow my clients to steal some time

83

from what a tightly timed and structured mediation process would dictate because I believe we will work better when we get back to the original tempo. I have come to feel I can rely on my sense of what that tempo should be with my clients, as I get to know them. Indeed, I often save them the trouble of stealing time by stealing it for them.

Talking about the tempo of the process reminds me that years ago, on holidays in Crete, my wife and I met a group of Swiss people, all middle-aged, all tough, who went on walking tours together. They took long walks, but always seemed relaxed and fresh at the end of the day. We wondered how they managed, until we were told that their rule was to walk for fifty-five minutes, and rest for five.

There is a message here for mediators. If we think of the process as a journey and of ourselves as guides, we should remember that the journey is hard, the path steep, and most of our clients are not in training for this kind of exercise. We should try to help them to get to the journey's end as soon as they comfortably can, but remember that they may droop from fatigue along the way, or feel like giving up. If one party finds the going easier at a particular stage in the journey and can walk on, but the other cannot, we should hold him back, because we do not want to be out of earshot of either party. If we work our clients hard at one stage in the journey, we may let them take a rest when they reach a suitable resting place. They may need it. They may also be inspired to further efforts if they have been allowed breathing-space, and a chance to realise how far they have come, and to admire the view. However, we should remember that they are with us only because they need us as guides on their journey. We are not doing what we are being paid for if we sit around chatting with them. We should let them have the rest they need and no more, and as soon as they are able to move on, we should start up again.

This reminds me of another essential truth: the tempo of the process, that is, the speed at which it should move, *should not be faster than the highest speed that the slower-moving party at that time can be persuaded to accept*. The word "persuade" is important. So are the words "at that time". A mediator should not pressurise his clients to move faster than they are willing to. And I say "at that time" because the slowest-moving party will not always be the same person. Differences of mood and feeling can influence tempo. So can differences of expertise in the subject under discussion. A mediator needs to keep an eye on both parties, and make sure the process moves at a speed that keeps us all in the same group.

Unbalanced bargains

There are situations where I think a mediator may become involved in the content of his clients' bargain. One is if they are on the point of agreeing something he knows cannot be the basis of an effective agreement, for example, if it is illegal. Under Irish law parents are legally obliged to maintain their children, and an agreement between parents to release one of them from that legal obligation would be illegal. If the mediator knows that, and they do not, he should become involved in content – perhaps by suggesting they seek legal advice.

What if the parties are about to enter into an agreement that is so unbalanced, so clearly loaded in favour of one party that the mediator knows that, as soon as the other party's lawyer sees the "agreement" he will blow it out of the water? (I try to ignore the likelihood that the lawyer will probably also remove my name from the list of people he recommends!) The mediator has to exercise judgement, and has little time to decide whether the agreement is merely unusual or so odd that there is no prospect of it passing through the legal process. The first is within the parties' area of expertise, and the mediator has no right to intervene. The other is closer to the "non-agreement" described above, which is ineffective from the beginning because it infringes legal principle. Luckily, I do not think the mediator has to decide on which side of that line the bargain falls, because his response will be much the same either way. The conversation might go like this:

> *Mediator:* "Let me be sure I have this clear. I think you are agreeing [summary]? Is that right?"

[Answer: Yes.]

> *Mediator:* "Okay. Fine. I have a concern, and perhaps we should take a few minutes to discuss it. I don't think Paul's solicitor will have any problem with that. I am worried about Eva's. Not many people I have worked with have made an agreement along those lines.
>
> "That is not my worry. Eva knows what she is doing, and has negotiated this bargain fairly with Paul, and is satisfied with it. What worries me is how Eva's solicitor will react? Will he advise her that the division of assets is unfair, and she should not agree to it?
>
> "Is there even a danger that Eva's solicitor will want to renegotiate the bargain? I have known that to happen. Indeed, I have worked with people who made a bargain they were satisfied with, and seen the entire thing unravel afterwards because lawyers disapproved, and tried to renegotiate it.
>
> Is there anything the three of us can do to try to avoid that happening? For example, is it worth while to spend a few minutes working out how Eva might explain this to her solicitor, so that he won't feel bound to throw a spanner in the works?"

The difference may be that in one situation the parties may find a formula that Eva can produce to her solicitor that will discourage him from reopening the negotiations, and in the other, they will not be able to find such a formula because it does not exist. If I have used similar language in both situations, I have not gone beyond my role by interfering in the content of their agreement. In fact, I have "reality-tested" the bargain (Chapter Eight). The result of the test is determined by the parties, and by the nature of the bargain they have made.

The eleven camels

There is an old story about an Arab who died, leaving eleven camels to be divided among his three sons. His will said his eldest was to get half his camels, the next one-quarter, and the youngest one-sixth. The three boys tried to work out how to give effect to their father's wishes, and, after they had reached impasse, decided to ask a wise man for advice. When they came to his home with the camels and explained the problem, he said: "This is a difficult problem, and I would like to reflect on it overnight. Put your camels in my paddock with my camel, and we will eat together."

The next morning they went to the paddock, and the wise man said: "Here are twelve camels. Let the eldest take the half his father left him, which is six. Let the next take three, which is the one-quarter his father left him. And let the youngest take one sixth, that is, two camels. That leaves one camel over. That camel is mine, and I will keep it."

The story is based on a sort of arithmetical paradox, but I think it has lessons for mediators. The first lesson is that a conflict may be more complex than it seems at first. Clearly, each boy wants his inheritance. But the story suggests that they also want to respect their father's wishes. And they want to find a solution which will enable each to say two things: "I have acted honourably", and "I have been treated honourably and fairly by my brothers".

87

In my work as mediator of family disputes, I have been very impressed by how many people want both of these things, as well as their rights. They want to respect the wishes and needs of other people affected by their dispute; they also, almost always, want to find a resolution of their conflict that will allow them to say the last two things: "I have behaved fairly" and "I have been treated fairly." It is striking and inspiring to find that most spouses in a mediation that goes well will not try to take an unfair advantage of the other.

It may not be sensible to read too much into the fable of the camels, but it seems to me that the wise man's camel, as well as a hump, a valuable coat, and a supercilious expression, has these characteristics: it supplements its owner's wisdom and goodwill towards solving the problem; it is an essential ingredient in solving it; it is brought into the solution of the problem; it is still in his possession when the problem has been solved and the disputants go away. In these ways the camel seems to symbolise the skills and techniques that a mediator brings to his work.

Outside advice

A problem some people have in accepting mediation is that the process requires people to make major decisions without an adviser present, and so they may not get expert advice at a time when they need it. I think the answer to this lies in the choice of mediator. If people go to a responsible, professional mediator with good standards, they will not be asked to make decisions without having an opportunity to take the advice they need.

I am told some mediators extract from their clients an undertaking not to consult a lawyer during the mediation process. In my view, this is inconsistent with good standards. The message I give my clients is that they will have to make decisions, but not snap decisions; that when decision-making time comes, they will have the opportunity to reflect before they decide; that if they feel they need advice, they should take it, and that even if they have recorded an agreement in my room they are free to change their minds, right up to the end of the process. I want them to get that message, partly because I want them not to feel pressurised by me or by the process – they are under enough pressure already – and partly because I believe people who need to make decisions should not be deprived of advice. But, even more, I believe that a considered, voluntary decision is one that will last.

Pausing for thought

The fable of the camels reminds us that it is sometimes helpful to allow yourself time to reflect on a difficult issue. Giving myself time to think was something I found hard when I was starting out as a young lawyer. I assumed any client who brought a problem to me would expect an instant answer, and if I failed to produce one I identified myself as incompetent. It took me years to learn to say: "This is not a straightforward problem. I will not advise you now, but will let you have my advice later", and if they objected, to say, "the advice you get from me later will be better than you would get from me now, if you insisted on an immediate answer." Much the same is true in mediation work. There are situations where clients need their mediator to respond at once. If he does not, the process may be endangered. There are also situations where the mediator will best serve his clients by changing the topic of conversation, so as to give himself time to ponder.

Of course, mediators are not the only people in the process who may need time to think. Clients often do, too. Two things I have often said and rarely regretted are: "This is a tricky problem. I suggest we all give it a bit more thought, and take it up again at our next session. Meanwhile, let's talk about . . . " and "this is a major decision for Valerie, and I do not think she should feel she has to take it now. I think she should have time to reflect on it, and, perhaps, take advice, and see what she thinks about it after she has slept on it."

Just in case anyone thought otherwise, I do not use the second of those two "lines" only when I think Valerie is taking a bad decision which she may later regret. I say it, too, when I get the sense that she will take her decision with more confidence, and be better able to put it into practice, if she will not look back on it later and wonder was it taken too quickly.

Incidentally, I have found that women usually welcome and accept the opportunity for second thoughts. Men may thank you for suggesting they take more time, but will say much more often than women: "No thanks, Michael. I don't need more time. I have made up my mind, and that's it."

And there are still people who believe women are more vain than men.

The journey

Going back to the analogy with a journey with the mediator as guide, where the clients determine the destination they have chosen, and their guide has no input into that decision, I think he may check that they understand what their chosen destination will be like. For example, I have often said:

> "Almost every family I have worked with has experienced a drop in living standards after their separation. It is inevitable, if the same income has to be spread over two homes."

and:

> "Most people I have worked with found that, as children grow up more, they cost more money. If people start out with an agreed level of support for a household with

young children in it, and agree to adjust the level of it only in line with cost of living changes, the household the children live in may have problems down the road."

I see these as equivalent to a guide saying "It can be pretty cold where you are going. Have you packed thermal underwear?"

In an extreme situation I think a mediator-guide is entitled to say: "If that is where you have decided you want to go, you will have to find your own way there or get another guide, because I am not willing to guide you there."

This is a very powerful statement, and a mediator should make it only if he feels ethically bound to stop the process. It would be a major misuse of a mediator's power and an abuse of his relationship with his clients if he terminated because he thought they were unwise in their choice of destination. In effect he would be saying: "Go where I think you should, or travel without my help." I would only say this if I had no other ethically acceptable choice, and had discussed it with a respected colleague.

How can a mediator be a guide over terrain that is different for each couple? It is notorious that Irishmen rarely answer a question, and prefer to offer a counter-question, and my answer to it is "How can anyone be a pilot on the Mississippi?" From Mark Twain we learn that the river constantly changes, and where there was a clear channel on the last voyage there may now be a mudflat, and where there was a mudflat there may now be a clear channel. The skill of the pilot lies in his ability to interpret what he sees and hears so as to understand what lies beneath the surface, and to guide his boat to its destination as quickly as possible but not risking ship-wreck along the way.

I understand that it is not easy to be a Mississippi pilot. Neither is it easy to be a good professional mediator. If it were, neither the pilot nor the mediator would need to take training, or to strive, hard and continuously, to do it better. An incompetent pilot will be found out quickly. A mediator can hide lack of professional competence for longer. It would be hard to say which of the two carries the greater responsibility. The consequences of pilot incompetence can be measured straight off, in money. If a marital mediator handles his clients' separation without professional competence the results will not be measured in cash terms, and his blunders may affect later generations as well as the people he works with.

He learns to be a guide over waters that are always changing, to read the signs on the surface in order to understand the depths, and to adapt himself to endless change, because he realises that is the sort of guide his clients need.

CHAPTER SIX

STYLES OF NEGOTIATION

A lawyer who works in the area of marital breakup once explained to me why he does not recommend his female clients to try marital mediation, by giving an example of a negotiation he had been involved in. His client was a tough businessman whose marriage had come to an end. The lawyers negotiated, and when the only outstanding issue was the amount of a lump sum he would pay his wife, this man told his lawyer: "Phone her lawyer and say she can have £50,000 provided she accepts it within 48 hours. Say if she doesn't come back with a response within that time, the deal is off and I'll see her in court. She won't have the nerve to hold out: you'll find she'll accept that offer." He was right.

Having learnt the lesson that some people buckle under pressure and that some businessmen exploit that weakness, the lawyer decided that if he were acting for a wife in a future case, he would not expose her to an unprotected situation, such as mediation, where she might be a victim of such pressure. I respect his reasons, but think he did not properly grasp how mediation works, and how a competent mediator would handle that sort of bullying negotiation.

I usually deal with it not by confronting it, but by pre-empting it. When I meet a couple for the first time, I explain my ground-rules, and that the reason I propose these rules is that I have found they enable me to give them the best service I can. We discuss and agree them, perhaps with modifications. They include being off the record, not interrupting, full disclosure of relevant facts, and so forth, but there are two other groundrules which, although not intended to be pre-emptive, make it hard for anyone to pursue hard-nosed negotiation.

First is when I explain the pattern I expect their discussions to follow. I usually say something like:

> "In this process, I propose we operate like this. First, we will identify the people affected by your decision to separate. I assume these will be yourselves and your children, and, perhaps, grand-parents and other relatives? Is there an elderly parent living with you? No? Then I assume the three of us will be working together for the four of you, that is, each of you, and your children, Maria and Peter. Right?

> "Next, we will identify what all these four people will need following the separation. Then we will try to identify the resources available to meet all those needs. Finally, we will see how best to share out the available resources to meet the identified needs so far as possible."

I usually describe another ground rule like this:

> "During this process, you will make decisions that may affect your lives, and your children's lives, perhaps for years to come. It is important that when you come to make these decisions, you are fully informed, and have whatever advice you feel you need. This may include professional advice from lawyers, tax consultants, and perhaps other experts, so that when you look back on what has happened in this room, you can be sure you have done all you could to ensure that your decisions

are wise ones. If you need separate advice, we may agree to put our work on hold while you get it. Neither of you will be asked to make any decisions in this room, without first getting whatever advice you feel you need.

"I also suggest that our work together should be based on open disclosure of relevant information either of you may need to make an informed decision. Each of you will put your cards on the table face up. No cards will be face down, and certainly, no cards up anyone's sleeve. Are you both happy with that?"

These are not my only ground-rules, but if they accept them at the beginning, it becomes much harder for either of them to engage in an intimidatory style of bargaining. If they don't accept them, it is unlikely that they will work with me as their mediator. The process would be a waste of time if it is not based on respectful behaviour and full disclosure.

Let us look now at how an attempt by one of them to start that kind of negotiation might play out, with a couple who have agreed to these "boundaries":

> *Paul:* "Liz, you can have £50,000, provided you accept it within 48 hours. If you don't come back with a response within that time, the entire deal is off, and I'll see you in court."

The mediator may pause, to see how Liz will respond. If she is able to stand up to bullying, so much the better for their current negotiations and those they will need to conduct in future. The mediator will let Liz deliver direct to Paul the message that such tactics won't work, now or in the future.

If the mediator decides to stay silent, and let them educate each other – and, ideally, a mediator hopes to become less vocal with each succeeding session, because he hopes his interventions will become less needed until he becomes redundant – he will be alert to intervene if their discussion shows signs of overheating. Harry Plunket Greene's *Interpretation in Song* has another lesson for us. One of his rules for singers is: "sing mentally through your rests". That is, even if you are not performing at a given moment, keep your concentration. A mediator does not cease to concentrate on what is happening and where the session is going, simply because he is not saying anything. Indeed, the fact that he does not have to think about what to say, and how to put it, allows him to concentrate even more intensely.

If Liz's oral response or body language shows she can't handle it, the mediator may say:

Mediator: "I don't understand."

That is often a good opening. Having used it to buy himself a second to think, he might continue:

"In fact, there are two things that puzzle me. First is: how did you arrive at the figure, Paul? Second is: what is the reason for the deadline?"

Paul: "Well, first of all, £50,000 is the absolute last penny I can raise, and that is the reason I am offering it now. The reason for the deadline is that I can't sit around here indefinitely, and if Liz won't accept my best offer, we must start moving into court. Besides, if I have to sit here much longer paying you, and then paying lawyers, I won't have £50,000!"

Mediator: "Okay. Thanks. I understand now. Let me take those two in turn. First, I don't doubt you when you say that you think £50,000 is your ceiling. You know more about your finances than anyone else does, and you are probably right. But it strikes me that we don't yet know what is the amount of capital needed to provide a home for Liz and the children. It may be exactly £50,000. It may be less, in which case your offer will be too much."

[Pause for this to sink in.]

"Or a home for Liz and the children may cost more. In which case £50,000 will not solve the problem.

"People I have worked with have found that, if they identified the needs of all the people involved and tried to find ways to meet those needs, they were able to come up with creative solutions. There may be a danger that, if you get stuck into arguing about how to divvie up a pie of fixed size, you may miss out on opportunities to increase the size of the pie.

[Pause again.]

"If we can do that, everyone's slice can be bigger. So, I suggest that, before we get stuck into trying to share out the pie, we look first to see how big it needs to be, and if the existing pie isn't big enough to go around, whether we can make it grow.

"I don't know if this will work for you, but if it does, everyone will gain. Perhaps it is worth risking wasting some time if the possible pay-off is worth it?"

If this gets through to Paul – and his body language will tell the mediator if it is getting through – the mediator might simply move on at this point, and ignore the deadline Paul had set up. If the £50,000 is off the table, the deadline has gone with it. Ignoring it may be a way of helping him to save face which can be important in negotiation – see below. If he feels it is necessary to respond to the deadline – perhaps because this is a tactic Paul has used in the past, and got away with – the mediator might say:

"The other thing is the time issue. I understand, Paul, that you need to get this sorted out, and get on with your life, and this interim period is frustrating for you. I am sure it is hard for Liz, too, and, in different ways, for Maria and Peter. What worries me is this. Very often, in my experience, if someone is told: 'Take it or leave it. Give me a yes or no answer. And give it now!' the answer will be: 'I'll leave it.' If you ask Liz for an immediate yes or no, and she says no, then I assume we three will stop working together. Because we will have nothing left to talk about.

"In fact, that was one of the reasons I asked you both to agree, when we met first, that you would both be free to consult advisers during the process, and that neither of you would be required to make any decisions in this room, without first getting whatever advice you felt you needed.

"If this process doesn't work for you, I assume you will both have to go back to your lawyers, and I imagine it will take you a longer time to reach an agreement. To say nothing of it costing more. Because, even if I were charging you as much per hour as your lawyers – and I should be so lucky! – two lawyers will certainly cost you more than one mediator. And, of course, however you divide up the money, there is only one pot it can come out of.

"In any event, I do not work to artificial deadlines, because I do not think sensible agreements come out of them."

If a husband insists on hardball negotiation after all of this, I would usually terminate the process, in order that the wife could be represented in negotiations by someone who could play the same game on her behalf. And I would think about whether to say something like:

"The deadline Paul put to Liz seems to me incompatible with the way of working that we agreed at our first meeting, and, even if Liz is willing to agree to tear up those rules and negotiate on a new basis, I'm not. You are free to negotiate on any basis that suits you both, but not in this room.

"We agreed the mediation process is confidential and

off the record, and I won't tell anyone else what I've just said about why we are stopping, but I thought I should make it clear to both of you."

If I decided to say something like that, I would offer Paul eye contact ninety per cent of the time I was delivering the message, with only an occasional glance towards Liz.

I can only remember two occasions, in my work as a mediator stretching over more than ten years, when I have ended the process because one person persisted in an approach to negotiation that I found "unacceptable". (The quote-marks around the last word are intended to draw your attention to other loaded words like "appropriate" and "inappropriate" that I talked about in Chapter Two.)

One of the attractions of mediation to separating spouses must be that it excludes "hardball" – confrontational negotiation, and operates at a problem-solving level based on co-operation, and aiming to build trust.

Leaving room for manoeuvre

If an issue has been, say, ninety per cent agreed and there are other issues still unresolved it may be good tactics for the mediator not to finalise the issue that is almost agreed but to leave it incomplete, and move on to the others. The ten per cent not agreed on the first issue may be useful later on in offering opportunities for trade-off. Although some of its advocates claim mediation offers win/win solutions, even its most enthusiastic supporters do not claim that, on each issue, both parties will win. Some issues are incurably win/lose issues, or zero-sum games, that is, a situation where one person's winnings is the measure of what the others lose. (A night playing poker is an example of the zero-sum concept. If the winners tot up their winnings, and they do not exactly equal what the losers admit to losing, the explanation is that

99

someone is lying.) We feel current pain acutely, and there is a danger that if one party has to complete the process by making a concession, and receives no reciprocal concession from the other side at the time he is feeling the pain, he may forget concessions he gained earlier on, and take away from the process the feeling of being a loser, and that it was unfair. If one party feels like that, problems down the road are almost inevitable.

Control of the process includes control over the order in which issues are negotiated. A mediator will usually not want to tackle an issue on which one party will have to make concessions, and on which he may see himself as a loser, until a pattern of mutual conceding has been established. However, a careful mediator will avoid leaving a win/lose issue as the last one to be resolved, because of the risk that the entire process may collapse if the winner on the last issue has no "consolation prize" to offer the loser. If there is a prior issue, incompletely agreed, with room for concession, whichever party is going to win on the win/lose issue can make a concession on the previous one, and help the other party not to feel a loser.

Positions, interests and "face"

People often take up positions, in order to protect interests. (Men do this more often than women, in my experience.) I played this game every day when I was a lawyer. A lawyer representing a plaintiff in a personal injuries claim, or someone seeking to sell a property (the two are not very different) will start with a demand higher than he expects to get, and more than his client is willing to accept. The lawyer representing the defendant or prospective buyer will either refuse with contempt, or come in with an excessively low counter-offer. Having thus created an artificially large gap between their demands, they negotiate to reduce it. Experienced lawyer-negotiators know they must go through this ritual, in which the words may have some meaning, but the initial figures are meaningless.

On each side, there is a gap between the *interest* each party is trying to protect, and the *position* they have taken up. (That gap is often called an "add-on".) Most "hard-nosed" negotiation takes place in an attempt by each party to discover what is the true position of the other, without disclosing his own.

Taking up a position and trying to defend it will often lead to entrenchment (Chapter One). A trench may be a good position in some ways from which to fight a defensive war, but it is a bad one from which to negotiate a truce, let alone a lasting peace. A position is immobile. In contrast, an interest is mobile. Once you have identified it, you can carry it around with you. And being mobile is the single most important attribute a mediator's clients can have in their attempts to reach agreement. Substituting interests for positions enables them to leave the trenches and get to the negotiating table, carrying their interests with them. A mediator will often spend a lot of his time trying to identify his clients' interests and in encouraging them to discard the positions they have taken up to protect those interests.

Surprisingly often, the main reason why people engaged in negotiation refuse to abandon hopeless positions is fear of losing face. Nobody wants to emerge from a discussion feeling humiliated. Good negotiators know people will resist a humiliating bargain and that if they do make one they are unlikely to honour it. A mediator knows that too. He also knows that people who feel strongly on an issue are very inclined to put themselves in positions they can not vacate without humiliation: "This is my home, and I will only leave it when I am carried out!"

Even more dangerous than one client's humiliation by the other in their mediator's presence is a client's perceived humiliation by the mediator in the presence of his or her spouse. Probably the worst example is a male client feeling humiliated by a male mediator in the presence of a female. Primitive feelings may take the process over. It does not matter that the husband has lost sexual interest in the female who sees his embarrassment. He will be determined to reassert himself, wipe out the humiliating defeat, and, if possible, cut that cheeky mediator down to size. While this is going on, the mediator can forget about all those pleasant things like co-operation, avoiding win/lose negotiations, and mutual problem-solving. They will not be available.

In contrast, let us look at a situation where the husband (let us say) has painted himself into a corner from which he cannot escape without loss of face. Many people – men in particular – will do this as a strategy: "if I paint myself in deeply enough, people won't dare to disturb me!" If it becomes clear that he is going to have to leave his corner, a mediator can create goodwill for himself and the process, if he helps the husband to escape from his corner, and clean himself of the paint, without drawing attention to what has happened. Even if the husband is not conscious of having been helped, he will be relieved. If he sees that he had dug himself into a hole (to vary the metaphor) and that the mediator had helped him to climb out and not drawn attention to what had been happening, he will be grateful and may feel some goodwill. I discuss this with an example in Chapter Eleven – "Joe & Bella".

In his essay "Looking back at the Spanish War", George Orwell describes how he felt unable to fire at a soldier in the other side, who had been interrupted while relieving himself, and had leapt from his trench, and started to run away, holding up his trousers as he ran: "I had come here to shoot at

"Fascists"; but a man who is holding up his trousers isn't a "Fascist", he is visibly a fellow-creature, similar to yourself, and you don't feel like shooting at him." I try to see anyone who has to run from a trench in which he has tried to shelter himself as a fellow-creature, not to be shot at. It does not matter how he wears his trousers, or indeed, whether he wears trousers at all. Nor does it matter that he himself dug the trench from which he is trying to flee. It is wise to give him a flag of truce, and time to "adjust his dress" before he leaves. He will be better company later when you sit with him at a conference table, and more amenable to negotiating a truce and a long-term peace, because you have saved him from humiliation. Orwell's prospective target, the man holding his trousers up as he ran, probably remembered the incident more vividly than Orwell did, but never talked about it. If he ever read the essay, I imagine his face went scarlet. But he would have been grateful to Orwell for not shooting him, and leaving him to be found dead by his own side with his trousers about his ankles.

I talk in Chapter Three about how our choice of words can give us away, unconsciously. That quotation from Orwell suggests to me that he may have been a less than ideal soldier. He talked about shooting "at" the enemy, where someone more suited to the military life would have said "shooting him". The use of the word "at" is probably unconscious, and suggests a soldier who, however effective he might have been on a rifle range, would have been temperamentally inclined to miss, in combat.

CHAPTER SEVEN

SOME TECHNIQUES MEDIATORS USE

Planting potatoes last year taught me a few things about mediation. I picked up a spade at random, and only later realised what a good choice I had made. You do not plant potatoes (I discovered) in the same way as you plant a rose: by digging a hole, putting in manure, and then sitting the rose-bush in the hole, and filling in the hole with earth. To plant potatoes, you first dig a straight, shallow trench, piling up a ridge of earth on one side of the trench, then you walk along the trench, putting seed potatoes in it, about fifteen inches apart. Next you cover the potatoes with earth by piling back into the trench the earth you have moved in creating the trench. Next, or at the same time, you heap up some more earth, so that the row of potatoes is now covered by a ridge.

The work would have been a lot heavier if I had not had the good luck to choose the perfect spade. It had a longer handle and a narrower blade than I was used to, making a trench just wide enough to plant the potatoes in, and saving me from having to shift more earth than was needed. The blade was bent slightly forward, so it was easier to dig a shallow trench than a deep one. In hard, impacted ground, the length of the handle was an advantage, because it was easy to lever the spade, and loosen enough soil to make a trench.

Of course, this was a spade intended for planting potatoes. I might have made a similar discovery if I had been shifting sand, and taken a shovel designed for that purpose. Its pointed end is designed to dig into sand, and its curved shape to hold sand in the highest possible hillock on the shovel consistent with stability. The same applies to a violin, whose convoluted, elegant shape is not designed for visual beauty, but to produce the maximum amount of agreeable noise, and to enable the player to vary the quality and volume of the noise it produces.

The shapes of these three implements were not devised overnight by a genius. They evolved over time, with modifications, as people noticed that a change of design made the implement easier to use, or more effective.

All of this is also true of the techniques I want to describe in this chapter. Over the years that mediation has been evolving, mediators tried various ways of helping their clients towards agreements and noticed that some of the things they did, perhaps contrived on the spur of the moment, perhaps borrowed from other disciplines, produced results. To make them easier to recall for their own use, and discuss them with their friends, they gave them names. When other mediators started to use them, they became labelled as "techniques".

At least, that is how I imagine "techniques" developing. A technique, like the design of a spade or a violin, is a common sense solution to a recurring problem. Nothing more. If you argue that it may have taken a genius to see the common sense solution to a problem that nobody else could solve, I will not disagree, but will remind you of Orwell's saying: "To see what is in front of one's nose needs a constant struggle."

Having quoted Orwell again, here is another quotation

from Harry Plunket Greene's *Interpretation in Song*, describing how we absorb and use the techniques we learn.

"Technique is easy to acquire; it is difficult to absorb. The one is a matter of months, the other of years. Technique is not uniform, and in its rules does not apply to each individual alike, but any man of intelligence can be taught the one that suits him best. It is the absorption of that knowledge into his very system so thoroughly that its application becomes automatic which is the difficulty. The physical use of his voice must be *the unconscious response to the play of his feeling.*

"Technique must be the singer's servant, not his master, and must follow his mind as automatically as his hand follows his eye . . . It is a long and wearisome business, for there are no short cuts . . .

"Finally, the singer should bear in mind that he is not the best judge of his own technique, and that that technique can never be left alone . . . no matter how high he may stand in his art, his technique is bound occasionally to grow rusty, or get out of control. In such cases he will do well to submit it to a master whom he can trust."

I will not list in this book all the techniques used in mediation. I am aware of twenty or more I have used consciously in my work. There may be another half dozen I have used without realising I was doing so, and others I do not know about that are used by colleagues with great success. While each of them may be simple, the process of becoming a mediator involves absorbing them into oneself, so that we use them *without realising we are doing so.*

The purpose of any technique a mediator uses should be to serve his *strategic plan*. And the plan is almost always directed towards inducing change, creating movement.

So let's look at a few techniques.

Listening

The first technique I want to talk about is listening. "Listening", you say, "he calls that a technique." Yes, indeed, he does.

James Thurber said of himself: "He never listens when anybody else is talking, preferring to keep his mind a blank until they get through, so he can talk". This is an accurate description of how a lot of communication works, or doesn't work. Practising listening, consciously at first, and then eventually, instinctively, is the first essential step in the evolution of a mediator.

A basic truth affects all human communication: we listen to someone's message if the speaker has first shown that he is willing to listen to us. If I want my clients to listen to me, I must first show willingness to listen to them. And it is not enough to show that willingness at a first meeting with them; I must never give them the impression that what they have to say is not worth listening to.

I learnt something about listening before I worked as a mediator, during a time when I was occasionally asked to write reviews of concerts for *The Irish Times*. If you had asked me, before I was offered this informal appointment, I would have said that what you got from listening to music was directly related to what you put into it: the more intensely you listened, the more you heard. But it was only when I started to review concerts that I realised how true this is. (An example of the difference I mention in Chapter Fifteen between knowing something and understanding it.) I covered a variety of concerts, not all of which would have been on my short list of musical events not to be missed, and came away from each with a deeper understanding of the music I had heard performed, and of the art of music. This was partly because I knew I would have to go to *The Irish Times* office when the concert was over, and type my review. Knowing I would have to write about the performances, I concentrated on what was played, and how it was played.

After a while I noticed that a description of what I was hearing might cross my mind as I listened. I was in danger of composing my review during the concert. But if my mind was on what I would write, it could not concentrate at the same time on what was being played. This was unfair to the performer, the composer, and to my readers. (The composer was probably beyond caring, but I felt responsible to him too, and think, in retrospect, that I was right – though pompous.) I disciplined myself by deciding that while I was at a concert I would not allow myself to think about the review I would have to write later, and, if a sentence or phrase occurred to me as I listened, I would not use it when I came to write the review. (I mention this here because it ties in with the question of using a "standard form" which I talk about in Chapter Thirteen.) I took from my stint as a part-time reviewer an ability to listen to music with a level of concentration I did not previously have. Although I eventually lost the job, I gained enormously from it, in the way I now experience great music.

This experience also made it easier for me to understand when I turned to mediation, that a mediator should listen to what his clients tell him, and listen so intensely. ("Intensely" is not a misprint for "intently". I am talking about intensity, not just attention.) He aims to understand what is being said, but he also needs to get a sense of how it feels to be the person who speaks the words he hears. He wants to know whether something unspoken lies behind what is said, in much the same way as deep emotion can lie behind musical notes.

One reason the mediator needs to listen so carefully is that, like the concert goer who writes reviews, he knows that when each speaker has told his or her story, he will probably be called upon to use the second technique I want to discuss – feedback.

But before I go on to it I want to say something else about listening. Years ago I read an analysis of a scene in *The Cherry Orchard*. The writer quoted the lines Chekhov had put in the mouths of the characters, offered his analysis of the messages that lay behind the words, and argued that it was the sense of unspoken messages that made Chekhov a great dramatist and *The Cherry Orchard* a luminous play. In much the same way, a mediator needs to focus on the words his clients speak, and to be sensitive to unspoken messages, too. He listens with his ears to what they say and to tone of voice, and he "listens" with his eyes to their body language. It is not as hard as it may sound. Most of us listen to tone of voice and observe body language, unconsciously. A mediator learns to do consciously something he already does instinctively.

Feedback

Someone unused to working with conflict might reasonably assume that each party to a dispute will be bound to hear what the other says. This is not so, and understanding why it is not so is fundamental to understanding mediation.

When I was a young lawyer, cynics said about a judge who sat in Dublin that having listened to a plaintiff presenting his case, he would switch off his hearing aid when the defendant started to present his, for fear of becoming confused. One of the most striking things a mediator notices in his work is that one party or both will in effect switch off their listening apparatus when the other is talking, so as not to have to listen to their complaints. This may be a healthy, even necessary, part of the process of disengagement for former lovers moving towards being strangers, but it makes

109

communication between them difficult. (see "dysfunctional communication" in Chapter Three.)

Sometimes, rather than switch off the hearing aid, a husband or wife will listen intently to what the other is saying, but only to pick holes in their arguments, and refute their proposals. We cannot say of these people that they are not listening, but they certainly are not hearing, in the sense that they are not trying to understand or share in the feelings and hopes being articulated.

So, after each party speaks, the mediator may feed back the content of what they have just said. Again, surely, nothing could be easier. Repeating back to a speaker what he or she has just said? A tape recorder could do it!

So it could, if all we needed was a repetition of what has been said. But the mediator wants to achieve a number of different effects when he offers feedback. First, what he says should assure the speaker that the mediator has listened to his words and understood them, and the feelings that lie behind them. It will also be heard by the other party – who may up till then have "switched off" when his/her ex-spouse was talking. You will find examples of feedback in Chapter Three including two examples, at the beginning of the chapter of feedback that did not work, and a more successful example in "the Button Factory War" in the same chapter, but I want to offer another example here, from a marital dispute.

Let us assume that I am working with a married couple, and the wife who does not work outside the home starts to describe her side of the history of the marriage, and what she wants to take from its wreckage. When feeding back what she has said, I may need to do something a bit like simultaneous translation at a multilingual conference. First, it is essential that the wife knows I have listened to and understood what she said. I want to establish a listening relationship with her so that she will trust me, and if the time comes for me to say things to her she will be ready to listen to them. I know she is more likely to listen to me with a receptive mind if she knows I have first listened, with understanding and sympathy, to what she has said.

But, of course, the husband is also present, and if I do what a tape recorder could do, that is, repeat her accusations, I am going to alienate him. He probably has not listened to what his wife said – he thinks "it is the same old record I have heard so often" – but he will listen to what I say, when I feedback what I have heard from her, if only because he wants to know whether I have bought into her views.

So I do not say:

"Mary, if I have understood you rightly, the drunken oaf you married, after years of treating you like dirt, has gone off with a slut from his office, young enough to be his daughter, and is now trying to starve you into submission."

I probably say something like:

"I understand from what you have said, Mary, that your relationship with Peter has come to an end. And in a way that has left you feeling sore and resentful.

"I understand Peter has moved out of the family home, and is living in a flat with another woman. You and the children are still living in the original home.

"You had been willing to try to stay together if it had been possible, for the sake of your children. You now feel this would be impossible, and intolerable for you. Peter doesn't seem to want to, but if he did, you would say no.

"You blame Peter very much for what has happened in your marriage.

"And at this stage, you feel the money arrangements that he has proposed will not meet your needs, and your children's needs. So there is another reason for you to

111

feel tense, on top of all the emotions that are always around when a marriage comes to an end: you also have major money worries."

I will probably next give Peter the floor, and offer him feedback along the same lines as I did Mary, in language that he will accept, and will not alienate her, but I want to focus on the feedback to Mary. I suggested it would not be good feedback to talk about drunken oafs or sluts from his office, but assuming that would have been an accurate precis of what she had said, please re-read the feedback I suggested above, and ask yourselves:

- does it seem to tell Mary that I have listened to what she has said?
- does it reassure Peter that, while I have listened to Mary, I have not necessarily bought into her views?
- whether you regard "non-judgemental" as a term of praise or an accusation of lack of moral sense, is the language "non-judgemental"?
- does it look like a basis for further discussion?
- does it look like a model for Mary and Peter, for expressing their views, in non-confrontational language?

If the answer to most of those questions is "yes", then it is probably pretty good feedback.

Remember, too, that when I offer feedback of what one person has said, that may be the first time the other actually hears what she feels or needs, for either or both of two reasons. If one party has always articulated her position in confrontational language, the other may have listened only to the language – in order to rebuke it, resent it, use it to put her in the wrong, or whatever – and may have blocked out the message. It is quite common to find that the person to whom a message has been delivered – perhaps over and over – may have heard the offensive language and ignored the content.

It is also quite common to find that a message has been "blocked" because the person to whom it was given was unwilling to hear it. Most of us have heard stories of people who have been told by their doctor they have a fatal illness and have come home and told their families that there is nothing wrong with them. Some sort of cut-off system operates between the ear and the intelligence, so that a message the "listener" cannot cope with is not heard. I could not count the number of times I have been told by a husband that his wife told him last week that she wanted a separation, and it was a terrible shock to him, and the wife says: "I told you last summer, reminded you at least four times since, and have been begging you for the last three months to make an appointment with a mediator!" She will usually assume he is lying. I assume he has simply "not heard" a message that, at the time, he did not feel ready to process.

Thus, feedback has a double, or sometimes treble significance. It assures the speaker that he or she has been heard and understood; it informs the other party about the issue, and perhaps for the first time about issues that had previously been blocked; finally, it may perhaps explain to the other party the feelings that lie behind the message.

Feedback should include all the essential elements in the speech that is being reflected back. If we make a mistake by omitting an element that one party says is essential, and have to be reminded of it, we can simply say: "Sorry. I overlooked that. Thank you for reminding me." But if this often happens it is a sign that our listening is defective.

Reframing

If I had to throw away all the tools in my mediator's toolbox except one, the tool I would keep would be reframing. Rather than give you a definition of a reframe, let me offer a few examples, staying with Mary and Peter. Let's assume Mary tells me that since Peter moved out, he is letting her have an amount per week that is insufficient for her and the children to survive. She has got by only by borrowing from her parents, and will have to pay back the loans. I feed back to her what she has said, omitting the accusations against Peter of meanness, indifference to his children, etc., and concentrating on the problem she is grappling with, which is that she cannot manage on the income she receives from her absent husband, and is sliding into debt.

Next, Peter tells me of his difficulty in making ends meet, and how incompetent Mary is at managing money. He goes further, and suggests she is more than unable to handle money: she is deliberately over-spending so as to get at him, and the reason she is borrowing from her parents is to humiliate him and wrong-foot him in their eyes. I offer him feedback, again without seeming to buy into his picture of her as an incompetent manager, or his accusation of deliberate over-spending.

I now want to reframe the problem, that is, to redefine it so that we can start to work on solving it. My first assumption is that I should not do so in the way that either party has asked me to. Each of them has presented it in a way that says: "Make the other person change!", which implies "so that I don't have to". If I buy into Peter's approach, I alienate Mary, and vice versa. Also, it is unlikely that either party is presenting a comprehensive, rounded, picture of the problem, so that if I adopt either party's description of it, I have started a journey in a wrong direction. So, I will not say: "We have to help Mary to manage money better" or "We must negotiate a higher contribution from Peter". I will say something like:

> "Peter's salary is £30,000 a year before tax, and it is the only current source of income for the four of you – Peter, Mary, and your two children, Deirdre and Simon. Mary and the children need support, and, at present, it seems that can only come from Peter. Peter also has to support himself.

(That is an example of summarising – a technique we will look at in the next chapter.)

> "You both want to maintain a reasonable standard of living, in Peter's household, and in the household consisting of Mary and Deirdre and Simon.
>
> "If belts have to be tightened – as they probably will, if an income that previously supported one household now has to support two – then you need to agree how this should be handled.
>
> "Is that a fair summary?"

As well as eliminating the conflictual language – which I dropped at feedback stage anyway – I have restated the problem in a way that meets what I think are the essential elements in a good reframe:

◆ it should be acceptable to the parties in conflict. This means it must include all the essential elements in the shopping list each has produced.

◆ it is more open to solution than the problem as they have stated it.

◆ it removes or lessens the conflict – the "him versus her" aspect.

◆ it focusses on what is to happen in the future. They may be able to exercise some control over how their lives will develop, but not about what has happened in the past. We cannot change what has happened, and if we start to discuss it we will be forced back into a non-productive conflict.

As regards the first – acceptability – it is hard for anyone to judge whether the reframe will be accepted by both parties when we have not heard them state their points of view. We can reduce the risk of our reframe being rejected as inadequate by effective feedback, before we reframe. If the parties have both accepted our feedback as accurate, it is unlikely they will reject a reframe based on it.

As regards being soluble, there is no way that a static

income can be stretched to support a second household without a drop in living standards. In this sense, the problem is insoluble. But it is, at least, easier to work with one question posed as "how do you share income so as to keep living standards in both homes as high as you can?" than with the original two: Peter's "how little can I get away with paying", and Mary's "how much can I force him to pay?"

On the third aspect – of lessening conflict – I think the reframe stands up. Instead of being a "him versus her" problem, I have restated it as one in which they have a shared interest, trying to maintain living standards for all the family.

It clearly passes the fourth test of being focussed on the future, not the past.

Before I leave that reframe, let me just mention something else mediators often do, called "bringing the children into the room". I mentioned the children by name, twice, to remind their parents that we are not talking about some abstraction called "the children", but about two individuals whom they both love, Deirdre and Simon, and who will be affected by what they decide.

Reframing can be useful at any stage in the mediation process after the parties have had their say and the mediator has fed back what each has said, but is usually most useful in the early stage. I have sometimes telescoped the process by offering a reframe at the same time as I am feeding back the message of the second speaker. I do not reframe when I offer feedback of what the first speaker has said, for reasons that I hope will be obvious.

Talking about the fourth aspect of a good reframe, future focus, let us look at another reframe about the same family, Peter and Mary, Deirdre and Simon. This one is about how Peter will stay in touch with Deirdre and Simon now that he no longer lives with them. Assume they have each complained about the other's parenting approach while they were living together, and about how his contact with the children has been handled since he moved out. Having fed this back carefully so as not to precipitate a "you did/I didn't" exchange, the mediator needs to reframe the issue of Peter's contact with the children. He might say something like:

> "Another issue is the time Deirdre and Simon will spend with their father, and how it should be arranged. When we look at this do we need to think about Peter's needs and availability?"

[Pause, for each of them to agree]

> "And about Deirdre's and Simon's needs and availability?"

[Similar pause]

> "And about their mother's needs, too?"

[Further similar pause] Then, having got a "yes" to all three:

> "I assume, given that Deirdre is a girl and Simon a boy, and Deirdre is five years older than Simon, they may not both need exactly the same things from their father at present? And that their needs will change as time goes by? Simon is still in primary school, and Deirdre has moved on to secondary, so I assume, too, that they may not always be available to spend time with him, at the same times?

> "I imagine, too, that there may be another aspect to this, for Mary. I get the impression that there isn't much cash around to pay baby-sitters?"

(Agreement from Mary)

> "I suppose that means Mary doesn't have much opportunity to get away from the children for a while, and either take a rest, or do things that grown-ups enjoy and children don't?

> "Is it worthwhile, then, to try for arrangements for Deirdre and Simon to spend time with Peter that will also give Mary time off?"

117

You will see that this reframe, as well as being future-focussed, has built in something for Mary, additional to the benefits for Peter of having time with his children, and for them of having time with their Dad: time to herself.

Let me just say a few more things about reframing. First, I assume a reframe will take the form of a question and that a useful form of question is: "How can you . . . ?"

Secondly, if a mediator reframes an issue, he should stick with the reframe and not let the parties go back to talking about the issue as originally defined by them, especially if the topic is not resolved immediately, and we will have to go back to talking about it at a later session.

You may have noticed that the second reframe above is not about Peter's contact with his children, but about "Deirdre and Simon's contact with their father". The result may be the same, but there is a difference from Mary's point of view. I am now putting it in terms of the children wanting to be with their Dad, not about his wanting to be with them. She might feel inclined, consciously or not, to punish him for his treatment of her by putting barriers between him and the children. She is much less likely to take this approach if the issue is stated in terms of their need to be with their Dad. Rewording the issue in terms of the children's interests, not Peter's, may in itself be a powerful reframe.

We are on thin ice here. When I reframe the issue of contact between father and children so as to put more emphasis on their needs than on his, my intention is to create movement. But its effect is to lead Mary to think of the issue in her role as the children's mother, rather than as Peter's estranged wife, and it may affect the content of their bargain. So how do I reconcile this approach with the concept that a mediator does not direct his clients? Am I not in breach of that principle, by reframing the issue in this way?

I think I am very close to it. But another concept is relevant here – the concept of what is possible. A mediator should not close his mind to a possibility that clients will make strange bargains. For example, he should not assume, even if the husband is a lighthouse keeper, that the children will live with their mother, and not with him on his lighthouse. But if he hears the mother saying that the children cannot live on the lighthouse because they must go to school, he may switch his focus to helping to save the husband from losing face by digging himself in over an issue he cannot win. So I think a mediator may justify using his control over the process to postpone or inhibit further discussion on that topic.

Something similar applies on the question of whether the children will spend time with their father. The mediator assesses from Peter's words, tone of voce and body language that he will not accept being excluded from their lives. He knows that there is no realistic prospect that a court would sanction such exclusion. In other words, he recognises that if Mary decided to fight this one she would lose. Accordingly, he helps the process and saves face for her by helping her to avoid painting herself into that corner.

But he intends to do more than that. By reframing the issue as he did, he intended to persuade Mary to make some movement. And his own values as well as his rational judgement will influence which of the parties he tries to mobilise, and how. I discuss this dilemma further in Chapter Twelve.

I would not reframe in terms of the children's wish to be with their father before I had done some exploration of what kind of children they were, how each parent saw their interests and temperaments, what contact they currently had with their father, and how they were reacting to the change in their lives that his departure had brought. To try to reframe this issue in terms of the children's interests, without first getting a sense of what those interests were, would be premature and presumptuous.

Feedback revisited

There is a problem about feedback that I think will be clearer to you now that we have talked about reframing. Like so many of the things mediators do, feedback puts us on a tightrope. We must not lean too far in either direction and we must keep moving. If we have to feed back a stream of insults, abuse or complaints that one client has uttered, we will sanitise the message. But we may want to follow the feedback with a reframe, and our reframe will usually be based not on what the clients said – which is often loaded and contentious – but on how we fed back their message. If the feedback was not accurate, how can we produce a worthwhile reframe based on it? It follows that feedback may dilute or soften the message we are feeding back, but must not distort it.

For example, let's assume that one spouse expresses concern about the safety of the children, in the other's care, because of lifestyle. Let's assume it is the husband, though it is more often the other way around, and that his name is Alan and hers is Sue. He says:

> "Sue has no judgement about how much liquor she can hold, and no capacity to say no. If she has a few drinks she is liable to do anything. She may bring some chap home, and the kids will find him in her bed next morning. Or she may light a cigarette, pass out and set the place on fire. She has been known to wake up the next day without a clue about how she got home. Someone like that can't be trusted with my kids."

Let us assume that while Alan has been saying this, the mediator, while listening to him, has also had his eye on Sue – as he should – and seen rising indignation from her as she listens to Alan. What does the mediator do? If he feeds back to Alan what he has said, he risks increasing Sue's sense of being under attack. She may classify the mediator as one of her attackers. If he ignores it, Alan will not feel heard. Furthermore, if the children really are in danger, that cannot be ignored. It is the parents' problem, not the mediator's, but mediators have reflexes – and children.

One thing a mediator should not do in that situation is to feed back to Alan something different from what he has just said. He may not soften the message by saying, for example: "you want to ensure that the children will be looked after by one or other of their parents at all times", because that is not the message Alan has delivered. His message is that one of the children's parents cannot be trusted to look after them. If we offer Alan feedback that does not reflect what he said, he will reject it. Even if he does not, it cannot be a starting point for addressing the problem, because it fudges it. A reframe based on false feedback will be useless, because it is based on pretending that the problem is something different from what it really is.

Moreover, a mediator who pretends to offer feedback of what has been said, while distorting the message, is not being truthful, and is running against what I consider to be a cardinal rule in mediation work – see Chapter Twelve.

So what does the mediator do? How I would respond would be determined by the impressions I had formed of the parties and the extent to which I had established a relationship with each of them and gained their trust. One possible response, which would not involve repeating Alan's accusations against Sue, and would give us all time to think, would be:

> *Mediator:* "I have listened to what Alan has said about this. It does not seem to me that he is saying it frivolously. It sounds to me like a serious issue. I get the impression, from watching Sue, that she does not accept what Alan says.

[Pause, to allow Sue to agree]

"We will probably have to put a lot of work into this issue. But, at this stage, I don't want to get into it, and I want to ask . . . "

Such a response would give Sue an opportunity to plan how she might respond to Alan's accusation. It would also give both of them a message that I had not sided with either of them over it. And it illustrates the concept that process control includes control over the order in which agenda items are addressed.

Of course, having said I will return to it, I must do so. One obvious reason is that it is a major issue which they will have to address if they are to make a bargain. The other is that it would be dishonest of me to make a promise and not keep it.

I don't know in the abstract how I would return to the issue. The answer depends on the people, the chemistry between them and me, and progress in other areas. One approach might be to raise the issue of the children's time with both parents, and their safety with both, and with any other child-minder, as a general issue, not as a direct accusation by one parent against the other. I think I would be less attracted to that approach now than I might have been some years ago, because I have come to believe that a conflict should be exposed as a first step to resolving it, and that looking the other way, and pretending it doesn't exist, does not produce results.

I might deal with it in two steps. First might be to re-raise the topic tentatively, to see how Alan reacted. If he showed he no longer wanted to pursue it, I would not speculate about whether this was because he had been satisfied by something else that happened in the process, or that he had raised it as part of an obscure negotiating manoeuvre which he had abandoned, or for some other reason. I would simply proceed on the basis that the issue was off our agenda and avoid asking Alan questions about it that might involve a loss of face for him.

If it was clear that Alan was still concerned, and wanted to pursue it, I might say something like:

> "I want to go back now to what Alan said earlier, about the children being safe while they are with Sue, if she went out for a few drinks and let her guard down."

This is feedback intended to record what Alan said, without making Sue feel I am putting her on the spot. I might go on to reframe:

> "It is not my place to decide the rights and wrongs of this, but it seems to me it may break down into a series of questions.
>
> "The first might be: are the children in a safe environment when they are with their mother?
>
> "Next, perhaps: is it important that their father should feel happy about this?
>
> "If so, how do we relieve his mind of any concerns he may have?

After a pause to let this formulation sink in and enable Sue to see that the second question – is it important that their father should feel they are safe with her? – answers itself, I might then say:

> "Let's look at the third question first. It may be the most difficult one, but if we succeed in answering it we may have disposed of all the others. So, let's see how Alan's mind can be relieved of any concerns he may have about the children's safety with their mother.
>
> "I think I have to break one of our rules here, about not going back into the past, and ask you something about past events. I assume something happened at some stage to make Alan feel, rightly or wrongly, that this was an issue he felt he should raise?"

How the dialogue will develop from here on will depend on Sue and Alan's history and personalities, and to pursue it further would be guesswork, as well as getting us further off the topics under discussion, namely feedback and reframing.

Let me just assure you, though, that I did not cook up the problem Alan and Sue presented. It is a situation that arises in family mediation, though more often the other way around, in gender terms.

I reversed the genders to illustrate that the problem is the same either way, and that a marital mediator needs to identify gender biases he brings into his work. If he starts with the mindset of looking at a concerned husband differently from how he looks at a concerned wife, or at a reckless wife differently from a reckless husband, he needs to recognise this fact, and work on himself to look on both in the same benevolent, non-judgemental way.

Why did I not invite Sue to produce counter-accusations against Alan? Simply, I would not need to. If she felt her children were in danger when with their father she would say so. Indeed, she might say so anyway, using attack as a means of defence. I don't have to invite her, or give her space, if she wants to attack him. And I will have got a good sense of how she reacts to the accusation from her body language.

Do I get a sense from her body language about whether Alan's accusation is justified? The answer is that if I am doing my job properly, I don't. Because I shouldn't. It's not my business. They have not asked me to act as a judge of Sue's sobriety and responsibility. They have asked me to help them to work out a bargain for the future which will meet the needs of Alan, Sue, and their children. My agenda is limited to that, and I am not doing my job properly if I speculate beyond my instructions. If they work out an arrangement that leaves Alan happy, my work is over. I should not even ask myself would I be happy with it if they were my children.

CHAPTER EIGHT

SOME MORE MEDIATION TECHNIQUES

In the previous chapter I mentioned some of the techniques that a mediator would expect to use every day of his working life. There are others that are interesting, and that I suspect many of you will recognise when I put a label on them:

Summarising

Dialogue with Joe and Bella about candlesticks that I describe below in Chapter Eleven offers two examples of summarising:

> *Mediator:* "So, it seems selling one candlestick would be a bad deal. Your choices are either to keep both, or to sell them as a pair. I recognise the second choice would not be welcome to Joe, and I will not ignore that, but I want to ask you both, now, are these the only two real possibilities?"

and:

> *Mediator:* "You agree the candlesticks are worth £5,000. Bella feels they should be sold, and you should use the money. And, clearly, it would come in handy at this point. For example, you could clear the arrears outstanding on the mortgage."

These may both seem like reframes (previous chapter) but they are not, and their purpose is different from a reframe.

The objective in each case is not to change the way the parties might look at the issue, but to summarise where they now stand. I see two merits in summarising from time to time in the mediation process. First, it reminds the parties that they have made progress, gives them a sense of movement, and therefore encourages them to move on. The second is that every summary is a marker. It says, "this is the point we have reached in our journey. We may not make more progress, but at least we will not regress behind the point where we put down the marker." So, after accepting the first of the summaries quoted above, Bella is not likely to return to the suggestion that Joe most disliked – splitting the candlesticks. And after the second, neither is likely to re-open an argument about the value of the candlesticks, or to deny that selling them is one possible method of producing needed cash.

A summary presented by the mediator and accepted by the clients records that they have completed one stage in the process, passed through the door that leads from it to the next, and politely closed the door behind them. Once they have passed through the door, it is hard for them to go back unless the mediator unlocks it for them. A summary may be thought of, harshly, as the mediator throwing away the key.

For all these reasons, it can often be a good idea for a mediator to open a second session with his clients by offering a summary of what they have discussed at the first:

> "Let me just say, before we get down to work, what I have understood from you both from our first meeting. If I leave anything out, or get anything wrong, please correct me. Okay?
>
> "Right. Peter is forty-three, and Angela is thirty-nine. You both work outside the home. Peter earns £45,000 a year as financial controller of a company. Angela is a legal secretary, and earns £18,000.
>
> "You live in a house in Monkstown.
>
> "Adam is sixteen and Susie is fourteen. They are both

in St Paul's school, and you are happy with the school. You want them to finish school, and hope they will go on to third level.

"You have agreed to separate, and that Peter will move out, but not until after Christmas. Angela and the children will stay on in the house. Peter wants to have a place where Adam and Susie can stay overnight with him.

"Neither of you has any immediate plans to live with anyone else, though you are both open in principle to doing so.

"You haven't agreed long-term money arrangements, but the plan is that Peter will pay the mortgage on the house, and pay some support to Angela in the short term.

"You both have pension rights. Angela doesn't think hers will be worth much because she left the paid workforce when Adam was born, and only went back two years ago when Susie went to St Paul's. You agreed to quantify your pension rights.

"You were also going to get the house valued, and find out how much is due on the mortgage.

"You don't have any major debts apart from the mortgage. Peter owns some stock options in the company he works for. He was going to find out how much they are worth, and whether they can be sold now, without either infringing the company's rules or being hammered for tax. You have no other assets of substance, apart from the contents of the house, the car Angela drives, and some life assurance policies which you have agreed should be kept up, for the children's benefit, in case Peter dies before they are reared. (Peter drives a company car.)

"The areas where you wanted my help were:

"What to do about housing. Peter wants to buy a place of his own and to start paying off a mortgage. You would like each of you to own a home when you hit

127

retirement. You want not to move the children, if possible, as they have neighbourhood friends, and school friends living nearby.

"Next is the level of income support from Peter's household to the household where Angela, Adam and Susie live.

"You are also keen to work out plans for Peter's role in Adam and Susie's lives.

"Finally, there is a question of long-term income security. Peter says he will support the household while either of the children lives there, but there is a question about what happens afterwards. Angela feels she may not be able to live on her salary when the children leave home. Plus, there is a longer-term problem about her income when she hits retirement.

"Is that a fair summary?"

If they say yes, they waive their right to fight about other issues. If they say no, that the mediator has left out something – for example, how to divide their furniture and other assets – he can say "sorry", and add it to the list. When the mediator has summarised, and his summary has been accepted, with or without changes, the list of issues is complete.

Partialising

The next technique I want to talk about is called "partialising". It is based on the concept that, if you want to build a wall you put a brick in place, and then another brick alongside it, and more on top, and continue to add bricks until you have a wall. Similarly, if you want to remove a wall an effective way is to keep on removing single bricks. After a while, you have a pile of bricks, and the wall no longer exists.

The easiest way to illustrate partialising may be by examples from marital mediation, where time is the wall to be built or demolished. For example, a husband says the family home must be sold, as otherwise he will never be able to buy a home for himself. The wife insists that it must not be sold. The mediator says something like:

"Your daughter Helen is due to sit her final exams in medical school, next autumn, and her brother Peter is to sit the Leaving Cert in June. Do you want to put the house on the market now? Or would you rather wait until after Helen sits her exams?

"Until after Peter sits his?"

If they say it would be better to wait until the children have finished, the mediator might then say:

"It is a pretty big house. I wonder, when both the children have moved on, and are no longer living with you, Nuala, will it be bigger than you will be comfortable in? Will you rattle round inside it? Is the garden big too? Will keeping the house and garden take up more of your time and energy than you may want to give? Is it likely that a smaller house might suit you better?"

Of course, that series of questions assumes that the mediator has had a positive response – probably by body language – to each question, before he asked the next one. If the response to any question is negative, he will stop. If Nuala says a smaller house, or an apartment, might well be more comfortable for her when the children have left home, she and Paul are no longer discussing *whether* the house will be sold, but *when*.

Partialising can help us to deal with timing, and can be helpful in other ways. A house can be broken down into its components: it is a home for mother and children; it is a potential burden for Nuala, when the children have left home; it may also be a source of income, at that stage in her life; an investment, with a cash value – and under Irish law it is an investment that differs from most others, because it can be sold at a profit without a liability for capital gains tax. Each

129

of these aspects can be looked at separately. For example: "Paul, if you could raise cash now, and invest it in a home for yourself, would this be worth more to you than a prospect of getting perhaps more cash at some future time?"

Here is another example of partialising. I worked with a couple some years ago, in October or November as it happened, and they both wanted to spend the first Christmas after they separated with their children, and without the other. Neither was willing to give way. The obvious choice of alternating Christmases would have left them both feeling they had lost. This issue became more central to each of them as we worked on it, and other issues were agreed. They agreed how to share time with their children on Christmas Eve and after Christmas Day, but both wanted to bring the children to their parents for Christmas dinner. All the families lived in the greater Dublin area.

We seemed to have an impasse, a wall we could neither climb over nor break down. It was called Christmas Day, and it started in the morning and ended at their children's bedtimes.

I asked: "Peggy, when do your parents have their Christmas dinner?" She said in the evening, and I asked Joe the same question. His parents (luckily!) ate their Christmas dinner in the middle of the day. I then asked: "How would it be for Peter and Anne this Christmas if they went to Joe's parents for dinner in the middle of the day, and then to their other grannie and grand-dad in the evening?"

Please notice two things about the wording of the question: First, I asked, "How would it be for Peter and Anne?" I did not ask: "How would it work for you, Peggy?" or "For you, Joe?" (by naming them, I "brought them into the room" – see previous chapter). Secondly, I did not say, "How would it be if you spent every Christmas this way?" I asked about Christmas of this year. I partialised in two ways: first, by breaking down Christmas Day into the first part of the day and the second part; and secondly, by separating the Christmas that was around the corner from subsequent Christmases.

That couple agreed to divide up Christmas Day for that year. They thought the children would manage, even if they got a bit bloated from getting through two dinners on one day. They each saw that, if they didn't compromise on this issue, there was a 50/50 chance that he or she would wind up "loser". They agreed to decide on how to handle subsequent Christmas Days in the light of experience.

This illustrates the concept of a "win/win solution". They could have agreed to an alternate Christmas plan, and it might have worked, but might also have left each feeling they had "lost out" every second year. And remember "winner takes all" means: "loser gets nothing".

I think it may also illustrate an advantage of a mediated agreement in marital separation over one negotiated by lawyers. I worked as a lawyer for years, and do not want to be unfair to former colleagues, but I doubt if many lawyers, negotiating a separation agreement for their clients, would discover that their respective parents ate their Christmas dinner at different times, and that this difference could be exploited, innocently and benevolently, to try to ensure that three generations could enjoy Christmas together every year, not every second year.

It reminds me to mention another difference between lawyer negotiations and mediation. Lawyers tell horror stories of representing separating couples who agreed everything, and the agreement collapsed at the last minute, over something trifling, like a china dog, or Elvis Presley records. This hardly ever happens in my experience as a mediator. I think there are two reasons. One is that the process moves at a pace determined by the parties, not by outsiders and they finalise their bargain only when they are both ready to do so. (See comments on tempo in Chapter Five.)

131

To understand the other reason clients in mediation rarely end the process over something artificial, I think you need to recognise why so many lawyer-negotiated agreements collapse. I would list the following reasons: wrong tempo, unwillingness on one side or both to let go of the relationship; feeling unheard, "unfinished business", and finally, a partly pathological state of mind in which to agree with your former lover becomes psychologically impossible. Unlike lawyers, mediators, who are in contact with both parties throughout the process, can detect each of these problems at an early stage, and address it. Only the last one, psychological impossibility with a partly pathological root, cannot be addressed in mediation, and we can at least recognise it and end the process without putting our clients through a long drawn out and useless negotiation process.

In fact I can remember very few couples I have worked with who had real difficulty in dividing assets, and in each case my assessment was that the difficulty arose from problems that could have been addressed only with psychological or psychiatric help.

Going back to Peggy and Joe: of course, when they had agreed to partialise the 25th of December, there were still lots of details to be sorted out. Where would the children sleep on the nights of 24/25 and 25/26 December? And subsequent nights? Who would transport them? When would the change-over take place? Could they trust each other to be punctual? But these were mechanical problems, not issues of substance, and if they dealt with these satisfactorily, they were well on the way to co-operating over Christmas in the following year.

I can hear someone saying: "Yes, but the luck was with Michael. What would he have done if they had both said their parents always ate their Christmas dinner at 7.30 p.m. and that other children and grand-children would be there too, and the timing could not be changed?" The answer is I would have grinned at them, and said "Oh well, back to the drawing board!" And they would have grinned back. The process would not have been harmed because I tried an approach that did not work. It might even have been helped if they got the message that looking for a solution to suit all of them was a worthwhile approach.

And, of course, if my idea had not worked out, I would not have told you the story.

Reality-testing

An agreement that looks good on paper, or that attracts clients because it offers a respite from strife, is useless unless it is going to satisfy their real needs, or can be modified to do so. It may be worse than useless if it breaks down after a short time, because it may encourage their mutual feeling that the other cannot be trusted. A mediator may be tempted not to explore how a bargain his clients want to make will work in practice. After all, the content of the agreement is determined by the couple, not by the mediator.

Yes, but. The mediator has experience that they do not have. In my view, he acts responsibly if he questions how a bargain they contemplate will operate, and he acts irresponsibly if he takes the soft option, and says: "Oh, well, they seem happy with it, so I will accept it, and won't ask questions." If he acts responsibly, as I see it, he may question their bargain, whether to help them to improve it or to help them to see that an idea that looked attractive was impractical. Or, best of all, he may explore it with a completely open mind, not caring whether his clients improve on their original plan, abandon it, or reaffirm it, provided they are both contented with whatever they decide. Of course, there is a danger that the mediator will unconsciously cross over the line, and start influencing the content of the decisions the clients make. As so often in mediation, we walk a tightrope. We must not push our clients into agreements that we think are right for them, but we do not want to watch them drive at high speed over a cliff, or even into a cul-de-sac. All we can do is to try to maintain a balance.

The characteristic questions in reality-testing are: "How would that work in practice?" "Can you be clearer (or more precise) about that?" "What would happen if . . . "

Let's take a break from marital mediation for a moment, and look at how we might test the reality of a bargain in a commercial situation. The "Button Factory War" between the production man and the salesman that we first talked about in Chapter Three might be a good one. Let us suppose that Tom, the production man, having admitted that he was wrong to take a swing at the salesman, Peter, offers an apology, which Peter accepts. I have known apologies to be offered and rejected, but not in the mediation process, and there is nothing like an apology gracefully offered and graciously accepted to improve the atmosphere. They next look at how they will co-operate in future, and agree to present a plan jointly to Owen, the managing director, to increase capacity by investing in new plant. Peter will take responsibility for selling the increased turnover and Tom for producing it, if Owen makes money available for the new plant.

They also agree that Peter will make sure that he always has a clear idea of production capacity in the plant for the following four weeks, and will not take an order that can not be filled. The mediator's first reality-testing question is "how will Peter be kept informed?" They discuss this and agree it will be Peter's duty to look for that information weekly – not Tom's duty to furnish it unasked, but Tom will have it available for Peter at 3.00 every Monday. At this point, the mediator feels he has done pretty well. He might sigh with relief, and decide to call it a day (or quit while he is ahead), but he decides he ought to test out their bargain, to make sure it will stand up in the day-to-day life of the business. So, he asks some more reality-testing questions:

"Peter, is it possible that a customer might come to you with a hard-luck story about needing special buttons in a crisis, you might feel this was an opportunity to cement relations or make a valuable new connection and book an order without consulting Tom?"

After thinking about it, Peter agrees that it would be bad business to make promises to the customer that might not be kept, and agrees that he should make encouraging noises, but consult Tom before making any promises. That disposes of that problem. The mediator then asks Tom:

"What happens if something goes wrong in the plant, and production comes to a stop? What do you do?"

Tom says the right thing to do is to notify Peter at once, because customer goodwill is Peter's responsibility. The mediator's next question may be:

"Who should be the point of contact if a customer wants to complain? Will this depend on whether he is complaining about quality, or timing? Should he be asked to contact Tom, because the customer sees Tom as responsible? Or do you want him to contact Peter, because customer goodwill is his responsibility?

Tom and Peter will probably agree that Peter, not Tom, is the person to deal with customer complaints. This relieves Tom of his worry of being bawled out over the phone because of a foolish decision by Peter, and relieves Peter of the fear that he may lose a good customer through Tom being tactless or aggressive. (Remember, Tom is the chap who punched Peter!) The mediator finally says:

"I think we are doing pretty well here, and it looks as though you two will be able to co-operate brilliantly in future. But let me ask you: is there anything I have overlooked, that could go wrong, and bring you back to square one?"

If they think of something, we will consider it. If not, the mediator may say:

> "We know Murphy's Law says if something can go wrong, it will. We may not have covered all possible problems this afternoon. What happens if you hit a problem along the way that we have not covered today?"

Perhaps they will agree that they will take any unforeseen problem to Owen, the managing director, but only together, never separately. They may also agree that if Owen consents, they will contact the mediator, but only as a last resort. At this stage, the process will be complete when they have both read and approved the mediator's record of their bargain. The additional questions he asked after the parties had agreed on the major issue may have been entirely unnecessary because the contingencies he asked about may never arise. But asking them and pursuing them represents the difference between a task well done and one left incomplete.

As we leave the button factory, let me ask you: does anything the mediator says to Peter and Tom require expertise in the making of buttons? Or only common sense and imagination? I hope your answers will illustrate a conviction of mine, which is a theme in this book: that a mediator is an expert in conflict-management, and does not need expertise in the family or industry in which conflict arises.

Mediators need to remember that while reality-testing is a very useful and valuable tool, it is potentially dangerous. Its main danger, for the clients and for their mediator, is that a mediator who explores the consequences of decisions his clients are taking may cross over a border, and start to influence their decision-making. The danger is greater because this could happen without anyone in the room being aware of it. I said above that a mediator may question his clients' bargain, either to help them to improve it or to help them to see that an idea that looked superficially attractive was impractical. In either

136

case, he uses the same technique: reality-testing. And, in each case, there is the same danger: of becoming directive.

The danger is probably smaller, and the potential for damage is less, where the purpose of the questioning is to help the parties to refine their bargain. The two areas in marital mediation where I have most often used the tool of reality-testing in order to help people to improve their bargain are, first, contact between a father and children who live most or all of the time with their mother, and, secondly, the machinery for paying financial support. When I talk about unpunctuality later, in Chapter Ten, I describe some questions a mediator might ask to explore what happens if a Dad is late in collecting his children or bringing them home. These are also examples of reality-testing.

The other issue I often reality-test is when and how support – for children, or spouse, or both – will be paid. One of the most common complaints of separated wives who receive support from their husbands is that it arrives unpunctually, and sometimes does not arrive at all. I do not doubt that some husbands use their power in this area to continue their marital warfare with their ex-wife, and that others get into arrear by accident, not design, because they have difficulty in managing their finances when they are living alone. But from the ex-wife's point of view it does not matter whether he has let her down intentionally or accidentally – she is now in money trouble. His failure as a provider to pay the money when it was due may put a strain on their relationship as parents trying to co-operate in bringing up their children. "Why should I let him see the children when he is not keeping his side of the bargain?" is a question we often hear.

An experienced mediator knows that the timing of the payment of money can be a major cause of strife between separated spouses. He also knows that if the party who pays support – usually the husband – has a wage or salary, it can be paid directly into a bank, if it is not paid that way already. It is not hard, either, to organise standing instructions to the bank to pay a fixed amount at regular intervals into his wife's bank account. This eliminates a lot of potential for fighting between the husband and wife.

Most husbands agree to this method of payment. I do not know – it is not my business to ask – whether it is because they recognise that they should honour their side of a bargain, or that to cut off income supply would be an abuse of power, not an exercise of a legitimate right, or that it might expose their children to hardship, or that they may be tempted to use the timing of the payment of money as an offensive weapon, and choose to deprive themselves of the opportunity. What I do know is that couples who put in place arrangements to ensure that money payable by one to the other will be paid regularly have a better chance of co-operating as parents than spouses who expose themselves to the risk of recurring rows over delay in paying.

An experienced mediator will often use reality-testing as a means to help his clients to make an agreement that will eliminate that bone of contention. Typical questions and answers might be:

"Maria, do you do one big supermarket shop every so often?" Answer: yes.

"How often?" Answer: every week.

"What day of the week?" Answer: Friday evening.

"So do you need to know on Friday that Peter has lodged money to your account, and that you can take cash out of the hole-in-the-wall machine?" Answer: yes.

"Does that mean that, from your point of view, he would need to have lodged it by Thursday evening?" Answer: yes.

"Peter, when are you paid?"

And so on.

We are in more dangerous territory if the purpose of the

reality-testing questions is to erode a bargain that the clients have tentatively made. Clearly, a mediator is not entitled to say to people who want to live their lives in one way: "You would be mad to do that", but we need to be aware of the danger that we may confuse the substance with the form, and make a statement of that kind, but pretend to ourselves that it was not a statement, but a question, because it had a question mark at the end. We are on a mediator's recurring tightrope. In the mediation process, he has earned the confidence of his clients, which means that anything he may say is going to be listened to with respect. The more trust the clients have in us, the greater our duty is to respect them, and their trust in us, and continue to earn it.

Let us take an example. A married couple are separating, and have agreed that the husband, Paul, will move out, transfer the family home into his wife Mona's sole name, and maintain the household consisting of Mona and the children, Anne and Tony, until the children have completed their education, when financial support will stop. Mona is in her early 40s and has a part-time job. Anne is 19 and in her first year in college. Tony is 16, and the parents expect him to go to third level education.

A mediator listens to this bargain, and wonders what is going to happen in Mona's life when the children move on. He asks a few questions:

> "Let's see. The mortgage has about eight years more to run. Tony is 16, and has – what? two years to go in secondary school. How long will he spend in university? Another four or five years? So, the mortgage will have just about a year or so to run, when he graduates, and the support stops. Right?

Having got their agreement to that, he continues:

> "Mona, I imagine that there is quite a good chance that you may be able to pay off the balance of the mortgage at that time. After all, it will then be a pretty small amount. What do you think?

139

Mona: "Probably."

Paul: "If not, I'll pay it off, so you needn't worry about that."

Mona: "Thanks. I appreciate that."

Mediator: "Great. So, at that point in Mona's life, she will be turning fifty, hopes she will still have her part-time job, and will own the house, free of mortgage. Will you be able to get by on that, Mona? Do you think at that point the job will pay enough for you to live?

Mona: "Perhaps. But it's not very likely."

Mediator: "Is there a possibility you might use the house to augment income? I mean, if Anne or Tony is still living there, and working and earning a salary, would they contribute to household expenses?

"If neither of them is living there, would you see yourself letting space in the house? Taking in lodgers, or students?"

Mona: "It's not something I have thought about."

(Pause for Mona to think)

"I don't think I'd want to. I will be in my fifties, and I'd find it hard to work every morning, keep the house and look after lodgers."

Mediator: "What about later, when you are coming up to retirement? Does your part-time job carry any pension rights?" Does it give you the right to any state pension? Does your employer stamp cards?"

The likely answer to these questions is that there will be no pension, or a much reduced one. The mediator continues:

"So, what does Mona live on, when the children's education is completed, and the support from Paul stops? That is, really, for the rest of her life?"

Mona may say that this is her problem, and she will deal with it when it arises, and, anyway, she may be dead by then. The mediator has done his duty by asking questions that push both of them to look at the consequences of the bargain they

140

are making. If Mona says she is satisfied with it, he does not push it any further. If he does, he ceases to be a mediator and becomes a participant.

The distinction is quite fine, and can be hard to maintain clearly in the mediator's mind. This can perhaps be illustrated better if we look at the issue I mentioned earlier, where the mediator asks reality-testing questions, to pin-point a possible problem about regular payments of support, by "him" to "her", or "them". But he needs to ask himself: why does he do this? Is he trying to help them to see a possible snag and eliminate it, like the Dirk Bogarde character in the Pinter/Losey film, "The Servant", saying to the painters: ". . . tell me of any problem, so that we can correct it before it becomes a fault." Or is he trying to get them to see that the solution to their potential problem is a bank standing order?

The first aim is legitimate; the second is not.

The problem for a mediator is that while he looks to the first he knows that if his questions lead them to decide there is a problem, he can produce a ready solution to it. To ask questions in order to expose a problem to which the mediator knows a solution, without trying to push his clients towards that solution, requires fairly remarkable mental gymnastics. There is an atmosphere of unreality about it all, like Chico and Harpo Marx in "Go West" agreeing, first that they would open the envelope, but not read the telegram, and then that they would read it, but wouldn't listen.

This is one of the many tightropes mediators have to walk, or pinpoints on which we have to dance, if you prefer. There is a way of keeping our balance on this one. If the parties decide that there is a problem, and that it would be useful to address it, such as the possibility of conflict over delays in paying support, I often say something like: "Another couple I worked with had a similar situation, and they decided that it would suit them to have the money paid out of his bank account into hers

141

by regular bank standing order, or whatever they call it. It might not suit you, but I thought it worth mentioning, since you are looking at a similar situation." I find that a good way of getting myself out of an artificial situation, where I know of a way out of the problem but am reluctant to mention it for fear they may feel they have to accept it because it comes from me. They get the message, but they do not feel any compulsion to follow the example of other people, presumably no wiser or more experienced in handling these problems than they are.

I said just now that the distinction was quite fine and hard to maintain clearly. To keep it clear in a mediator's mind may seem especially hard in a line of work where the dialogue is continuous and we want to maintain an appearance of spontaneity. But to me, as a fairly experienced mediator, the appearance of spontaneity now seems less important than it used to. I am now quite comfortable about saying to people I am working with: "Let me take a minute or two out, to think about that". I find people accept that, appreciate that I want to put time into thinking through problems, and are willing to sit quietly while I do so. It can often be useful to them, too, to be given a chance to ponder quietly.

Before leaving Mona and Paul I should mention that throughout this dialogue with Mona the mediator will have kept his eye on both of them, and observed Paul's reactions. Does Paul seem concerned? If so, is it on Mona's account? Is he worried that the mediator is encouraging her to reserve the right to seek support from him in years to come? The dialogue I have sketched assumes the mediator does not pick up negative signals from Paul. If he does, the line of questioning will change – probably to include Paul.

Process-interruption

If you took a sample of mediators, you would find most of us had started in a different line of work. John Haynes says most

142

mediators when they get stuck fall back on their profession of origin. Lawyers begin to give legal advice, psychotherapists to practise therapy, and so on.

If trained professionals react to uncertainty by falling back on their old-established certainties, it is hardly surprising that our clients react in the same way, when they feel confused or disoriented. That is exactly how most of them feel when they come to mediation. People come to mediation when their marriages have recently collapsed, more often than not with bitter hostility, and frequent, savage rows in which they have torn what was left of their relationship to shreds. It is understandable that many spouses do what John described professional mediators doing. They fall back on the pattern they are used to. They fight.

When his clients fight, a mediator has choices. He can ignore the fight. But that will allow it to continue. While it rages, no progress is being made, and progress to date may be unravelling. He can join in the fight, and hope to manoeuvre it to an end. But it is hard to get involved in a fight between other people, even with the intention of breaking it up, without giving one or both of the fighters the impression that you have taken sides. It doesn't much matter whether they both feel the mediator has weighed in on the other side, or one feels he has become her ally. Either way, he is no longer seen as an impartial mediator.

Another choice is to use the technique called "process-interruption". This is a concept that everyone who looks after children uses every day, even if they never put a name to it. If a child is about to have a tantrum, or if two children are about to start hitting each other, the adult interrupts with something extraneous to the business in hand. It doesn't always work, but when it does, the child or children subside, and the world goes on, instead of coming to an end.

Process-interrupting involves saying or doing something that stops the parties in their tracks. If I am working with a marital couple, and they start to fight about which of them should keep their old car and which should buy a new one, I might say, "tell me more about Frank. What kind of kid is he?" or "Is it next summer or the summer after next that Maria is due to leave secondary school?" If I have started the process effectively, and gained their confidence, and some level of process-control, then one of them is bound to answer any question I ask. They cannot answer a question about Frank or Maria and at the same time go on fighting about the car, so the answer suspends the fight, if only for a moment. I have resumed control over the process, and moved my clients from an unhelpful mode of communicating and negotiating. The next step is to get them into a helpful one.

But I recommend any mediator who decides to interrupt a fight by asking a question not to ask a cul-de-sac question. "What time is it?" is a cul-de-sac question. When it is answered, there is nowhere else to go. Parents will probably not answer "what kind of kid is Frank?" in one word, but if they do it can lead on to "which of you will tell him you are going to separate?"

Breaking up a row by asking a process-interrupting question on an unrelated topic has another attraction. It gives the couple a message: "When you get back into that stuff about your spousal conflict, I know I have heard it before, and I stop listening to you and start thinking about something useful."

I suggest that if a mediator interrupts a fight by asking a question, he should try to choose one that meets two criteria. One is that the interests and emotions of his clients in answering it should at least be congruent, for example their children. There is little merit in getting them to stop fighting about who will keep the old car and who will get a new one, and start them fighting about whether they should sell the family home.

The other is that it can be discussed in a future-focussed way. This is not as difficult as it may sound: when we are in a session with our clients, there is usually no shortage of future-related topics, and it is not hard to choose one. "Is it next summer or the summer after next that Maria is due to leave secondary school?" is an example.

144

CHAPTER NINE

PROBLEMS IN MEDIATION

I want to talk in this chapter about some of the things that can cause problems for people trying to resolve their conflicts amicably, and to describe how a mediator may help his clients to get over these problems, or around them, so that they can reach agreement. Unlike the next chapter which will talk about problems specific to marital mediation, this one will be about problems that can arise in trying to resolve any type of conflict, though some of the examples will be drawn from marital conflict, because it offers good illustrations.

Imbalances

In any negotiation, if one party is more skilful than the other he may negotiate an unbalanced bargain in which he gains too much and gives too little. This may look like a good day's work for the more skilled negotiator, but it will not always turn out that way, especially in those situations where mediation is most likely to be useful: where people in dispute have a continuing relationship, and cannot walk away from each other. The unequal bargain may poison the relationship. Even if it does not, a bad bargain is unlikely to work in practice.

If the bargain is not fair (of course I mean by the standards of the parties, not of the mediator), sooner or later the penny will drop for whichever party failed to negotiate effectively, and he (or she) will feel "Why should I carry on with this deal, which gives her (or him) everything, and me nothing?" The person who has used superior skill to get a "good deal" may wind up wishing he had been less grasping. Or, to put it another way, wiser. The other party at that stage will probably recognise three things. First is that he made a bad bargain, first time around. Second is that he did so because the other party took advantage of greater negotiating ability. Third is that he himself walked into it – allowed it to happen. He will feel embarrassed, angry at the other party and at himself, and suspicious – a mixture that will not make him easy to deal with.

Being reasonably detached from the content of our clients' bargain (none of us can be completely detached) mediators can see that danger, and can often do something to avert it. The smarter negotiator may feel at the time that we interfere too much, but may be grateful later, if he winds up not with a bargain that will collapse in a few weeks, but "a good one that will last".

Imbalance in skill or power?

It is legitimate for us to intervene if we see a danger that a more skilful or dynamic negotiator may foist on the other party an unbalanced agreement that we judge will not work in practice. It is not legitimate to intervene if our motive is to steer the parties into making a bargain that meets our sense of what is fair. The distinction is clear on paper, but a mediator who is tempted to intervene in a way that may shape the outcome needs to keep asking himself about his motives.

Indeed, there are two problems, not one. We need to look at the imbalance and see what causes it. Is it an imbalance in

146

negotiating skill, which it is legitimate to try to balance? Or does it arise from the fact that one party is in a stronger negotiating position than the other – what I will call, for convenience, a power imbalance?

Deciding which it is can be harder than it sounds. We often come across situations where one party is in a stronger position than the other (power imbalance) and also has greater negotiating skill (skill imbalance). Indeed, in negotiation, people who realise they have more power than they thought will often develop greater negotiating skill. Conversely, the ability to negotiate effectively can drain away through the soles of our feet when we realise we have very few cards in our hands. If a mediator recognises an imbalance in the negotiating abilities of his clients, he needs to be able to sort out how far it is caused by their positions and how far by their respective skills, and to what extent the relative positions increase the skills of one and decrease those of the other. This is often a delicate judgement to make and it has to be made in fractions of a second. More often than not, an experienced mediator will make it instinctively. (Though an American friend, a mediator whom I admire, made an interesting comment to me recently. Someone else had just said that she worked on intuition, not theory, and my friend suggested that this might simply mean that her internal computer was faster than other people's.)

All this is very abstract, so let's take an example. Let's assume a man is applying for a job, and his prospective boss, who is interviewing him, is a woman. If the man is unemployed, or under notice, he may be desperate to get the job. Unless he has exceptional acting ability and self-control, or she is lacking in insight, she will soon realise that he needs her more than she needs him. If she spots his weakness, she may decide to look for a "bargain" and offer him a salary less than his true value, and he may feel he has to accept. On the

147

other hand, if he has a satisfactory job, and she is head hunting, he will recognise, however hard she tries to hide it, that she is negotiating from weakness. This puts him in a strong position, and he may insist on being paid more than his value in the marketplace.

In either case, they will have started their relationship on a bad footing. If it is a short-term appointment, that does not much matter. If they both want it to be a continuing one, the opening imbalance may cause problems. If the man is under-paid, this is probably less serious because his boss can remedy the under-payment by offering him a raise. Moreover, if she does it voluntarily and gracefully, it may help to cement their working relationship. However, unless this happens he will be resentful as soon as he gets over his relief at having a job. His sense of being undervalued may sap his initiative. He may become unable to rise above the status to which he has been relegated, even if he has the inherent ability to do so.

If he is over-paid, the resentment will be on the other side, but he may become complacent, and, again, his performance may suffer. His boss may also expect from him a level of performance related to his pay rather than his capacity. The mixture of a complacent employee and a demanding boss promises an even worse working relationship than that of a contemptuous boss and a resentful employee, and it is harder to remedy.

Let's make another assumption, this time a rather far-fetched one: that these two people agree to ask a mediator to sit in on their interview. The mediator will start with an assumption that people who use him will put their cards on the table face up, and that neither will keep secrets from the other. So if he does his job according to his lights and training, he may start by asking the applicant: "How badly do you need this job?" Or, by asking the employer: "Do you need to fill this position quickly? Have you alternatives lined up?" Either way, he may expose weaknesses that each may want to conceal.

I exaggerate. A competent mediator will not go rushing into negotiation in that ham-fisted way. However, it is true that we seek to identify our clients's needs, and inherent in that search is a risk that we may expose negotiating weaknesses that the parties may want to conceal. In this unlikely scenario, the mediator will probably try to augment the negotiating capacity of the disadvantaged party, so that their bargain will reflect their respective positions and bargaining strengths, not their abilities. But as I said earlier, he must not try to change the power they each have at that time. If he does, the bargain that would emerge would not reflect the relationship and would be unreal. And he should remember that however healthy a bargain may look in the mediator's cosy room, an unreal one will not long survive when it is exposed to the cold air of the outside world.

How would a mediator try to adjust negotiating skill? There is no one answer to this question. I have never been asked to mediate in the negotiation of an employment contract, as distinct from its termination, and I hope I would have enough sense to decline if I were asked. One scenario, using skills we have been discussing, might play like this, if it seemed that the prospective employee was going to be taken on at a low level of pay:

Mediator: "Okay, Geraldine, you are offering Ignatius £15,000 a year. That is £10,000 a year less than he had in his previous job. I suppose it is about half what he was getting, if you take into account benefit-in-kind in the previous job, which you are not offering.

"It looks to me, from what Ignatius said, that he may be inclined to take it. If he does, it won't be because he thinks it is a good offer, or fairly values his

149

qualifications and experience, but because he badly needs a job, and, although he has valuable skills, they are not currently in great demand.

"I imagine that if Ignatius does take that size drop in salary, and is paid less than the market says he is worth, he will stay in the job only for as long as it takes him to get another?

(Pause for assent from Ignatius, or, at least, for him not to dissent – and for Geraldine to see that he does not dissent.)

"If so, Geraldine will have to replace him as soon as he gets another offer. I'm not asking either of you to comment on whether I'm right, but doesn't it seem to be the kind of thing an outsider might guess?

"I am also wondering about Geraldine's job specification and the level of ability it calls for. Is the job Geraldine wants to fill one that a £15,000 a year employee can be expected to do? If she rates Ignatius at £15,000 a year, and pays him accordingly, is she giving him a message that she doesn't really expect the level of competence – and dedication – that her ad talks about?

"I wonder is Ignatius going to be able to do even a lower level job than he is used to, and work as an equal colleague with the other people in the company, if they get to know that he has been hired on terms that say he is not their equal?

"So I am thinking about a few things. First is: will the job be done to Geraldine's satisfaction by someone who is paid £15,000 a year? Second is: is Geraldine going to have to be in touch with me again, in six months' time, either to fill a vacancy because Ignatius has left, or to renegotiate terms, because Ignatius isn't willing to stay on at £15,000, and Geraldine doesn't want to lose him? And will the boot then be on the other foot, with Geraldine needing Ignatius more than he needs her?"

150

This is an example of reality-testing. It may lead Geraldine to think again before she offers Ignatius insultingly poor terms. It may also lead him to recognise that he is not as helpless as he thought he was, and this may help him to negotiate more effectively in his own interests.

Unfortunately, it is also an example of something a mediator should never do – becoming involved in the content of his clients' bargain. I give it partly to illustrate another problem in mediation work. After I wrote it I realised that it describes aspects of my own working life. In the early '60s, I left the law firm where I was a salaried assistant to work in what I thought was a better firm where I might have better prospects, though at a lower starting salary. My bosses in my new job did cement our relationship by voluntarily offering me a raise before we were due to review, because they realised I was worth more than they were paying. Twenty-five years later, I changed career and resigned what had meanwhile become a partnership in the same firm to work as a mediator. My decisions first to join the firm and then to leave it both resulted in a drop in income for me, and I have never regretted either.

I offer this slice of biography at this point because it shows something we will look at in more detail later: the need for a mediator to be aware of how his experience may affect his attitude to his clients' needs. If I were involved in this interviewing process (unlikely as that might be) and if I did my duty of putting myself in the shoes of each party in turn, I might be in danger of thinking that the prospective employee would prove his value and be promoted, and encourage him to take the job at a lower salary than he should be paid, because that is what I had done and good consequences flowed from it. He might be in danger of following my lead, to his detriment. Worse, I might be guilty of encouraging him to do so. This raises a separate but related topic, unconscious mediator bias, and we will return to it in Chapter Fifteen.

In marital mediation you might think – as has often been said to me – that a woman who has spent her life at home rearing children will be no match in negotiation for a man used to negotiating business deals every day of the week. The opposite is often true. Much of the man's perceived advantage derives from experience in business negotiation. He will probably be accustomed to a confrontational style, with his cards close to his chest. His experience in that style of negotiation may be of little use to him in an environment and negotiating pattern based on both parties identifying the needs of all involved, disclosing resources, and then co-operating in trying to stretch resources to cover needs.

I remember a husband who was trained in negotiation and used to tough commercial dealing, and his wife, who was a full-time mother and home-maker and had no training in negotiation. After I had watched them negotiate for a short time, poised to come to her aid, I recognised the pattern of their negotiation, and, in the interests of helping them to negotiate a rational agreement with some prospect of lasting, started to intervene to correct an imbalance in negotiating skill. Each time, my intervention was to help the businessman husband.

I have no doubt he continued to perform effectively when he was not negotiating with his wife, but with her he was out-classed. I think this was partly because the negotiating style which I see as inherent in mediation is different from what he was used to. Instead of negotiating with cards held firmly to the chest, and using bluff and threats, we were trying to identify the needs of each person in their family, and see what could be done to meet those needs.

The traditional, hard-nosed negotiator faces another

problem. If a poker-playing negotiator fails to disclose his needs, he is in danger of losing out, because they will not be met. Of course, he can exaggerate them, but that seldom works, as a couple of examples will show:

He: "I need to keep my present car, because I do a lot of driving, and it is important that I am seen to drive a good car. It is part of my image. It enables me to earn the income you will depend on."

She: "Are you saying I have to drive the children around in a clapped-out 14-year-old rust heap, that costs a fortune to keep on the road, so that you can drive this year's Series 3 BMW? What will the people you are trying to impress with your flashy car think when they see my rust-bucket stalled on the side of the road, and you sail past in your Beamer?"

Or:

She: "I will hardly have any fun time with the children during the week, and I am the disciplinarian, so I should spend Saturdays with them, and take them places, and we can have good times together."

He: "They will be with you, Monday to Friday. Sunday is a dead day. Most places are closed, they have to get their homework finished for school on Monday, and I have to get ready for work. I need to spend time with them on Saturday, at least as much as you do, if not more. Plus, they need more time with me, and to have fun with me, as they will hardly see me from Monday to Friday."

I have seen similar patterns – lawyers who were tough and demanding on behalf of their clients, but incapable of pushing their own interests, and mediators who in Yeats' splendid phrase would "ride among the arrows with high heart" in their work for clients, but run a mile from aggression in their own lives.

Powerlessness and fear

Paradoxically, it is not unusual in mediation to find that both parties feel powerless. This is usually obvious in marital separation, where the lower income earner – usually the wife – is afraid of penury, while her husband is terrified of losing contact with his children. But the same is true of Peter and Tom, from the Button Factory War, coming to mediation. Both are afraid of being fired; being ostracised by their fellow-employees; being denounced by the other, or by their mediator, or both; what happens when they go back and tell Owen, the managing director, that the process has failed; and when the other lays the blame at his door.

If parties share feelings of fear and powerlessness, they are unlikely to make a good agreement. Most of us give back, in one way or another, what we receive. On a basic social level, if someone buys us a drink, we are likely to want to buy him one in return, and if we feel someone has treated us badly, we are likely to want to reciprocate. This is the instinct that leads some separating spouses to conduct amazingly prolonged and vicious warfare. The success of mediation and the lasting benefit some people get from it often grow from one person making a gesture or a concession that is seen to be generous, and that starts a cycle of generous responses.

Generous instincts and the ability to make generous gestures do not come out of fear, but may be stimulated by generosity from others, or from feelings of relief when our fears have been dispelled. Very often, the first thing a mediator should do is to relieve the fears that he finds in his room.

He can do this in a number of ways. One is to establish, openly, what each party is most afraid of, and get the other to promise that it won't happen. (I describe this in Chapter Two, where I talk about the merits of face-to-face mediation.) This can be useful, but it can be even more effective to relieve fears, *without* exposing them. For example, Tom may apologise early in the process to Peter for hitting him, and Peter may accept. They then both feel they are no longer in imminent danger of a confrontation that will lead to one of them being fired.

I think there is another, more subtle way, in which a mediator may dispel, or at least reduce, the tensions his clients bring into the room: by showing himself to be calm, quiet, and rational. If he can induce a feeling that, while he is around, nothing very awful is going to happen, the irrational fears, and the unconscious fears that all his clients, especially those who are facing marital separation, carry into the room, will begin to reduce. Once this starts to happen, he has a better chance of being able to work on the rational, conscious fears, by addressing their causes.

Getting "hooked"

Most of us have some experience of fear and intimidation in our lives. We are more aware of what we have suffered than of suffering we have inflicted. This is certainly true of the pain that goes with a failed marriage, and I think it is also true of intimidation. We remember being intimidated by others and may not realise we have been intimidating, or gained our wishes by actual or implied threats. This is the experience against which we assess any symptoms of intimidation we observe in our clients, and our instinct is to protect the frightened, and to down-face the bully.

That is an instinct we would not want to change, but working as a mediator involves controlling our instincts and not allowing them to dominate our work. A mediator who automatically grabs his lance, vaults on to his white charger, and rushes to the rescue of someone he sees as intimidated will be useless with a client who probes for his weaknesses – clients do – detects that one, and exploits it – clients do. As part of the process of becoming a mediator we need to confront our own feelings about intimidation, bullying, and domestic violence, recognise them, and not allow them to affect our work.

I should probably say "infect" not "affect", because if we do not recognise our own feelings and their influence on us, they will become like an infection that spreads and corrupts the health of the process, without our recognising what is happening. They are also like an infection because when we are aware of the danger we can lessen it by frequent applications of disinfectant. But we can never be sure we have killed the source.

Violence and intimidation are by no means the only issues mediators need to confront, in order first to recognise our own feelings about them, and then to ensure those feelings do not affect the process. For example, how do we feel if we are told that a long-standing marriage has come to an end, because the husband has "come out", and wants to live with another man in a homosexual relationship? What are our instinctive responses, when he says he wants he wants to continue to play a big role in his children's lives? Will we have a different response if it is the wife who has "come out", and wants to live with a another woman as her lover, while playing a big role in her children's lives? In either case, will our response differ, depending on whether the children are boys or girls? What if one party has been sexually promiscuous? If he or she has infected the other with a sexually transmitted disease? Again, will our reaction differ, depending on whether the husband slept around and infected his wife, or the wife slept around and infected her husband?

To me, the answer to all these questions is simple but harsh. If I sympathise with one, and not with the other, I am in danger of not being a mediator. I may even become, unconsciously, an advocate for the person who has won my sympathy. So I have had to learn that if I am to be a mediator between two people, one of whom has complaints against the other that if I were not in my mediator role might sound legitimate, I must be able to give the same sympathy and understanding to both.

I have worked with couples who had passed through serious domestic violence. I felt entitled to mediate, when it became clear that the wife, on whom the violence had been perpetrated, was not currently exposed to danger, did not feel intimidated, and was capable of negotiating with her husband, although he had treated her in a way that endangered her life. I think I served them reasonably well, and if I did it was because I strove to have for both the same level of acceptance and understanding. I did not find it too hard to understand her physical and mental pain and the feelings of impotence and fear she had felt when confronting someone out of control and much stronger physically than she was. I had some sense of how that experience coloured not only their relationship, but, perhaps for the rest of her life, her sense of the world she lived in, and her attitude to the other fifty per cent of its inhabitants, (including me) who were, presumably, capable of treating her in the same way.

I tried to understand the husband, too, and what dark, uncontrolled impulse had led him to use violence to his wife, but found identifying with him much harder. It was a line from *Julius Caesar* that came to my mind, and helped me to make a partial breakthrough into the husband's. The conspirators have decided to kill Caesar, and gather round him, apparently to implore him to rescind the banishment of Publius Cimber, but really to isolate him from his friends, and have a pretext for attacking him when he – inevitably – refuses. The last words spoken, before they fall on Caesar and hack him to death are Casca's: "Speak, hands, for me!"

These four words helped me to an insight into what had happened inside the skull of the man who had struck his wife – more than once. He carried inside himself a dangerous, potentially lethal combination. He had huge anger, which probably went back to his childhood; he had a lot of emotional needs of which he was unaware; he was less articulate than most people, and much less intelligent and self-aware then his wife. The potential to explode that was part of his personality meant that he needed, more than most of us, to be vigilant, to prevent it escaping. The lack of self-awareness meant that he was less likely than most to understand the need to be disciplined. Emotional needs he was not aware of made him vulnerable to disappointment, and his inability to articulate frustration and anger when his needs were not met, or even acknowledged, meant that if his anger did break out, it was likely to do so through physical aggression: "Speak, hands, for me!"

Once I had a sense that I could understand him better, and see the loneliness and pain that lived inside him and controlled him, I was able to sympathise with him, and work with them both, in a balanced way.

Indeed, I was in danger of being more sympathetic towards him than towards her. Before you dismiss me as a male chauvinist, and throw this book away, let me explain. She was an intelligent, poised woman who had made a major mistake in marrying him, had recognised her error, left the marriage, and, though emotionally scarred by the experience, was about to get on with her life in a positive way. He had acquired no understanding or awareness, did not recognise the problems in his own psyche, and carried around within himself a poisoned seed that would probably ensure that any other relationship he might have would founder in the same way that this one had. Which would you feel more sorry for?

High conflict

Another big problem mediators meet is "high conflict". You might assume that the anger people bring into the mediation process is part of the conflict that needs to be addressed, and the mediator must work with it and resolve it. Often this is not so. If a business partnership is breaking up, and one partner is furious with his ex-partner for leaving the joint venture, his anger has no relevance in valuing work-in-progress, or deciding which of them should represent specific clients. If a wife is full of rage and shame because her husband has been sleeping with another woman, and he is furious with her because she has blackened him to his family, none of that affects their children's needs, or how income should be shared.

Angry clients make for tense mediators, and unfortunately angry people represent a large part of our work. Calm, placid, reasonable people have less need of a mediator.

Colleagues often say that the people they most dislike to work with, and who tire them most, are angry, rowing people. Funnily enough, I do not feel that. I do not handle conflict in my own life well, but my background as a lawyer has accustomed me to conflict and helped me to handle with detachment conflict to which I am not a party. The fact that I worked as a commercial lawyer may have helped me to become relaxed about conflict around me. The conflicts I dealt with were about money, not about things of real importance, so it was easy for me to learn to take part in the fight but be detached from its results. When I am asked what gets to me most in my work as a mediator, I answer, "unshed tears".

High conflict is very common in marital mediation. I have worked with people over whom I could exercise no control whatever. Almost the entire session was taken up with

159

needling, abuse and threats. I usually listen with interest to the first "round" because it can teach me a lot about my clients, but when it is repeated with no variations it has nothing more to teach. What to do, if faced with something like this? I could assert my authority, as "chair" of our meeting, and say:

> "It seems to me we are wasting our time here. You are using this room to fight in, not to solve your problems. It is not available for that purpose. Neither am I. If you want to fight more than you want to address the issues, please go and do it somewhere else."

Another way would be to ignore them. When the same fight broke out again I could turn away, or – extreme measure – picked up a book and start reading it. That is pretty well guaranteed to stop the fight. People who fight in this way in their mediator's room do so because they want an audience, and if they see the audience leaving the theatre they will change the show. The problem is that it humiliates them, and they will see me as the person who inflicted humilation on them. My ability to help them further will be in doubt.

It is worth knowing that most people in high conflict will absorb as much time as they are allowed in fighting, and devote to problem-solving only the minimum amount of fighting time they are forced to yield up. A good way to deal with high conflict is to impose strict time limits on the fighters:

> *Mediator:* "OK, folks, we have twenty minutes left in this session. You have wasted the last forty in calling each other names. Do you want to try to achieve something in the twenty we have left?
>
> "And they are probably the last twenty minutes we will have together, because I am not going to let you go on using my room as a boxing ring. This is probably our last meeting. It certainly will be if you use the next twenty minutes the way you have used the rest of the time.

160

"So do you want to try to achieve something, in the little time we have left?"

If I say something like this, it is partly to push them into doing some work instead of airing their grievances. But I mean it. And I will not say it unless I am going to be willing to say to them, twenty minutes later: "I don't intend to make another appointment with you, because I don't believe it will do you any good, and it certainly doesn't do me any."

I may change my mind during the last twenty minutes, but I mean what I say, when I say it. And I will bear in my mind something else I have learnt about people who are engaged in conflict at that intense level. In order to have built up that level of hostility, they must have got to know each other pretty well. And over the time they have known each other they have built up an ability to communicate without needing words. Faced with a common foe – a mediator who is about to spoil their game by taking away the opportunity to fight – they will often unite in a strikingly co-operative way. Their unspoken bargain may be: "We will be very good and constructive for the next twenty minutes. We may even agree on a few minor issues. After all, if we do there is nothing to stop us from repudiating the agreement when we have our next row. By showing this poor mediating fool how good we can be, we will trap him into giving us another appointment. Which we will use to continue the row. Indeed, we may be able to repeat this trick at the next session, by reverting at the end of it, because he seems pretty gullible."

I am not cynical enough to suggest that this kind of collusion goes on at a conscious level. But I have no doubt whatever that it operates at an unconscious level. Nor have I any real doubt that it has been operated successfully by high conflict clients I have worked with.

161

Staying detached

Many mediators start with an unconscious assumption that actually makes it harder for us to operate effectively. It is that it is our duty to bring our clients to a resolution of their conflict. It follows that if they go on fighting we are to blame. Another mediator, more skilful or more understanding than us, would have "succeeded", where we have "failed". I am not saying the second part of that is always wrong. What I do say is that the first part, that it is our duty to bring our clients to a resolution of their conflict, is wrong. Conflict can be resolved only by the people engaged in it. An outsider may try to help them to resolve it, but he does not resolve it for them. Nobody can. (As we discussed in Chapter One, a judge can determine a conflict, but cannot resolve it.)

Indeed, it is often helpful for us to remind the people we work with of this basic fact, and it can be useful for a mediator to remind himself, as well as his clients. Some of the people I worked with over the years may remember my telling them this "joke". (The inverted commas are because I don't think it is funny.)

> *Client:* "I have been accused of fraud. What do we do?"
> *Lawyer:* "We defend the charge."

(Later)

> *Client:* "I have been convicted. What do we do?"
> *Lawyer:* "We appeal."

(Later again)

> *Client:* "The appeal has been dismissed. What do we do?"
> *Lawyer:* "*We* don't do anything. *I* go back to my office. *You* go to jail."

I have never had to explain that "joke" to any client.

When I worked as a lawyer I was retained by my friend (as he became) Laurence Crowley, the leading insolvency accountant in Dublin at the time, who was winding up a

162

company. As we toiled through the terrible mess the directors had left behind, Laurence said to me, "I could not do this work if I did not constantly remind myself that I am not responsible for making the mess that I have to clear up."

The lawyer "joke" and Laurence's comment remind a mediator that while three people are dealing with a set of problems, they are the problems of the parties, not of the mediator. Even if you believe that one party to a marriage may be totally to blame for everything that went wrong, and the other wholly blameless (do you also believe in the tooth fairy?), the blameless one, not the mediator, made the mistake of marrying the monster.

If thinking along these lines leads me to feel I come between my clients as they fight, or to give up my relentless search for a solution to their problems, it may lead them to stop fighting, and start looking for their own solution. And their solution is likely to be a lot better for them than one I might give them, because it is theirs.

It is often better for a mediator to knock off from doing the clients' job, and to sit back, physically as well as mentally, and let – or make – them do the work. A group of aspirant mediators I trained some years ago included a woman of whom I was rather in awe, because her qualifications as a marital therapist were high, her intellect impressive, and her demeanour – or so it seemed to me at first acquaintance – formidable. (I became less nervous, though no less respectful, as I got to know her better.) We did a role-play in which she was the mediator. She was finding it difficult, and I noticed that she was leaning forward in her chair, towards the couple, more and more as she tried and failed to get movement from them. Two things were happening. She was being sucked into their conflict as a participant, and a pattern was created by which she made suggestions, and they united in shooting them down. Since

163

they had no incentive to set about solving their own problems, the process was heading rapidly towards impasse. (Remember, she was only a learner at this stage, not even a beginner.)

Rather diffidently, I came up behind her, placed a hand on each of her shoulders, and gently drew her backwards, until her spine was against the back of her chair. She continued to work with the couple, noticeably more effectively, and told me later that my pulling her back had been the single most valuable learning experience in the training for her.

So, high conflict need not bother us or prevent us from getting on with our job. It is a bit like mowing a lawn. If the grass is short and easy to mow, the job will not take long or be very exhausting. If it is long and tough we will have to work harder, it will take longer, and we may need more frequent rests. But we are working in their garden, not our own. And, if we still find it getting to us, we remind ourselves, with a touch of cynicism, that we are paid by the hour, not by results.

CHAPTER TEN

MORE PROBLEMS IN MEDIATION

I want to talk in this chapter about problems that arise in mediation with separating spouses.

"Family ties"

The words "family ties" usually describe the ties of affection or consanguinity that bind families together. They are also a statement of fact, as expressed in Bacon's essay "Of Marriage and Single Life": "He that hath wife and children hath given hostages to fortune; for they are impediments to great enterprises, either of virtue or mischief". Here are some of the ways that separating spouses can find their children "impediments to enterprises".

Children of separating couples more often have their home with their mother than with their father. Many fathers feel this as a loss, but it also inhibits mothers. It is hard for a woman to pursue a career, or to return to paid work if she has left the paid workforce, if children are making demands on her time and energy. It is hard for a woman living with young children to re-establish a social life, an emotional one or a sexual one. It is hard for her to get out of the house for the evening, and it is very much harder for her to invite people, especially men, to her home if there are children around.

Children inhibit their father's sexual and romantic activities after separation, though less than they do their mother's, if they spend less time with him. A working Dad will usually want to spend time with his children at weekends, which is also the time when he has the best chance of socialising and meeting unattached women.

Children can also inhibit what, but for them, would be sensible decisions about the family home. A husband will often start with a demand that the house should be sold to raise money so that he can have a home, too. In his role as a father he will withdraw that demand, if he feels that having to leave their home at the time their parents split up might be more than his children could handle. (This is a sacrifice, but depending on family finances, it is often possible using a little imagination and a problem-solving approach, to find a way of raising a stake for the husband to buy, without displacing the wife and children.)

Something similar can happen about pension rights. A husband may want to ensure that any pension payable to his widow will pass to a prospective second wife, not his present one, but change his mind when he recognises that if his present wife is unable to support herself in old age, the burden may fall on his children. The "enterprise" of enticing some woman to become his new wife – and perhaps using his pension as an extra encouragement to her to take on that role – suffers an "impediment".

Having mentioned protecting children from financial responsibility for an impoverished parent, let me just say something about how people usually tackle it. The first stage is for parents to recognise the problem in those terms. If they do, they may be able to solve it in one of a number of ways. If the husband is self-employed and well-paid, it can be comparatively easy, since most tax regimes offer quite generous tax reliefs to encourage people to save for their retirement, and if he has a job with a decent pension plan, they can usually agree how to handle a widow's pension, in their children's interests. Of course, if the husband is already in a new relationship it becomes more difficult, though not insoluble.

The pension problem illustrates how family ties to children can affect decision-making about all phases of the lives of parents, and how hostages to fortune may inhibit him that hath wife and children even after his children's mother has ceased to be his wife.

Tribal warfare and the Absent Warrior

Family feeling, the loyalty that people feel for their own family, the support we get from our siblings, the ability of children to forgive their parents' faults and love them in spite of their failures, and the unconditional love parents have for their children, are beautiful and precious. I value them, but as a mediator am more impressed with them when they do not interfere with my efforts to help spouses to agree how to handle their separation. I do not know how often I have heard a wife say: "my mother thinks he shouldn't be allowed to see the children", or a husband say: "my dad says I shouldn't support her, since she walked out on me". Even when they are not quoted I know the views of parents and siblings underlie and support a lot of the conflict I hear.

I have also come across a reverse situation where both families, and nearly all friends, unite behind one party, and reject the other. This is a hard and painful situation for the person ostracised, and he may react by saying: "If you all cast me as the villain of the piece, I will not disappoint you!" It takes wisdom and a lot of character to avoid this trap.

In the more usual situation where the families of origin of a separating husband and wife close ranks in support of their own blood relation, and in bitter hostility to his or her ex-spouse, the description "tribal warfare" is accurate. Where the support comes from friends, we cannot strictly call the problem "tribal", but from the point of view of the mediator the result is not greatly different. Crudely, we are trying to help our clients to reach sensible agreements while their "support systems" are working against us.

Family are not the only people who influence separating spouses. When I hear a wife, for example, saying: "I am very lucky to have good friends who have stood by me at this time, and been a great support to me", I am pleased to know she has support when she needs it, but apprehensive that she is going to take up positions fed to her by a sympathetic friend.

My fears are based on something I have noticed over the years about helpers who emerge when someone is in crisis. I have often heard clients say: "My own family were too busy to help me, and friends I thought I could rely on were no use either, but some people I would never have expected to rallied round me, and gave me great support." Most of these helpers are genuinely kind and well-meaning people whose only conscious motive is to help someone in distress, but I am convinced that some people who volunteer support to friends in trouble do so in a way that expresses their own needs and feelings more than the needs and feelings of the person they are supporting. This applies more often, and more powerfully, to people who emerge unexpectedly as supporters, not having previously been close friends. A woman supporting a wife whose marriage is coming unstuck is the scenario I have most often observed. In my experience, the unexpected supporter is often motivated, perhaps unconsciously, at least as much by her own feelings – based on her own experience or by what is currently happening in her life – as she is by what is happening to her "sister".

"Sisterhood" – the strong sense of solidarity that women have for other women in difficulties – is, like family love, beautiful. Like family love, it can also be a major problem, if the supporting "sister" encourages the supported one to engage in a war from which nobody can emerge a winner. Sometimes the supporter has herself been through a marital separation. If she shows hostility towards her friend's husband, and anger at how he has treated her friend, he may not be the true target of that anger. It may be her own anger, directed at her own husband but transferred to her sister. Or hostility may come from the childhood of a supporter, perhaps remembering conflicts between her parents. If the supporter is married and not separated, there may be unaddressed issues in her own marriage, which she feels more comfortable acting out in someone else's.

Whatever their motive, people who take sides in a marriage while the couple are in mediation can be a danger to the person they are supposedly supporting, to her husband, and to their children, if they are more intent on making war than in negotiating peace.

The distinguished therapist Brian Cade dislikes labels because they "thingify", but I find it useful to label the warmongers behind my clients, and call them Absent Warriors. I also label them "colonists", as described in Chapter Two.

People in mediation will often quote advice given to them by lawyers or therapists. I have no way of knowing how accurate their quotations are, but if a wife says: "my lawyer says I should keep the family home, and it should be put into my sole name, and John shouldn't get a penny from it!" or: "my counsellor says the children should not see their father more often than once a week, and for not more than three

169

hours at a time", the lawyer and the therapist are from my point of view Absent Warriors. It does not matter to me whether they have really given the advice quoted, because they represent the same problem, either way. What is happening is that the decision-making process, instead of being under the control of the two parties, involves someone the mediator cannot talk to.

Dealing with the Absent Warrior

So how do mediators deal with Absent Warriors? I have two ways, both of which I learnt from John Haynes. One is to push the Absent Warrior out of the room, and the other is to invite him in. Two examples of pushing the Absent Warrior out:

> "It must be frustrating for you to have your brother always interfering and telling you how to run your life."
> "I am puzzled by what your mother says. How far is her judgement affected by her hostility towards Tom?"

Each of these invites the person on whose side the Absent Warrior has enlisted, to take a critical look at the support she is getting.

An example of bringing the Absent Warrior into the room would be:

> "I wonder how your Dad would react, if he was here, heard what was being said, and realised how much his grandchildren, Kate and Peter, miss their Dad?"

I find the second approach – bringing the Absent Warrior into the room – more effective. It is less confrontational. If the children's mother "brings her father into the room", and if she recognises that her children miss their father, she will probably decide that her father would see that too. If she realises that he would not, she will probably throw him out herself, because she realises he has nothing to contribute.

And if he is going to be thrown out, she can do it more effectively than I can.

What if the Absent Warrior is a lawyer, as in the example quoted above? We may be able to bring him into the room, by saying something like:

> "It seems from what you are both saying that the only prospect John has of getting a home of his own, where the children can stay overnight with him, without Anne and the children having to leave the present home, would be by remortgaging the house. Anne, do you think if your lawyer had an update on what we have talked about today, and realised that this was the only prospect of John being rehoused where the children could stay overnight with their Dad, might he take a different view?"

I have no way of knowing whether Anne has quoted her lawyer accurately. Even if she has, he may have given her this advice as a tactic.

If the Absent Warrior is a lawyer, and I can neither "bring him into the room", where he will have to see reason, or exclude him altogether, I may say something like:

> "I don't think this process is going to get you two anywhere. Anne says her lawyer advises her not to yield on the issue of the house, and John says he could not agree to what Anne's lawyer advises. It seems to me Anne is saying she will not agree to anything her lawyer doesn't approve. Understandably. She is not willing to ignore the advice of someone she trusts. If his advice is therefore effectively governing Anne's decisions, then it may be best for John to be in the same position as Anne, and for the two of you to get your lawyers to do the negotiating."

If I say the above it is not some subtle ploy to get the wife to abandon her lawyer's advice, or to undermine her

171

confidence in it. I would say it because the reality now is that the negotiations are taking place between the husband and the wife's lawyer, not between husband and wife, and I thought fairness to the husband required that their negotiations should be carried on through both lawyers, not one, from then on.

The mediator might also invite the Absent Warrior into the room if he anticipates (using that word in its correct sense, of expecting something and taking steps to deal with it in advance) resistance to the bargain the parties are making, from the lawyer advising one of them. I will sometimes say:

> "I have been wondering how Mary's lawyer will react to this bargain. Don't misunderstand me: I have no problem with it. But it is a bit out of the normal course, and it occurs to me that when you bring it to your lawyers to have it made binding, Mary's lawyer may raise an eyebrow when he/she sees what you have agreed about . . .
>
> "It would be a pity if your bargain was upset because one of the lawyers took a negative view of it. Would it be worth while to look at this possibility, and discuss whether the three of us, together, can do anything to avoid this happening, or what Mary can say to her lawyer?"

I will sometimes say this as a way of balancing unequal negotiating skill – effectively, bringing Mary's lawyer into the room to supplement her as a negotiator. Or I may do it because I see a problem looming, and feel three heads are better than one in solving it. It may also help my clients to co-operate in their future dealings, if they recognise that this is a problem for both of them, because if they are both satisfied with the bargain they have reached, it is in neither's interests to have it unpicked, by her lawyer or his, or anyone else. The lesson, for this and future problems is: a problem for one is a problem for both.

Bringing up the children

People I work with will understand me more readily, and be more involved with the question, if I say: "How do you want to handle bringing your children up when you no longer live together?", than if I say: "Now, I suggest we talk about parenting." I involve them even more intensely, if I say: "I want to ask you about Alan and Amanda, and your ideas about how you want to bring them up, when you no longer both live in the same home with them." I do not like the word "parenting" but it is probably the biggest single problem, as well as the most important, for separating couples.

Parents who are contented with each other, want to stay together, and have roughly congruent attitudes on most issues, often disagree about how to bring up their children. For example, on how late a teenage boy or girl should stay out on weekday nights and at weekends. (Often the answer will differ depending on the gender of the child.) If contented husbands and wives disagree – not necessarily about principles, but about how to apply them – think of what room for dispute these issues may offer to separating couples. Remember, too, that there may be all sorts of reasons for them to disagree:

♦ they may be looking for something to fight about;
♦ they may have genuinely different attitudes on the perennial debate about freedom versus responsibility for teenagers;
♦ one of them may think: "I want to become more popular with the children, and encourage them to live with me, not him/her. Giving them greater freedom than he/she is

173

willing to will be a good way of making them want to stay with me";

◆ if one of them is thinking along these lines, it is likely that the other is aware of it, and resentful;

◆ their children may already have started to play one off against the other: "Can I stay out until three on Sunday morning, for the disco? . . . Why not? . . . Everybody else is going to! . . . If you won't let me, I'll go and live with Mum/Dad. I know she/he will let me!" Most children, whether their parents live together or apart, play one off against the other in this way, and most parents, whether separated or living together, can write the script.

How does a mediator handle conflict between separating spouses about how to rear their children? I have no answer to that question. It is not a mediator's job to work out "parenting" arrangements for his clients' children. That is the job of the parents. Remember Larry Fong's: "He's not my kid!" which I quote in Chapter Two. What we do need to do is to ensure that whatever arrangement they may make will at least have a chance of working, because we have ensured that it is properly reality-tested before it is adopted. So, we will ask questions like: "How will that work in practice?" or:

> "How will you answer Stephanie, if she comes up to you on Saturday evening, when she is staying with you, and says all her friends are going to a sleepover in Monica's house, and she wants to go too? Will you ask her whether Monica's parents will be there, and, if she says yes, will you check? What will you do if you say no, and her eyes fill with tears?"

I usually explore whether what I think is a particularly invidious parental tactic will be allowed, or outlawed – when the children ask the more easygoing parent for permission to stay out until some outlandish hour – and you can be sure they will pick the one they think is more likely to indulge them – he (let's assume it is Dad) will say: "It's okay by me, but you'll have to ask your mother." This one really puts it up to Mum. If she says no, she gets all the blame and has to deal with a disappointed, sulky teenager – perhaps for weeks. (It's amazing how they can keep it up!) If she disapproves but says yes, because she doesn't feel she can handle the vibes, her sense of how children should be brought up has been set aside.

My sense is that children whose parents show a common front in face of their demands get a better start in life than kids whose parents give them a "divide and conquer" message. I also recognise that very few separated parents can maintain that level of consistency. It is hard enough for parents who are not separated. Learning how to manipulate their parents is part of the process of growing up, and one parent will be identified as more indulgent or more easily manipulated than the other. My function as a mediator is to explore the possibilities, ensure that they recognise the consequences of any decision they take, reality-test it – and cross my fingers.

Unpunctuality

Unpunctuality emerges as a problem in marital mediation in three ways:

◆ if one party is consistently unpunctual in coming to mediation sessions;
◆ if one (let us assume, Dad, as this is how it most often happens) is consistently late in collecting the children when they are due to be with him;
◆ if one (again, assume Dad) is consistently late in bringing them back.

Let us take these in turn.

Some people are naturally unpunctual. Others, even if they are normally on time, may turn up late for a first meeting

175

with their mediator. (This may be a signal that they don't want to be there. Who does?) The first rule I give myself is not to allow myself to become irritated or be triangulated (Chapter Two) if a client turns up late. My second is to end the session at the same time as it would have ended if we had started on time. Thirdly, I charge the clients for the full time, and fourthly, I do not apologise or explain.

A useful fifth rule, if your physical set-up allows it, is not to keep the punctual one waiting in your waiting-room but to join him or her at the appointed time and chat while waiting for the other. This needs discipline, as the punctual one will often want a tete-a-tete about issues in the mediation, but it is worth staying, and avoiding talk about issues. If the unpunctual one arrives to find the other chatting with the mediator, unpunctuality will probably not be a recurring problem. And I find the punctual party does not insist on pursuing a topic of substance if I say: "I'd rather not talk about that until Joe arrives."

Let's look at unpunctuality in the family, and the two patterns I describe above, of Dad being late in collecting the kids and late in bringing them home. I often deal with both by reality-testing. Let's assume Mary has just said that Peter is always late in collecting the children, or that he is always late for everything, and that he is bound to be late collecting them on Saturday morning:

Me: "What will happen if he is late?"

Mary: "We have to hang around until he turns up."

Me: "How long are you talking about?"

Mary: "It could be up to an hour."

Me: "Peter?"

Peter: "She is exaggerating, as usual. I admit I am sometimes kept back, by a crisis in work or something like that, but it would very seldom be for as long as an hour."

(I asked him to comment because he has been accused and I don't want him to feel unheard, but I do not let that one develop, because it is going to bring them back into their past conflict – and because a work crisis blowing up on Saturday morning without any early warning on Friday sounds unlikely.)

Me: "Mary, what happens if you have made plans to go out and Peter is late?"

Mary: "I suppose I have to cancel."

Me: "I don't suppose that would please you too much? I was also wondering, would you usually have the children ready? Say, if Peter is due to collect them at ten-thirty in the morning, would you have them ready by then?"

Mary: "Yes, if they are due to go out with their father, they will be ready and waiting."

Me: "How will they react if they are expecting him at ten-thirty and he turns up at eleven? You haven't been doing this for long, and I don't suppose, Peter, you can compare their mood for the rest of the day if you have turned up late, versus if you have been on time?

(Pause)

"I have been told some kids take Dad turning up late as a message that he didn't much care about being with them. I don't know if any of yours would feel that way?"

Peter being late in bringing children home at the end of a day out is a much more serious issue than unpunctuality in collecting them. If they are due back at 8.30 p.m., and arrive at 10.00 their mother has probably been getting more frantic with each minute. She will likely have phoned hospitals, or the police. She may even have phoned airports, to ensure he is not taking them out of the country. When the children come bouncing in – or straggle in, tired and fractious, after an exhausting day – she is so furious, and so relieved, that she doesn't know whether to hug them or whack them, but she is

177

in no doubt which treatment he should get – and she is just about ready to give it to him.

I find that if I put this scenario through my reality-testing projector, her head will nod, and he will look thoughtful. I do not know the outcome, because people I work with seldom come back to me and never give me progress reports after our work together is finished, but my sense is that most people operate reasonably punctual arrangements after being exposed to this kind of reality test.

On this topic, there are two other things that I sometimes say. One is:

> "People in your situation can make arrangements for both of you to play a role in your children's lives, but it does require co-operation. And co-operation is a two-way street."

The other is:

> "Peter: would it ever happen if you were going to be delayed unavoidably in collecting the children that you wouldn't be able to get to a phone, and let them know you were held up? And if you were going to be delayed in returning them that you wouldn't be able to let Mary know you were held up?"

Notice the wording. I asked Peter about letting the children – not Mary – know, if he was going to be late in collecting them.

I mentioned the phone. I think when parents separate, and children live with either one parent or the other, a telephone link between the children and their absent parent becomes a necessity. It is important to them that they can phone their absent parent whenever they want. It may be even more important to them that he phones them, rather than their having to phone him. I try earnestly not to tell my clients what to do, but, if they are thinking of saving money by not having a phone in each home I will spend some time reality-

178

testing with them, so that they get a sense of how phone contact with the absent parent can enhance the lives of their children, and how the absence of that contact can hurt them.

This illustrates again the tightrope I have been talking about, where a mediator is determined not to tell his clients what to do, and at the same time hopes, more and more fervently, as he grows to like and respect them, that their decisions will be good for them and their children.

Intimidation

I have talked so far about fear as something people carry within themselves, and bring into the process of meditation, not about fear that the other party engenders. If one party is afraid of the other, the problem should not be labelled as fear. It should be called intimidation. There is one essential and universal rule for a mediator when he recognises a level of fear that prevents one party from negotiating with the other in his or her interests: the mediation process should stop.

If someone – say a wife – says "he intimidates me" it can mean "I feel intimidated by him", or it can mean "he imposes his will on me, and make me do things I don't want to because I'm afraid not to". The words: "he intimidates me" remind me of a story called "The Lady or the Tiger?". Its main character was a princess in a primitive land, whose ex-lover, at the climax of the story, was in the gladiatorial arena, while she sat above. He had to open one of two doors. If he opened one door, a beautiful young woman would emerge and become his bride. If he opened the other, a hungry tiger would leap out and devour him. The princess signalled to him, and he opened the door. The story asked, but did not answer, whether the lady or the tiger came out. You couldn't know, because the author had failed to give you enough information about the character of the princess, and her relationship with her former lover, to enable you to assess whether she would prefer to see him chewed to death or married to another.

On paper, the words "he intimidates me" are like that. Lacking either the tone of voice or the context, it is hard to know what they mean. And, of course, it will be essential for a mediator to know, because his first decision will be whether to work with the couple. So how does he respond? Let us make a few assumptions. First, let's assume that the tone of voice implies an accusation, rather than an admission of weakness. And let's assume that the speaker is a married woman accusing her husband. The first piece of information the mediator needs is one that I make a point of establishing in the first five minutes of my first meeting with almost every couple, even before I start to explain to them how mediation works, by asking: "Are you living under the same roof at present?"

Digression on language

Note the form of my question: "Are you living under the same roof at present?", not "are you living together?" The question seeks only information about whether they are both currently living in the same home. I need to know because if they are, and plan to part, my explanation of what mediation offers will have to be different from what it would be if they were already apart. If they no longer share a home, they will not need to discuss how to handle a move, or how to break the news to their children that they are going to separate. The form of the question, "Are you living under the same roof at present?", does not encourage an answer like: "We are living together, if you want to call it that, but we might as well live a thousand miles apart, because . . . " I will need to know about that stuff, and I recognise that they may have a compelling need to talk about it. But later. My first and current task is to prepare to explain to them what mediation has to offer, and help them decide if it is what they need. The form of the question discourages discussion of major issues until I have dealt with the preliminaries. This is an example of how the mediator's choice of words helps him to control the process.

Back to intimidation

When we have gone through the preliminaries and started to talk about the issues, I know whether they are sharing a home. I needed to know, anyway, but will want to use that information in an additional way if intimidation is mentioned.

My first thought, if I hear the words "he intimidates me", will be that one of the signs of being intimidated – in the true sense of your will being overborne by fear – is that you will not identify your fear to anyone, especially in the presence of the person you fear, precisely because you are afraid of the consequences. So if the wife says, "he intimidates me", that looks like a signal that she is probably not intimidated, within that meaning of the word, and it is unlikely that I will have an ethical issue about whether I should stop working with them. Unlikely, but not certain. Warning systems within me that have been alerted are not switched off. I will offer what is, on its face, simple feedback "you feel intimidated by Liam?"

Again, it is not possible to express the nuance in my voice on paper, but I have tried to suggest it by putting a question mark at the end of the sentence. "You feel intimidated by Liam", without a questioning inflection means that I am simply recording what she has said, but first (as normal in feedback) deleting its accusatory content: "I understand you feel intimidated." "You feel intimidated by Liam?", with a rising inflection, adds: "Tell me more."

She may say she feels intimidated between sessions but not during them. Or she may find his physical presence in the room intimidating – and many people who have been subjected to any kind of violence or other abuse will feel fear in the presence of the abuser, even though she is not put in what law books quaintly call "present fear of violence".

(The phrase, "present fear of violence" comes from a leading case that law students have to study. A man had put his hand on his sword, and said: "If it were not Assize time, I would run you through!" The judge decided that the – presumably unarmed – man to whom this was said by a man with his hand on his sword was not put in "present fear of violence", and that the speaker had not "assaulted" him, because the words indicated he was not going to be skewered at that moment. If any of you who are not lawyers sometimes get the feeling that lawyers are out of touch with reality, bear in mind the kind of nonsense they have been exposed to in their student days, and feel sympathy, rather than disdain.)

If the couple share a home, she may be subjected to intimidation between sessions. If not, it is possible that she was intimidated by him while they lived together, and, even though they may now be living apart, she feels the same fear of him as she did. Primo Levi said of his time in a Nazi concentration camp that torture is not over when it ends, but continues in the mind of the victim for the rest of his life. Much the same seems to happen in the mind of someone who has been intimidated. The fact that intimidation has ceased because she no longer shares a home with the intimidator does not mean that her autonomy is automatically restored. It may take her months of being physically safe before she can recover her ability to stand up for herself, especially in the face of the person she fears. She may never be able to do so.

If the message is: "I feel intimidated" rather than: "I accuse him of deliberately intimidating me", then the mediator will be even more on his guard. The first message, if it is accurate, signals that mediation should stop. The second is an accusation, and, although it sounds more serious, it suggests that however much of a big bad wolf the husband may be, the little pig who married him and is now accusing him is not really afraid of him. If she were, it is unlikely that she would be able to utter those words in his presence.

So a mediator who hears an accusation of intimidation will ask the accuser to expand on what she has said. He will listen carefully to her answer, and will "listen" even more carefully to the body language that accompanies it. If she says she feels intimidated by his presence, I will probably end the process. I say "probably" only because I will listen to her tone of voice and try to read her body language as well as listening to her words. If they tell me that she is not really afraid to negotiate with him and is, perhaps, trying to triangulate me, or gain a negotiating advantage, I may explore this further. If she tells me that she was bullied by him in the past but is not afraid of him now, and I know they are living apart, I may postpone a decision. A decision to stop is irrevocable. If I decide to continue, I can change my mind at any time if I feel I should, and stop the process.

If intimidation is mentioned and they are living in separate homes I will ask: "Does Liam have a key to Annette's home?" Again the body language in response to that question may tell me a lot, including giving me an insight into whether there has been violence, physical or mental, and whether there is intimidation. If I am told he doesn't have a key, and he shows anger, and she relief, that is a clear "tell". I will need to explore it further, to see if I can be satisfied that she does not currently feel intimidated and is able to negotiate in her own interest. If he has a key, and if he, not she, answers the question, that may suggest continuing intimidation. If I get a matter-of-fact answer from her, it is less likely that she is incapacitated by fear.

But I do not switch off my warning systems. Indeed, they should always be switched on. Even if intimidation hasn't been raised, it should be in my mind, if only at the back of my mind. And I should remember that, if I continue to work with a couple while one of them is intimidated by the other, I give a cloak of respectability to a process that is the reverse of respectable, by recording as a freely negotiated agreement something that one party imposes on the other by fear. I may also in effect conspire with the intimidator to continue to intimidate, because so long as she is in mediation, she will not seek the support and protection she needs from the legal system, or retain a lawyer to take whatever court proceedings might be needed to protect her.

Terminating because of intimidation

If I terminate because of intimidation, I face at least one and probably two ethical problems. First, I should not do it in a way that buys into her view of her husband as a bully and intimidator. If I did, I would be acting as a judge. They have paid me to be a mediator, and I have no right to put on judge's robes.

So, I may say:

"This is something I have come across. People in your situation often feel afraid. Sometimes the wife is afraid of the husband, sometimes the husband is afraid of the wife. Sometimes they are afraid of each other – as well as being full of fear about what the future holds for them."

"Annette says she feels intimidated by Liam's presence. I have to accept what she says.

"Liam says he has never done anything to intimidate her, and, again, I accept what he says. And, as I'm sure you have both found, somebody who has a strong personality, perhaps even a forceful one, may seem

184

intimidating to other people, even though he may have no intention of intimidating them.

"I have to decide what I should do. As I say, I am not questioning Liam's good faith in saying he has never aimed to frighten Annette or intimidate her, or Annette's good faith in saying that, even so, that is how she feels. If it is, it seems to me I must stop working with you now. And you might all be better off as a family if the two of you stopped working with me.

"This does not necessarily mean you have to go to court. You can consult lawyers and they may negotiate a separation agreement. That may be better for both of you than trying to negotiate face to face, if one of you feels intimidated.

"Going that way will probably cost more and may take longer than if the three of us continued to work together. I can see, Liam, for you that is a pain in the neck. However, it may not be a complete disaster if you look at it from this point of view. If we were to continue with this process, and reach an agreement, and you went away with it and got it turned into a formal legal document and signed it, I assume it would be open to Annette, at any time down the road, to say that she had been intimidated by you at the time, and she should not be held to anything she agreed while under intimidation. So from your point of view, Liam, any bargain you made with my help might be built on sand.

"If you negotiate your bargain through lawyers, without having to be physically in the same room, you can be much more confident that you will have a lasting arrangement that cannot be set aside down the road."

I can imagine some of you, reading this speech, and asking a few questions: "Does Michael really believe that Liam didn't intimidate Annette? And, if he doesn't believe

185

that, how can he produce all that stuff about not questioning Liam's good faith in saying he has never aimed to frighten Annette, or intimidate her? What about all that uplifting stuff in Chapter Twelve about telling the truth? Is that all for the birds?

No, it's not. But I keep my theories about what has happened in my clients' lives where they belong, and they do not belong in my room when I am working with them as their mediator. Their past is none of my business, and I have no right to speculate about it, still less to make judgements about it. I do feel entitled to form what I call hypotheses rather than judgements about what is happening between my clients, but only to the extent I must, to help them move forward. If Annette tells me she feels nervous of Liam, and he says he has never done anything to cause her to feel afraid of him, I do not need to question the good faith of either in order to decide whether to work with them, and if so on what basis. I accept at face value what each says to me, until it becomes clear that they will not reach an agreement on this basis. With some couples this never arises, but if Annette is not able to negotiate in her own long-term interests because of her fear of Liam then I will not work with them, and would be very critical of any colleague who was willing to.

The second ethical question about terminating is whether mediators have a duty to protect the safety of the spouse they think is threatened, whether in how they terminate mediation or after they have done so. This is something each mediator must decide for himself. Decisions are influenced by the temperament and instincts of the mediator, and his or her assessment of the perils and mental state of the intimidated party. It is a matter for individual judgement, and is so subjective that I do not believe there are universal rules. It is one of those "on the one hand . . . but on the other hand . . . " things. On the one hand, the mediator should not terminate in

186

a way that will mean Liam will beat Annette up that night, as punishment for letting the mediator discover she is afraid of him. On the other, he should not betray his principles by lying to either party – and his duty not to lie to Liam is not affected by whether Liam is a wife-beater. The speech I have put in my imaginary mediator's mouth, beginning "This is something I have come across . . ." and ending "that cannot be set aside down the road" is not ideal, but I have failed to invent one I like better.'

Addicts

I am not going to offer a definition of addicts, addiction, alcoholics or alcoholism. It is enough for a mediator to recognise that certain people who are labelled "addicts" come to mediation with their spouses, and to know that if one of the parties carries that label the prospects of mediation being useful to the couple diminish.

To date, I have identified four kinds of addicts I have worked with: alcoholics, drug addicts, compulsive gamblers, and sexual addicts. I have also worked with people who had broken free of their addiction but whose personality was still addictive.

I do not refuse to work with addicts. To do so would be to make a judgement of a very severe kind. But my experience is that very few addicts reach agreement, and, of those that do, few honour it. So once addiction is mentioned the question: am I taking their money with no real prospect of giving them value? is in the forefront of my mind. I might say:

> "Margaret, you say Bill has been diagnosed as an alcoholic, and that he is still drinking. Bill says his drinking is under control, and that he does not drink to excess. He doesn't see himself as an alcoholic.
>
> "I don't know whether Bill is an alcoholic or not. I have no expertise to make that judgement, and it isn't

187

my place to try to make it. There are two things I do know. First, which is pretty well known, is that a lot of people who are addicted to alcohol deny their addiction, and, in any family where there is an alcoholic the alcoholic himself is usually the last person to admit to it. So if someone who is qualified has said Bill is an alcoholic, the chances are he is right, even if Bill says no.

"The other thing I know from doing this work is that it is very rare for people to make a bargain in mediation, and to carry it out in practice, if one of them is an alcoholic.

"So from what you have told me, I feel I should tell you I am willing to work with you, and take your money, but you should both know I believe it is likely that what Margaret says is right, and Bill is an alcoholic. If he is, the chances of the two of you reaching an agreement in this room with my help, are a good deal less than fifty/fifty.

"And if you do, the chances of your being able to put it into practice are less than that. That means the time and money you spend here may be wasted."

This is hard talk. I don't think it is harsh, but it is hard. For someone like myself, who is nervous of conflict (like most mediators) and who handles badly conflicts in which I am directly involved (again like most mediators) it does not seem easy to say. In fact until I heard myself saying something very like that, I would have doubted if I could. Having found I could say it once, I have had no problem in delivering the same message again. It has not yet made any alcoholic turn against me or become aggressive.

I am not sure it has been much use to any couple who have heard the speech, but I do not think it has done harm. And I feel that to say something like that is consistent with the ethical duty of being open and honest with my clients, and treating them with respect, both of which we will discuss in Chapter Twelve.

Pending court hearing

Quite often people make an appointment to meet me shortly before they are due to go to court. It is easy to understand why this happens. There are hundreds of reasons to start down the road to the courthouse that may seem good when you start the journey but less convincing as the day of the court hearing draws nearer. When fear begins to take over from rage as the dominant feeling is the time in a court process when a negotiated settlement is most likely.

One way of avoiding a court hearing while not losing face is to agree to go to mediation. After a predictable dialogue ("If you had suggested this months ago, we could have avoided all these legal bills!" "Why didn't you suggest it yourself?"), they make an appointment to see me. It might seem that someone like me, an ex-lawyer turned mediator, would be delighted to have clients coming to him when the prospects of an agreement are at their best. If I wanted to increase the proportion of my clients who reached an agreement with my help, wouldn't these clients be extremely welcome?

Of course they would, if that was what I wanted. But it isn't. Remember, mediation is conflict *resolution*. A conflict is not *resolved* by people agreeing a treaty under unbearable pressure. It is merely driven underground. It may be a mediator's duty to bring to the surface a latent conflict so that it can be identified, addressed, and resolved, and the last thing I want to do is to drive a conflict underground, where it will not be acknowledged. So I do not want to work with people who are going to reach a truce because they have no choice. Nor do I think I serve their long-term interests by doing so. Let their lawyers deal with that situation. It is not part of conflict-*resolution*.

I am sometimes told during the first session that a court hearing is on the way, a date has been fixed, and if they don't reach agreement with my help they will go into court. I am often told this during the last few minutes of the first session, but let us assume that the husband complains early in the first session that his wife has issued a summons, and that it is due for hearing in three weeks time. The wife says: "I have told my lawyers that if we reach a satisfactory bargain here, the proceedings can be called off."

They are putting it up to me – demanding that I make an agreement for them, and that I do it within a specified short time. It is like one of those chess problems: "White to play and mate in three moves, against any possible move from Black." If Eric Beirne had worked as a mediator instead of a therapist his book might have included this as another example of "Games People Play". It is a game I am not willing to play. I will say something like:

> "I am willing to help you to negotiate an agreement. That is my job. But I am not willing to help you to produce something that looks like an agreement, but is not really one.

> "It sometimes happens that people come to me when their backs are to the wall and they will make any bargain they can, because they are so much afraid of the alternative. I don't think a bargain negotiated in such stress will stand up when the stress is over. The person who has caved in under pressure is reluctant to honour a bargain that he – or she – feels was imposed. The person who got what he or she wanted on paper finds that it isn't delivered, except on paper.

190

"So, am I right in thinking that you are here now because the court hearing is due in three weeks?

(Pause, for assent)

"Does that mean that if you make a bargain here it will be to avoid having to go to court?"

Assuming I get a yes to the last question, I will probably continue like this:

"Right. I think we all have decisions to make at this point. You have to decide if you want to continue with me as your mediator. I have to decide if I am willing to continue to work with you. I am, provided I am being used to help you make a genuine bargain. I am not, if the mediation is going to be used to make something look like a bargain that isn't really one. And this is not just for my own sake. I do not think I would be helping you, or your children, in the long term by helping you to cobble together some kind of deal dictated by the court hearing if it would not address the problems that brought you to the door of the court.

"So your choices are: you can look for another mediator who is willing to help you work out a deal in the next three weeks. Or the three of us can work out a way of reducing the pressure, in the hope that if a bargain emerges from our work together it will be a genuine bargain. Or you can go to court."

If they decide for the second option, we will start to work out a way for us to continue with the pressure reduced. What do I do if they decide to leave me and go to another mediator? First, I will not try to stop them. I don't want to, but even if I did, it would be a waste of time: once either of them has said they don't want to work with me, I owe it to both of them – and to the reputation of my profession – to get out of their lives as soon as I can.

If I withdraw do I recommend another mediator? Do I seem heartless if I say I do not? I am terminating my relationship with them because I think it would be unethical to continue it and help them to disguise their truce as a peace treaty. If it is unethical of me to work with them, how can it be ethically okay for someone else? If I recommend someone to them, my message to them about my replacement is: I feel ethically obliged to withdraw as your mediator, but my colleague has no such inhibitions, and will be glad to work with you. I do not see how I can recommend to my clients someone whose ethical standards I assess so harshly.

If I continue to work with the couple, what do I do to eliminate the pressure? The answer is that I don't do anything. Once they have identified their problem, or agreed with me that it exists, it is for them to work out their solution to it. I will help them, but the problem is theirs, and it is for them to shift it. I am a helper, not a principal.

But unlike topics of substance, where it is fundamental to my code as a mediator that I should not intervene, and influence their bargain, I may contribute more to the solution of a problem of this kind than I would to an issue of substance. Let's take an example. Let's assume a court is due to hear an application in three weeks time by Mary for a barring order to have her husband Peter forbidden to enter the family home. This puts both parties under huge pressure. Peter is afraid that the judge will order him out of his home on threat of being put in prison if he enters it. Less obviously perhaps to a male mediator, Mary is terrified that the judge will refuse to make the order, and that evening Peter will swagger into the house and say: "You tried to get rid of me, and it didn't work. It's my turn now and I won't be asking a judge to help me."

Let's assume they agree the court hearing is putting them both under such pressure that they will do almost anything to avoid it. Having told them the conditions under which I will continue with them, I will then ask them how those conditions can be met, and the conversation may go like this:

Peter: "She should withdraw the summons."

Mary: "No way."

Me: "Would that be right? If the summons is withdrawn and the mediation process doesn't work, Mary will be in a worse situation. When she has withdrawn the summons she may not be allowed to start it off again. If she does, the judge may not be very sympathetic. She could be a lot worse off.

"Is it possible to get the summons out of the way, but in such a way that, if you don't reach agreement with my help, neither of you has put yourself into a worse position?"

Mary: "Maybe it could be adjourned. But might that put me in a worse position later if I went on with it?"

Me: "I don't know. I think you should ask your lawyers." (A mediator should avoid answering a question on which the parties need legal advice.)

Me: "But what strikes me is that a judge might not be prejudiced against you because you tried to resolve the problems in mediation, and only went to court because mediation didn't work.

"Would you lose your place in the queue for a court hearing, if the summons was adjourned now? Or would it be put back into the court lists, not at the end of the queue, if mediation didn't work for you?"

Peter: "Is there any point in adjourning the summons? If it is not going to be withdrawn, aren't we better off to go on with it, and let a judge decide?"

Me: "Maybe, if that is what you feel is best. I suppose what you would get by adjourning would be a bit of time, to explore whether you can reach an agreement. The heat would be lowered even if it isn't switched off altogether for either of you. It is up to the two of you to decide if that is enough. You should probably talk to your lawyers before you make that decision."

Usually, a summons can be adjourned to allow time for mediation and re-introduced if mediation fails. For most people, that is as good a solution as they can find.

Lawyers' involvement before mediation

I want to make another point about the prospect of a couple working out an amicable agreement in mediation. I have not collected statistics or even tried to analyse figures from my own work, but my sense is that the prospect of a couple reaching an agreement with my help are greatly affected by how far they have gone down the road towards litigation. Few people who had court cases pending reached an agreement with my help. The proportion of those who have been able to reach agreement after the lawyers have written letters but a summons had not been issued would be higher, but not as high as the proportion who came to me without any prior legal steps, including a lawyer's letter. I could not prove that the prospects of mediation succeeding are worse if the legal process has been invoked, but my own experience, what colleagues have told me, and commonsense all leave me with little doubt about it.

If this is true, there may be a lesson in it, for lawyers and for their clients. For a lawyer, the lesson may be that if you believe there is a possibility that a client and spouse may be able to work out an agreement in mediation, it may be right to consider whether any action you may now take on your client's behalf may damage that prospect. "Any action" would obviously include issuing a summons, but could also include writing a letter setting out your client's complaints.

For clients, the lesson may be: if you feel you may want to try mediation, think carefully before authorising your lawyer to take any step that might damage the prospects of the process working for you including writing a "letter before proceedings".

I hope some lawyers may read this book, so let me say to them please do not feel I am telling you how to do your job. I realise you may be obliged to take speedy dramatic action to protect your client, like seeking legal protection against a violent spouse, or preventing children from being taken abroad. I also realise that you have to do what your client tells you, and that your first duty is to your client. I was one of you for years, before I became one of them.

A well known Dublin lawyer, now no longer with us, after issuing a summons would write to his client: "I have today drawn the sword, and thrown away the scabbard!" One of the problems about any step a lawyer takes in a marital dispute on behalf of his client is that it will be seen by the other party in just that way. In a marital row, if you do anything other than advise, you may be closing off the prospects that your client and his or her spouse will be able to reach an amicable constructive agreement. You may be able to negotiate an agreement on behalf of your client with a lawyer representing the other spouse. You may even, perhaps, be able to negotiate a constructive agreement, including sensible arrangements about children and money. But you can not negotiate an agreement that will be amicable and constructive.

"Stable-combative" couples and "trap the mediator"

There is a certain kind of couple that I call "stable-combative" – a description I don't think you will find in any textbook, but you will if you work as family mediators. Sydney Smith, the great Dean of St Paul's, who had a wonderful gift of teaching by making his hearers laugh, described this kind of marriage perfectly: "it resembles a pair of shears, so joined that they cannot be separated; often moving in opposite directions, yet always punishing anyone who comes between them."

Mediation seems to attract "stable-combative" spouses, for perhaps four reasons:

- mediation is a logical escalation of their combat;
- to refuse to go when advised to by an outsider might imply backing down in the continuing war with the other spouse;
- it is a process that they can terminate, usually in a way that enables each to blame the other (or the mediator), for its not having worked;
- unlike litigation, mediation is cheap, and will not force them to separate – something they have no intention of doing. (In fact, one of the characteristics of stable-combative couples, when we meet them outside the mediation room is that they live together, in an atmosphere of hostility, until one of them dies, and the survivor usually dies shortly afterwards.)

These couples have some things in common: determination – usually emphatically expressed – to separate; this never gets translated into irrevocable action; they will go to more trouble than most to triangulate their mediator; they will try, harder than most others, to involve him in their continuing combat, not the (purely hypothetical) question of what they would do if they separated; and sooner or later they will leave the process; usually they will do so either "because the other was impossible" or – an attractive alternative – "because the mediator was no good".

Such a couple make heavy demands on a mediator's energy. A mediator who does not recognise a stable-combative couple will put a lot of time and effort – perhaps more than another couple might call from him – into trying to help them, and feel a failure when his efforts come to nothing. If he hypothesises early enough in the process that they are stable-combative, he will work hard with them, but will be less likely to allow their problems to invade his leisure time, or to feel inadequate when they terminate.

CHAPTER ELEVEN

JOE & BELLA — SOME CONCEPTS ILLUSTRATED

In this chapter I want to illustrate a few things we have talked about, including how a mediator might go about saving face for a client who has painted herself into a corner and needs an escape. I wanted to produce a fairly trivial conflict, not something that might stir up major unhappy memories in some of my readers. My first thought was to offer a simple example, but when I tried to construct one, complications seeped in. When I simplified, the effect was to distort. When I cut something out, the picture was not just incomplete but misleading. The essence of good mediation is to be ready for whatever may happen, and if I want to show you how the process might work in practice, there is no point in my trying to make it look simple. It rarely is.

So let's look at a segment from a session with Joe and Bella. They are separating. Both have paid work. They have agreed arrangements about their children, income-sharing, and support for the children. They are now looking at division of capital assets, including contents of their house, and have agreed a fifty-fifty split is fair, in principle. Joe inherited a pair of silver candlesticks from his father. Bella says she should take one, and Joe keep the other. Joe says they are a pair, came from his family, and must be kept together and passed on to one of their children. Let's assume, also, that on this issue Joe argues well, as most people do when they feel they have a good case. He is getting irritated with Bella, and, in a moment of anger hints that if she is going to be unreasonable about his family property, he may claim the right to reopen other issues, already agreed. Finally, let's assume Bella is flustered and bellicose, and accuses Joe of being greedy.

The mediator sees a danger that the process may break down – over a pair of candlesticks. He is also alive to other possibilities. One is that he has failed to spot the importance of the candlesticks at an early stage in the negotiations, and they are emerging now, when room for concessions on either side is limited. If so, he has blundered, because it was his job to manage the negotiations in a way that would ensure that a major win/lose issue was not left undetermined, with no room for compromise on another issue, to compensate the loser (see Chapter Six). A second is a danger that issues already agreed and removed from the agenda will be reopened, and agreements already reached on those issues will come unstuck. The last is that one or both of his clients are playing a jolly game – which clients, especially stable-combative ones (previous chapter) sometimes play – called "trap the mediator", and unlike the mediation process, it is a game whose objective is to have one loser.

Finally, he is influenced by his own value-system. An other mediator would have a different set of values, but mine would give me a number of messages. First would be that Bella's and Joe's new homes have electricity. So at one level I would ask myself: "What's all the fuss about? They don't need candlesticks!" Second would be some sympathy with Joe's feeling about wanting to keep in his family things he has inherited and his upset at the idea of the candlesticks being sold or split. Third is that I know if I were in Joe's shoes I would say: "Thanks, ancestors, for the candlesticks. This is when your descendant really needs the money, so he is going to sell them."

As well as having his own set of values about the issue, a competent mediator would bring into the process some hypotheses about what lay behind the conflict over the candlesticks. For example, he might wonder if the conflict was real for Bella. Maybe, consciously or not, she is using Joe's feelings about them as a pressure point to get a concession from Joe on another, unrelated issue. Or as a pleasant spot for her to have a skirmish with Joe in their on-going warfare as spouses – what could be a more attractive issue for her if she wants to fight with him, than one that he would be all steamed up over and upset if he lost, but on which she could lose or yield without giving a damn? Or maybe she is using the candlesticks to express her anger at Joe.

And of course his talk about the candlesticks being heirlooms may be a smokescreen – for almost anything. So our mediator starts cautiously:

> *Mediator:* "These candlesticks seem more important to both of you than I had realised?"
>
> *Joe:* "They are certainly important to me. They've been in my family for years, etc."

The mediator might pause here to offer feedback if he felt Joe needed to be reassured that he has been heard. He might then continue:

> *Mediator:* "And to you, Bella?"
>
> *Bella:* "I don't think it would be fair for Joe to walk off with both of them. They are the most valuable thing we have ever owned – worth at least £5,000. None of our other things is worth anything like that. Why should he always have the lion's share of everything? In fact, they are worth more than all our other stuff put together.

"Joe goes on about how they came from his family, but who polished them for years?

"I want one of them. I am not looking for both, but I am entitled to one."

At this point, the mediator has to choose between a number of options, any one of which may seem a good idea and any one of which may lead to disaster.

First, he can try to establish whether they both see the candlesticks as family heirlooms, to be kept in the family and handed down to their children. Joe will probably say yes. If Bella agrees, he may be able to ask: "If you agree they should be kept in the family and handed on to the next generation, does it matter whether the children get them from their father or mother?"

That question will end the controversy if Bella has accepted the heirloom concept. But if she has not, the mediator will not ask it, because it would open up another issue: are the candlesticks heirlooms? and agreement is even further off. Moreover, the question might lead Bella to accuse the mediator of taking Joe's side. If she does so to his face, that will be better than if she thinks it but doesn't say it, because if she accuses him openly of bias the accusation can at least be looked at. But if she thinks he is biased but doesn't say so, that is potentially at best a distraction and at worst a disaster. So this is a question he will not ask unless he is certain Bella accepts the heirloom concept.

Next, he can try Solomon's trick, and say something like: "Some people feel that when money is very tight is the time to sell any valuables they have, because they will never need cash more. Do you want to think about selling the candlesticks?" There are a few problems with this. If he says it in Solomon's spirit, of trying to catch out someone (Joe) who is pretending one thing, while meaning another, he has abused his position, and will alienate Joe, who has said he

200

wants to hold them for his children. And there are two further dangers. He may come on strong in advocating something he believes is sensible, and substitute his preference for theirs. Or Joe may interpret it as an attempt to push him, and resent it.

He knows that if a negotiation is to produce a reasonable bargain, each side will have to be ready to make concessions. (If one of them makes all the concessions, and the other makes none, it is possible to find a number of different names for what will emerge, but "reasonable bargain" is not one of them.) The extent of the concessions on each side will depend on a number of factors, including whether the parties took up initial negotiating positions, and, if they did, how much "add-on" (Chapter Six) each adopted. The one who took up more extreme positions will have more room for concessions, and will probably make more.

Where both parties have legitimate interests and there are no issues of principle it is not hard for each to make concessions. It is much harder to make a concession in a situation where (a) your cause is important to you, (b) you believe it is just, (c) you believe the other party's cause is unjust, (d) you cannot see real benefit to yourself from giving up something you see as your right, (e) you could do so only at the expense of someone else to whom you feel an obligation. All of which is a fair summary of Joe's stated position. If the mediator guesses there is not much difference between Joe's stated position and the interest he wants to protect he will not want to ask him to make a concession against his principles.

So what does our hypothetical mediator do? I think he will compare Bella's negotiating stance and skill on this issue with how she argued and defended her position when she was arguing for something important to her, like financial support for the children. If she seems flustered and bellicose on this issue, compared with her calm, forceful, logical argument on the issue of support, this may suggest that she isn't herself convinced by the case she is making.

The mediator begins to hypothesise that Bella may need some help fairly soon in saving face, if she has got into a conflict that she cannot win. Furthermore, if she recognises, first that she needs help, and then that she got it from the mediator, that will probably increase her disposition to co-operate with the process. The unspoken dialogue goes:

Mediator: "You were in the manure, and I dug you out."

Bella: "Thanks! I won't forget it!"

Without being there, it is hard to know what I would do. I would be fairly sure the next thing I said would be in the form of a question, for reasons described later in this chapter. I might ask:

"What about you, Bella? If you owned one of these candlesticks – or indeed if you owned both of them – what would you want to do with them?"

With this question, the mediator has moved Bella to a position where saving her face should no longer be a problem. She can move to whatever ground she chooses, without loss of dignity.

Bella's next answer will determine the mediator's further strategy. This is true not only of this dialogue, but universally. Strategy should be open to change in response to what each client says, each time either speaks.

If the mediator thinks Bella is playing "dog in the manger" about the candlesticks – doesn't want them herself, but doesn't want Joe to keep them – he may be tempted to add another question, when he asks her if she wants to keep them: "And go on polishing them?" He does not ask it, for a number of reasons. It suggests he is taking sides with Joe; it may be a useful question, at a later stage, and he doesn't want to throw it away prematurely; and his focus may have shifted from saving Bella's face, but he does not want to slap it.

Let me break off here to say that when our mediator speculates that Bella is being "dog in the manger", that is a tactical hypothesis, not a judgement. He does not say: "Bella is trying, out of spite, to deprive Joe of something he wants and she does not. Tut-tut. I will not help her." He says: "I wonder is Bella really interested in holding on to these candlesticks, as Joe seems to be? If they aren't really important to her, then the scope for the two of them to resolve this issue is much greater than if they were both locked into keeping them."

Bella may now say she doesn't want the candlesticks, since they are so important to Joe, or that they should be kept and passed on. In either case, the problem would be solved, and the only question left would be a mechanical one of where they would be safer, and who would be better at taking care of them. This is too easy, so let us take the tougher option: she wants a sale and Joe wants them kept.

I chose candlesticks at random. The fact that there are two of them and that Bella is claiming one gives the mediator a chance to ask a useful question:

> "Suppose you divide them up, and Bella gets one and Joe the other, and suppose, Bella, you decide to sell yours, do you think you will get half of what you would get for the two if they were sold together?"

There is only one credible answer to this question. If the candlesticks were not valuable, Bella would not be involved in an argument about her having one. She would be happy to trade the washing machine, dryer and iron against the fridge and the candlesticks. If they are "good" enough to be heirlooms, a pair of them will be worth a lot more than double the value of a single one. So the effect of the question is to identify that it is not in anyone's interests to split the candlesticks. Either they will both be sold or they will both be kept. We have eliminated one scenario that would have been unacceptable to Joe. He and Bella will not wind up with one candlestick each. And to anyone who argues that this is still a theoretically possible outcome, I reply that I do not work as a mediator in a world of theoretical possibilities. I work in the real world, where if Bella is interested in cash she will not diminish the value of an asset by splitting it, and if Joe wants to keep the heirlooms, he will not agree to split the pair. So we have reduced the possibilities to two. The candlesticks will be sold as a pair or they will be kept as a pair.

If they are sold, Joe and Bella will have to decide how to handle the money. If they are kept, in theory Joe and Bella have to decide which of them will keep them, but this is really not in dispute. Bella does not want to hold on to candlesticks that come from Joe's family. Nor does she want to be responsible for them. She may also have in her mind that if people – including her children – see her in possession of candlesticks that they know came from her ex-husband's family, eyebrows may be raised. Remember, this is in the real world.

At this point, the mediator may remember the question he thought of previously, and decided not to ask: who is going to polish them. He won't ask it. He won't need to, and he won't want to ask an unnecessary question, and risk annoying Bella or being stuck with an answer he doesn't want to hear.

As we look now at the two possibilities, the mediator will have in his mind a distinction between a course of action that can be reversed, and one that cannot. A decision to sell the candlesticks is like a decision to get married: once it has been implemented, it cannot be changed. A decision not to sell them, on the other hand, like a decision not to get married in April, can be reversed in May.

What the mediator does now will depend on Joe and Bella's finances. (I assume he has followed my advice in Chapter Five, and that before he allowed them to get into a debate about the candlesticks, he got a clear picture of the full agenda, including their finances.) There is no challenge for the mediator if they have lots of cash, so that the sale price of the candlesticks is immaterial, so let's assume money is needed and selling them would make a real difference. The first thing a mediator might do, in this situation, is summarise. If he doesn't, he is leaving the door open for them to go back into their old fight, and unravel the progress he has helped them to make (see Chapter Eight). He might say:

> "So it seems selling one candlestick would be a bad deal. Your choices are either to keep both as a pair or to sell them as a pair. I recognise the second choice would not be welcome to Joe, and I will not ignore that, but I want to ask you both are those the only two possibilities?"

He knows the parties must agree to his summary, but he gets their consent to make sure they have passed through that door, and closed it behind them. After saying "yes", neither can now plausibly re-open the debate about splitting the candlesticks and selling one. He continues:

> "Do you know what they are worth, if you sold them now?"

This question is designed to identify and exclude irrelevant dissension. Opinions each may have on what the things are worth are irrelevant. They may want to spend hours arguing about it, but the mediator knows those would be wasted hours. What is relevant is their actual value. If they do not agree on it he might say something like:

> "You have different views on what they are worth. Neither of you is likely to convince the other, and you are paying me to listen to you fighting about something you are not going to agree on. Do you want to get them valued?"

This is an example of an intervention intended to prevent useless conflict. If there is a piece of factual information which can be ascertained, that information is what we need, and time spent speculating about it is wasted, and may be worse than wasted if it pushes them into entrenched positions, (Chapter One). I prevent speculation about facts that can be ascertained, and am usually pretty brisk about it.

If they decide to look for a valuation, the mediator may ask:

"Will you nominate a valuer to give you both an expert opinion?"

Assuming "yes":

"Will you agree in advance to accept it?"

Let's now assume the candlesticks have been valued at £5,000, that neither disputes the value, and that this is a significant amount for them. At this point, the mediator may produce another summary:

"Right. You agree the candlesticks are worth £5,000. Bella feels they should be sold, and you should use the money. And, clearly, it would come in handy at this point. For example, you could clear the arrears on the mortgage."

Here is where he may feel entitled to get tough, and say:

"Joe wants them kept. He feels strongly about them. Joe, does this mean you are saying they are worth more than £5,000 to you?"

This is a hard question for Joe, and there is probably only one answer to it: yes.

The mediator has put Joe on the spot by making him acknowledge that these candlesticks are worth more to him than their sale value, and he can now put Bella on the spot without seeming unfair, by a series of questions:

"Bella, you favour selling them, and sharing out the money?

"Do you think fifty/fifty would be right?

206

"Or more than half to you?

"Or more than half to Joe?"

He can be certain that she will say yes to the first question, about selling them. He can also be reasonably confident that she will not claim more than half their value. She may perhaps concede that Joe should get more than half, because they come from his family, but she is unlikely to claim that she should have more than half. (In the real world, if she does intend to argue for more than half for herself, the mediator will have picked up a signal from her to that effect before he comes to this point, and he will not ask the question in that form.) So, either at best the question will lead to a concession from Bella that she is entitled to less than half the sale price, and improve the negotiating climate, or at worst she will have put in a claim for half of the sale price, and the climate will not have been damaged.

However she answers it, the mediator's next question may be much the same, subject to an adjustment in the figures if she has conceded that Joe's share is more than half:

> "Does that mean, then, that if Joe keeps the candlesticks and you get £2,500 you will feel you have got what was fair?"

A "yes" to that question is not inevitable. Bella may say:

> "If they are worth more than £5,000 to Joe, I think he should pay me half what he thinks they are worth."

I think a mediator could justify shooting that down, and would not need to ask himself later if his own prejudices intruded:

> "If they were sold to an outsider, you would get £5,000. If you agree a fifty/fifty split, it seems Bella's share would be £2,500."

The implication of this is tough. The next stage, if we had to take it, would be to suggest that the only way Bella could screw (harsh word, but justified) more than half the market value of the candlesticks out of Joe would be by blackmail – threatening to force a sale.

I would try to avoid even a hint of such an accusation, but if I had to say something like that, it might take the form of:

> "Are we looking at a scenario in which Joe has to pay Bella more than the maximum amount she could hope to get if the candlesticks were sold to an outsider, in order to persuade her not to insist on a sale?"

If something like that enters the process, an experienced mediator would start to speculate about how soon he should bring the process to a close, for two reasons. He would not want to become an accessory to Bella's blackmail of Joe, and he would read Bella's attitude as reluctance to use mediation constructively, and a signal that the process was unlikely to get anywhere.

Assuming this does not have to be said, the mediator turns to Joe, and, with Bella still in his sight, so that he can be sure she goes along with what he is saying, he says something like:

> "Joe, if I have understood Bella, she is saying that if you don't want to sell the candlesticks, she won't insist. She feels that if you keep them, she should get £2,500, as that is what she would have got if they were sold. After that, what you do with the candlesticks is up to you. You can keep them in your family and pass them on, or you can sell them later if you decide to. And if you make more than £5,000 that is your good luck.

> "And I assume – correct me if I am wrong, Bella – if Bella gets £2,500 she can take it in cash or in other ways. For example, perhaps, by increasing the value of what she takes from the contents of the house.

> "I don't know how you feel about that?

An issue about ownership of candlesticks has now been changed into a much more manageable one, about how the other contents of a house, in which neither party has a sentimental investment, will be shared out, or what money adjustment may be made between separating spouses, so as to produce a division they can both accept.

Their real problem has not been solved: that they don't have enough money to buy all the things they need. But the row over the candlesticks is over, and if belt-tightening follows a decision to hold on to the candlesticks, the only belt that will be tightened is that of the person who makes the decision. And as I said earlier Joe's, decision not to sell them today can be reversed tomorrow.

About questions

Apart from pausing to summarise, the mediator in that dialogue proceeded by asking questions only. I have two working rules about questions. First is I will not ask a question unless I really want an answer. Second is if I have asked a question, I will usually persist with it until it is answered. If I don't, I have effectively handed over control of the process to the person who doesn't answer my question, and I have been seen by the other to have lost control. However, I modify the second rule. If I ask a question and the person who should answer it becomes evasive, I ask myself is there a hidden reason, and should I take a hint, and not insist on an answer. If my answer to that question is yes, that means I should not have asked the first question and have no right to seek an answer. But I do not change my mind and withdraw a troublesome question unless I have cause to reasses it. I assume that an answer that is hard to give is likely to be important. Furthermore, if I exercise self-discipline, and do not ask irrelevant questions, I can be fairly certain that a question I asked was one I was right to ask, and is therefore one I should insist on being answered.

I went to a workshop some years ago given by John Haynes and Larry Fong when they argued in favour of mediators asking questions, not making statements. As John said, if the mediator makes a statement the clients may either accept or reject it. But if he asks a question and gets a reply, the person who answers takes responsibility for what he has said, or as John put it, he "owns" the answer. I was impressed at the time by what they said, but daunted. I could not see myself working on that basis. I felt making statements was something I would have to go on doing, and couldn't stop. However, I decided that I would try to increase the number of my interventions that took the form of questions, and reduce the ratio of statements. Some years later, most of what I say as a mediator, apart from techniques such as feedback, summarising and reframing, is in question form.

Most of the questions the mediator asked in this scenario were ones the answer to which he knew in advance. Indeed, to many of them there could be only one answer. It used to be said that a lawyer in court, questioning a witness, should ask only questions to which he already knows the answer. I am told it is not possible for a lawyer to abide by that rule all the time. He must sometimes take a leap in the dark. The same is true for mediators, but more often than not when we direct a question at either party we have a pretty good idea of how it will be answered.

We can be wrong. Here, carefully edited to ensure there is no danger of the people being identified, is an extract from notes such as I always write after a session:

"I ask Mary a careful question: if Paul needs capital for a deposit on a place of his own, and can't raise it elsewhere, would you be willing in principle to agree to an increase in the mortgage on your home, to help him raise the cash, provided you had absolute security that it would be repaid, and you couldn't suffer any financial exposure?

"I thought this was a fairly safe question, but Mary said no, and explained it was because Paul had . . . [material omitted.] Paul got into this with defence and counter-accusation. I said I had asked Mary a question, got my answer, and had to accept it: she was not willing to agree to an increase in the mortgage on her home."

I had asked a question that I had thought was safe in the context. That is, I thought the answer would be yes. Its wording included elaborate safeguards for Mary, but I still did not get the answer I hoped for. "Yes" from Mary would have meant she was willing to help Paul to get a home for himself, a sign that they could co-operate, and perhaps a cue for further co-operating between them - something their children needed from those parents. My job is helping people to look at their conflict more productively, and reach an agreement. The answer moved them backwards instead of forwards. It would have been better if I had not asked the question.

If you should sometimes feel I am boasting about successes in this book, please remember this description of how I tossed a pancake into the air and it landed on my face. Please also note that I made a mistake in my work, and wrote it into my notes to remind me of the mistake, and ensure I would learn from it. And, I hope, for the sake of future clients, not repeat it.

There is a distinction between the sort of questions mediators ask at the beginning of the process and questions asked later. The purpose of the first sort is purely to gather information: "How many children have you? Their names? Ages? Where is your home? What is it worth? Is there a mortgage? How much?" These are fact-gathering questions. The questions we ask later on, as shown in the dialogue with Joe and Bella, are really interventions by the mediator, intended to produce movement.

211

There is an ethical problem here. If a mediator asks only questions to which he knows the answer in advance, and the purpose of his questions is to produce movement on the part of his clients, how does he defend himself against an accusation that he chooses their destination for them, and then steers them towards it by selective questioning? My response is that the answers to his earlier fact-gathering questions show him how the current is flowing, and when he understands it he can guide them to their chosen destination by his later questions. (Of course, if the current is not flowing at all, and he cannot help them to work out a rough direction for it, the process will end without agreement.) It is like saying: "If they start from here, and are looking for a milder climate, they will head south. I know they can cover ten miles a day, so I can work out roughly where they will be after two weeks."

In his dialogue with Joe and Bella, for example, he clarified that Bella did not claim more than a half interest in the candlesticks. Similarly, if the topic is child support, a mediator may put a clarifying question to a husband, so that the wife will hear him say that he intends to pay a fair share of the cost of supporting his children. He will not ask the husband how much he plans to contribute. Still less will he say: "Would £125 per week seem about right?"

I think it is legitimate to ask questions the answers to which begin to build bridges, provided the clients recognise the existence of the gap and want to bridge it. It may be useful to get them to acknowledge that some points in the chasm are not suitable for the building of bridges, but we leave it to the clients to decide where, within terrain they identify, the bridge should be built, of what material, and how wide it needs to be. Of course, the width of the gap to be bridged will determine its length.

We are on the edge of being directive at all times, and, like someone standing near a cliff, we may be attracted towards the edge. Using a questioning form rather than making assertions may help to protect us from going over the edge. But as I said earlier content is what counts. If what we say pushes our clients in a direction we have chosen for them, then we are being directive, even if the form of words we choose demands a question mark at the end.

Mediation a rational process

The conversation between Joe, Bella and their mediator all took place on a rational plane, without our getting involved in the clients' emotions. The mediator took at face value Joe's position that the candlesticks were heirlooms, to be kept and passed down in the family. He did not question or try to assess Bella's motives for claiming a candlestick. I go into the "foul rag-and-bone-shop of the heart" only if I find that I must, because something there will block progress if it is not addressed. Otherwise I deal with issues at a rational level, acknowledging feelings, but not letting them get in the way of the work that my clients have asked me to help them with. I keep a box of tissues, and if either party starts to cry, I give them the tissues, and carry on with the work. If someone is crying so uncontrollably as to be unable to go on with the work, I suspend it for long enough for him or her to regain control, and then we continue.

If after a few sessions my clients do not make progress, I start to ask myself why. There may be issues left unresolved in the relationship. If one of them still feels married to the other, he may be psychologically unable to finalise an agreement, and let go of the person he still sees as his wife. "Unfinished business", in Kubler-Ross's phrase, may first need to be addressed and resolved.

If this seems to be the explanation, I first test it by asking questions. How else? What I do then will depend on my assessment of the depth of the problem. I may say:

"I think we are getting nowhere in this process. You have asked me to help you reach an agreement, but it seems to me that you are no closer to agreeing than you were when we started.

"I am not a counsellor or therapist, but I pick up strong feelings between you as spouses, or former spouses, and I suspect that what is blocking you is those feelings, and the fact that they have not been dealt with and resolved.

"For example, the first time we met, Mattie said she didn't understand what had gone wrong between you, or why Peter had left. Peter said he had explained it all, and Mattie said his explanation had explained nothing, and left her as puzzled as ever. I didn't allow you to pursue that subject then, because it didn't seem to be what you had come to me about. That may have been a mistake.

"I now feel that so long as there are unresolved issues in your relationship you are not going to reach agreement, and I think you are wasting your time here at present. My sense is that you will have a better prospect of reaching an agreement if you take time to sort out the personal stuff.

"If you then want to come back here, I'll be happy to try again."

Some people say:

"But, Michael we've got to know you, and you understand us. Surely, if we have to work on this other stuff, we can do it here, and not have to go to someone else? We've been to so many experts – therapists, counsellors, psychologists, you name it – I don't want to go to anyone else!"

What does the mediator say to that? I avoid changing my role from mediator to therapist, for the same reason that a responsible oculist will decline to remove an appendix: there are other people qualified to do the job, as I am not.

Suppose I were qualified to offer separation counselling? Should I be willing to take time out from mediating, work as a separation counsellor with a couple, and then return to acting as mediator when they no longer needed me as counsellor? The question suggests its own answer: I may not be an effective separation counsellor to the couple, if they have already got to know me as a mediator. And having acted as their counsellor may disqualify me from being their mediator later.

In the same way, when clients who know I was once a lawyer ask me for legal advice, I am willing to open a law book and let them read a section of a Statute, but I do not advise, and if they push I tell them that they can have me as mediator or as legal adviser but not as both.

The only exception I can think of, at present, to the rule that a mediator should not take on another role in the lives of his clients arises where they need other help, and there is nobody else available. In *A Short Walk in the Hindu Kush* Eric Newby describes meeting the explorer Wilfred Thesiger on an expedition. Thesiger told him he used to carry out primitive surgery on Bedouin. "I give them powders for worms and that sort of thing." I asked him about surgery. "I take off fingers, and there's lots of surgery to be done; they're frightened of their own doctors because they're not clean." "Do you do it? Cutting off fingers?" "Hundreds of them", he said dreamily, for it was very late. "Lord, yes. Why the other day I took out an eye. I enjoyed that."

Thesiger may have been justified, because his Arab patients were unlikely to be worse as a result of his efforts, and there was no better alternative available. This does not apply to a mediator who has no therapy training or qualifications, in a country where there is no shortage of qualified therapists.

215

CHAPTER TWELVE

ETHICAL PRINCIPLES

The concept that the mediator controls the process, and the clients control the outcome is clear, but the distinction can get blurred. If I say during a session, "we have made some progress on the question of income support for Vera and the children, and I now want to talk about Peter's contact with the children" it is because I want to change the topic for tactical reasons, to help them continue their journey, but what I say may affect its destination – the outcome of the mediation.

Indeed, when I change topic I intend to do something that may affect the outcome. Perhaps I feel if we stay with the topic of income support it may end in an impasse. Or I might decide to leave that topic partly agreed to leave room for trade-off with some other issue. Or I might decide to change the topic in the hope that if they sort out Peter's contact with his children their chances of agreeing about support for Vera and the children would improve. Or I switch topics in the hope that talking about the children – in whom they have a shared interest – will create a more constructive atmosphere for their tough negotiations about money. My intervention is intended to help them make a bargain, and I accept that it may also affect the content of their bargain. I hope to create a better climate for their negotiations, but my intervention shifts the location within which a bargain may be found, which means it may influence what their bargain will be.

I remember from my childhood that Catholic teaching, looking at the moral content of actions based on their results, drew distinctions between a result that was intended, and one that was not. I was told suicide was sinful, but a soldier carrying dispatches and pursued by the enemy might jump from a cliff in order to keep the dispatches from the enemy, even though it meant he died, because that was not his purpose in jumping. Fascinating stuff, I'm sure you will agree.

There is a parallel with a mediator who does something that was intended to help his clients to make a bargain, but which influences what that bargain will be. It is all right for him to intervene with the intention of facilitating a bargain. That is what he is paid for. If, in doing so, he helps to shape that bargain, then I think he is not out of line, provided he does not aim to shape it, and provided he can see no other way of achieving the desired result. (If the soldier could have eaten the dispatches, but jumped over the cliff instead, theologians would probably classify him as a suicide, not a hero . . .)

Because a mediator walks so fine a line between controlling the conflict of his clients and influencing the outcome of their discussions, he has big responsibilities, should be aware of them, and should always act in a way that is ethically acceptable. The difficulty is to know what is acceptable. I think there are tests. First, for me, is: what does a code of ethics to which I subscribe have to say? Does it prohibit what I have in mind? Does it specifically prescribe it – say it is my duty? Or does it leave the decision to me? I then ask a second question: whatever the code says, does my conscience and sense of what is right agree with it?

It would be pleasant for me to say that I have never done anything that was not permitted both by my conscience and by an acceptable ethical code. Unfortunately, it would not be true. For example, the Code of Practice of the Academy of Family Mediators provides:

"A mediator's actual or perceived impartiality may be compromised by social or professional relationships with one of the participants at any point in time. The mediator *shall not proceed* if previous legal or counselling services have been provided to one of the participants. If such services have been provided to both participants, mediation shall not proceed unless the prior relationship has been discussed, the role of the mediator made distinct from the earlier relationship, and the participants given the opportunity to freely choose to proceed."

Some years ago, I was consulted by a man – let me call him Fred – whom I had met in my days as a lawyer, as one of a group that sought advice from me. It was a one-off problem, I advised the group, and never saw him again until he turned up asking for my help as a mediator, following the collapse of his marriage to (let us say) Ursula. If there had been another mediator available, I would have referred Fred and Ursula on. But at the time mediators were thin on the ground in Dublin. It was clear that they needed help, and needed it urgently. I cannot now remember if the Irish Government-funded Family Mediation Service was available at that time, but if it were, the waiting time for an appointment was much too long for this family.

Luckily, Ursula was an outstandingly sensible woman, had good legal advice, and we worked out an arrangement. Because I had already met Fred, I met Ursula on the understanding – which she honoured strictly – that we would not discuss the substance of their disputes, and that our meeting would have two purposes only. The first was to enable her to decide whether I would be acceptable to her as a mediator, and me to decide whether, having met her, I was willing to act in that role. The second was to ensure that, if we did work together, Ursula would not feel at a disadvantage, because Fred knew me and she did not. Ursula and I met, and I went on to act as their mediator.

When I looked again at the AFM code some years later I realised that I had been in breach of the code in working with this couple. That does not bother me. Nobody was misled: we all went into the relationship of mediator and clients with our eyes open. And I felt throughout that what I was doing was right.

I consulted the AFM code again when one of my clients accused the other of having had an affair with a therapist who had worked with them on problems in their marriage. This seemed to me to be an accusation of professional misconduct against the therapist, but when I looked for a specific condemnation of such a change of role in the AFM code, I failed to find it.

So if a mediator is to function ethically I think he should be guided by two sets of principles. First are ethical rules drawn up by a professional group and second is his own conscience. He should respect both. If he finds that the rules allow him to do something his conscience tells him not to, he should look for a new set of professional standards. If the rules forbid things that his conscience tells him are okay, he may need to replace his conscience – or, at least, upgrade it.

When the AFM code describes how a mediator should operate, I agree. When it talks about such things as Impartiality, Neutrality, Confidentiality, Self-determination, how to deal with Conflict of Interest, and so forth, I say, with no difficulty at all: "Yes, that's right. I agree with that." If I were thinking of becoming a mediator now, and looked at AFM's standards, I would say to myself: "That looks like a body with good standards." And it is.

My problem has been that no set of professional standards I have studied, including AFM's, has been much help when I needed to decide how I should behave to be fair to my clients, protect myself, and maintain the reputation of my profession. I have looked at three sets of "standards of practice", each produced by a reputable organisation, and obviously the result of hard work by thoughtful people. Each has described the mediation process in a way that I accept. Unfortunately, every set of standards I have seen seems to have been written for a mediator's clients, or prospective clients, to assure them that if they consult a mediator who works to these standards they will be fairly treated. None of them has given me useful guidance when I have needed it.

Maybe I have been hoping for too much from the professional rules. It may be unrealistic to expect any set of rules to answer all the ethical problems that may arise in a mediator's life. Perhaps their function is to give general guidance to mediators, and assure clients that their mediator operates to a respectable code of conduct.

In any event, I have evolved my own set of rules governing how I work, approaching it in this way. First I ask myself what are the ethical principles underlying the practice of mediation? What duties do I accept when I begin to work with clients as their mediator? Having listed them, I state a series of "commands", each of which would follow from an identified ethical principle – in much the same way as theorems in geometry have "corollaries", or, in logic, "conclusions" can be drawn from "premises". If I look at a situation, and feel ethically bound to act in a certain way, but cannot see what ethical principle is involved, I try to identify a principle that impels me in that direction. And then, if it seems to be universally valid, I expand my list of principles to include it.

In this way, I hope, my own standards are based on logic. Every rule about what I should do is based on a principle I

220

have identified, and seems valid for that reason. This gives authority to the rules. I cannot disregard them without ignoring a principle that I believe should govern my conduct.

So, what are these principles? I thought, before I started to write this book, that I had them clear in my mind. When I got down to this book, I realised that my list of ethical principles was longer than I had thought, and I added two that were not previously on my conscious list. Since I am open to adding to the list, I obviously don't claim my list is exhaustive, but it includes:

1) Respect

We treat our clients with respect. We aim to feel the respect that we show. That may sound difficult, but it usually is not. I can remember only one person that I have worked with during eleven years as a mediator for whom I was not able to feel respect. (In case any of my former clients reads this, and wonders, like the disciples at the Last Supper: "Is it I?", if you are reading this book you are not the person I am speaking of.)

It is sometimes hard to feel respect early in the process, when people act out their aggression and hostility. With experience and more understanding, we recognise their aggression, sniping, and hostility are expressions of their pain. And as the process continues, and we continue to show respect to our clients, we begin to feel the respect we show. This is partly because we recognise that they deserve it, and partly because we continue to show it.

There is a paradox here. In Max Beerbohm's story "The Happy Hypocrite", Lord George Hell, a deeply debauched man, falls in love with an innocent girl. She is repelled by the ugliness she sees on his face, printed on it by the life he has led. To woo her, he buys and puts on the mask of a saint. When, later, the mask falls from his face, no change is visible.

His face has changed, and is now the face of a virtuous man, indistinguishable from the mask. In much the same way, I start with an assumption that people who come to me for help in sorting out their problems, taking the hard course, rather than the easy way of asking their lawyers to negotiate for them or a judge to make decisions for them, are worthy of respect. I treat them with respect, accordingly. After a while – and, as I say, the time is getting shorter, not longer, with experience – I usually feel for them the respect that I show.

Respect dictates that while first sessions with different clients may start similarly, they always end differently. I think too, that respect for our clients is one of the convincing arguments against a too-structured approach to mediation. To keep the clients under rigid control is to treat them disrespectfully.

And, of course, "empowerment" comes from respect. This is an imprecise word for a complex concept. When colleagues talk about "the E-word" as though we graciously bestow on our clients the power to decide how to live their lives, I disagree. At most, we return to our clients something that has been stolen from them. The word reminds us that the trust clients develop in their mediator gives him an ability to influence their decision-making. For me to impose on my clients my view of what is right, either in principle or in their circumstances, would involve failing to treat them with respect. This includes not acting as adviser.

Being empowered to negotiate also includes not being disabled from doing so – for example, because one of them is so skilful or dominant, or the other so timid and uncertain, that they cannot negotiate on reasonably fair terms. It is the principle – though not necessarily the only one – that directs a mediator to terminate the process if he detects intimidation. It includes the concept that, if people are make decisions, they must have whatever information they need, and that nobody should be pressurised into making a decision without having time to reflect and to take advice.

2) Neutrality

We may lean towards one party or the other, and may even get out of our chair and sit with them in theirs for a while. Indeed, as I said earlier I have come to believe that joining each person, and sitting with them, inside their skins, is the core of mediation. But we are like the cyclist I mentioned in Chapter One, who leans in to keep his balance going round a bend, and then returns to his natural flexibly upright posture, not leaning towards either party, but ready to lean in either direction at any moment if that seems the right thing to do.

3) Confidentiality

The mediator keeps his clients' secrets, except in specific, clearly defined circumstances. The only exceptions I accept to the rule of confidentiality are:
- where not to reveal information would involve a breach by the mediator of local criminal law, and leave him open to being prosecuted. Please note: "breach by the mediator". It is not my business or my right to interfere if my clients cheat on their tax, or smoke pot. In some counties, not currently including Ireland, certain professionals are obliged to report any allegation of child abuse. Failure to do so is a criminal offence. In such countries I assume the legal obligation overrides the duty to keep clients' secrets.
- where the mediator feels that in order to serve the clients well he needs to consult a colleague. It is possible that if I consult a colleague about a couple, the consultant will guess who my clients are. I think I should take that risk, provided three conditions are met: consultation during the

223

case is essential to serve the clients properly; my consultant-colleague accepts the same duty of secrecy as I do, and I know my consultant well, and trust him to honour his duty of secrecy.

4) Availability

People consult a mediator because they have a dispute they need to resolve, but cannot, without help. If their dispute results from the collapse of a marriage with children, the decisions they need to make will affect their children, their children's spouses, and their children's children, their spouses and children. It is also likely that any agreement ending this marital dispute, and influencing all these generations, will need to be reviewed as time passes. This is a big responsibility, even though the mediator does not take decisions for his clients. If we agree to work with people in dispute, who may need to return to us, there is an implied obligation on our part to be available to them. In my view, unless it is clearly agreed by all parties that the clients will never, in any circumstances, return to the mediator, a mediator should not voluntarily do or allow to be done anything that might make him unavailable to them in the future.

My exception is that a mediator is entitled to retire, and is not bound to emerge from retirement at the request of former clients.

Availability also dictates what goes into in a mediator's appointment diary. If I start working with a couple, the frequency of appointments is – within reason – governed by their needs. If I plan a holiday during the time I expect to be working with them, I tell them so before our first appointment, and let them decide whether to come to me or go elsewhere. Availability and respect – from which it derives – dictate that a mediator should limit his appointments to what he can manage and meet his clients' reasonable needs. Most clients need an appointment fairly soon (unless, of course, there are reasons for postponing, such as one of them needing recovery time) and to move through the process at a reasonably fast and consistent tempo. If a mediator cannot give them a reasonably early appointment, or, once they have started the process, cannot meet them at intervals that meet their needs, he should tell them so at the outset, and recommend a colleague.

5) Professionalism

Professionalism governs our relationship with our clients when they are with us, and when they are absent. We are hired to act as professional people, and we behave accordingly. All the time we are "on duty" the question we constantly ask, and the answer to which determines what we do is "does this serve the interests of the clients?".

My friend Brian Boydell once told me a story that illustrates the meaning of being a professional. When he was a young man in London he wanted to take singing lessons and the doyenne of teachers agreed to take him as a pupil. She asked when he could come, and he answered, "any time except the morning. I can't sing in the morning." She said, "I'll put you down for nine on Tuesday mornings. If you are going to be a singer, you must be able to sing at any time."

Among other things, professionalism dictates that we go into each session with every set of clients properly prepared. For every session except the first we have all relevant facts at our finger-tips, and a clear sense of the personalities we are about to work with. This requires us to make detailed notes about every session, and keep the notes for a reasonable length of time.

Another reason for writing notes is the sense of confidence the clients get from their mediator if he is seen to be well-informed.

"Tuesday week will be Peter's eighth birthday, won't it? Will he expect you both to be involved? Have you worked out plans for how to celebrate it? Or do you want to talk about them here?"

Some mediators say they work with clients over a short time, and don't have time to forget them. To which I answer: how do you know? What if the clients decide to take time out from mediation to try separation counselling? Or one of them gets ill? Or you do?

The value of comprehensive notes is proved if the clients need to come back for a review of their bargain, years later. If I say something like "How is Gloria? She must be seventeen now. Is she still at school?" it is not intended to fool them into thinking I have total recall of all that passed between us. They are not so foolish. They know I relied on notes, not memory. But they get a message that I keep notes, and they don't have to start again at the beginning. That is, that I offer a professional service.

Another reason for writing up notes carefully and conscientiously is that it forces us to address our mistakes. For example, here are two extracts from a set of notes I prepared, in which I used the opportunity given by writing the notes to question the quality of my work (names and background changed):

"Is there a gap here? I have heard something about Peter's relationship with his two younger daughters, Grace and Maria, but not with Anne. Is this because I haven't asked? Or is there more to it?"

After describing an exchange between Peter and me:

"I think I pushed this. And I was seen by both of them to do so."

In each of these notes, I was rubbing my nose in the fact that on specific issues, I had not done my job as well as I want to. I was also reminding myself of things I had to do next time, or of the need to regain trust I had put at risk.

226

Not all mediators treat note-taking as seriously as I do. It is a choice for each of us. But if someone says he doesn't bother with notes, that tells its own story.

Professionalism also dictates that a mediator should be sensitive to the possibility that his actions, though ethically acceptable, may attract criticism to the profession of mediation. He will not allow this principle to override others, and do something that he thinks wrong, in order to avoid criticism, but he may decide on a course of action that he would not otherwise feel bound to follow, in order to preserve the reputation of his profession. If other mediators had been available, I might not have agreed to work with Fred and Ursula, not because I could not be a balanced mediator, but in order to ensure that people would not think ill of my profession because they thought I was acting unethically.

Finally, a professional mediator, like any other true professional, constantly strives to become better at doing his work.

6) Integrity

This should really be at the top of my list. The embarrassing fact is that it was not included in my initial list of principles governing the conduct of mediators. I woke up one morning, after I had started to write this chapter, realising that I had overlooked it and wondering why? Was it that I had assumed it? Or – depressing thought – was I like John Proctor in Arthur Miller's play *The Crucible*, who could remember all the commandments except the one he had broken?

It should be at the top, or at least number two after respect, because everything else should be viewed in the light of a mediator's duty to be honest at all times.

Obviously, it includes being rigorously truthful, but there is more to it than simply avoiding falsehood. A mediator will never engage in half-truths. He will hate the expression "white lies". He will avoid situations where there is a danger of his integrity being questioned. For example, if a prospective client phones him to make an appointment, and then starts to tell him the history of the marriage, he will interrupt and say: "I think it will be better if we don't talk about the problems until the three of us are all in the one room. I like to get both sides of the story at the same time, and I don't think it would be helpful if the three of us were talking, and I seemed to know things that hadn't been mentioned."

Similarly, if he gets a phone call from one client between sessions, he will not discuss the specifics, and will only make appointments and the like. He will not respond to questions like: "What do you think I should do about the children?"

Few clients resent their mediator refusing to talk about the problems in the absence of the other party. They may have contacted their mediator with a view to getting him on to their side – "triangulation" (Chapter Two). And, yes, he has disappointed them by refusing to be triangulated. But they may even feel a little relieved, because their mediator has at least reassured them that their spouse is also unlikely to be more successful than they were in getting their mediator to take sides.

To illustrate the importance of truthfulness, let me tell you about a couple I worked with recently. At the second session, the wife talked about something that had happened at the first. She said she had started to say something, and I had said: "Let's not go into that, now, Anna. I want to finish talking about . . . We'll come back to that issue later." She complained that I had not gone back to the issue she had raised, and she felt, thinking about it afterwards, that when I had promised we would, it was only to shut her up, and that my attitude was patronising.

Of course, she was telling me that I had blundered in a major way during the first session. If she mentioned a topic she wanted to raise, and I had not come back to it, or she felt

228

she had not been allowed to air it, then I was at fault. If she felt I was patronising her, I was doubly at fault. However, she also felt that I had done something else, which I was able to tell her I had not: namely, promising to come back to a topic without meaning to do so. Luckily, because being scrupulously truthful and not practising half-truths or evasions is a universal rule with me, I was able to say:

"Anna, I am really sorry not to have come back to [whatever it was], as I promised to. I should have made a more careful note that you wanted to raise it, and made sure we came back to it, before the session ended. I do apologise for that. I apologise even more for making you feel patronised. There is no possible excuse for that.

"However, I want to assure you that I did not pretend to postpone it in order to avoid discussing it. If I said we would come back to it, I intended to, and if I failed to, it was through an oversight, not on purpose. I did not pretend, because that would not be truthful. And, whatever mistakes or blunders I may have made in my work with you, or may make, I have not lied to you. Nor will I."

She accepted what I had said, and our work went well. But what about other clients, whom I may have treated in the same way, and who may not have felt confident enough to confront me?

I learnt a few lessons from this. First, clearly I had handled this client, and this issue, badly. A mediator makes a judgement call any time he stifles or postpones discussion on an issue, and this time, clearly, my judgement or my memory or both had been at fault.

Secondly, I needed to be more vigilant. If I stifled discussion on a given topic, I needed to remember that I had done so and to return to that topic later. Even if the topic had been discussed under a different name, later I should have said:

229

"Anna, I think this what you wanted to raise back there when we were talking about . . . and I cut you short? Has it now been dealt with to your satisfaction?"

These were the areas where I had to criticise my work. Against them, I was able to draw some consolation from two other thoughts. If I had not made it a practice to be always and undeviatingly truthful with my clients, and not engage in any subterfuge, I could not have told her that I had been guilty of carelessness and forgetfulness, but not of trickery. And, secondly, since she felt ready to tell me where and how she felt critical of me, I must have established at least a comfortable environment for her to do so, and some level of trust and rapport.

Perhaps the only time I say something like: "Let's leave that now, and come back to it later", but not come back, is if one party has got into a position on a topic which I assess he (or she, but let's say he) may want to abandon, but feels he cannot without exposing himself as a bluffer, a bully, or a fool. My aim is to help him save face – avoid humiliation, as discussed in Chapter Six. If I am trying to help a client out of a hole he has dug himself into, or (like Orwell's temporary non-fascist) to escape without embarrassing exposure, "Let's leave that now, and come back to it later" can be helpful. The change of topic allows him to drop his demand or change his position.

A mediator should be grateful to a client who says to him something like what Anna said to me. If a couple come once to me, and do not come back, it may be because they decide the process does not suit them, or for some other reason, not related to the personality or skill of their mediator. Or it may be because I have failed to gain their confidence. People like Anna, who tell you where you have blundered, help you to avoid making the same mistake again.

Thank you, Anna – even though that is not your name.

Mediators' integrity counts, too, when we are involved in that awkward exercise I mentioned earlier – trying to help our clients to narrow the gap between their positions, but to avoid pushing them towards a specific bargain. Like the soldier who killed himself by galloping over the cliff to prevent the dispatches from falling into enemy hands, we aim to help them reach an agreement – any agreement – but recognise that we may unintentionally influence what their agreement will be. If we walk this fine line, we owe it to our clients to do so with all the honesty and integrity of which we are capable. Sometimes, we need more honesty and integrity than we have, or realise we have. We can be helped, here, too, I think, by Beerbohm's "Happy Hypocrite", and by the thought that if we try hard enough to do what is right, we may eventually become righteous.

Of course, for those who succeed in crossing that tightrope, and becoming righteous, there is another problem: how do we continue to be righteous, without becoming self-righteous? I have not got to the stage where that presents a problem.

Integrity will sometimes put us in a difficulty – which is perhaps why some people consider "social lies" acceptable. I mentioned my friend Laurence Crowley, the company liquidator, in Chapter Nine. I learnt another lesson from him when he was liquidator of a company, I was his lawyer, and we were due to meet trade union officials to try to persuade them to encourage their members to stay on at work and turn raw materials into finished goods. The day we were due to meet them, Laurence received a letter. I cannot now remember what it said, or who it was from, but I remember that Laurence was going to have to disclose it to the trade union representatives, and it would not make his task easier. One of his colleagues said: "Could we not produce the letter tomorrow, and pretend it arrived after the meeting?" "No," said Laurence. "Why not?" "Because it wouldn't be true."

My last word on integrity is that it is like a certain kind of hardwood. The grain is close throughout the tree and any plank cut from the tree will show the same closeness of grain.

231

It is not like a softwood, where tough, solid wood alternates in the tree and in the plank with sections of soft timber. Trying to find a way of expressing this, I turned to the Oxford English Dictionary, which defines integrity thus: "wholeness, entireness, completeness . . . the condition of having no part or element taken away or wanting . . . unimpaired or uncorrupted condition . . . soundness of moral principle . . . the character of uncorrupted virtue, esp in relation to truth and fair dealing . . . uprightness, honesty, sincerity."

We may never get there, but the journey is worthwhile. Indeed, for a mediator, it is compulsory.

7) Humility

This seems to fall naturally into place after integrity. It relates to how we look at ethical issues in our working lives, and whether we should involve other people in our decisions about ethical problems. It relates, too, to Cromwell's plea to the General Assembly of the Church of Scotland: "I beseech you, in the bowels of Christ, think it possible you may be mistaken." We need (the reverse of what I was told, in school, on a different topic) not merely to permit the principle of humility to enter our minds, but to entertain it. And I mean "entertain" in the normal sense. That is, to invite it to stay, try to make a comfortable place for it, and encourage it to make itself at home.

The principle of respect that I talked about earlier dictates that we are also humble in the presence of our clients. It is not hard to feel humble with marital clients. They are people who in spite of all the rage pain and hurt they feel, come into a room and sit down with the person they see as most to blame for their hurt, and try to negotiate face to face with that person and a stranger arrangements for the benefit of their children. We *should* view them as heroes, because that is what they are.

Humility governs how far we rely only on ourselves in looking at ethical issues. I think a mediator faced with an ethical dilemma should decide on his own sometimes, but most times he should consult a colleague. If he decides to do something because to act otherwise would offend his sense of what is right, or break an ethical rule that he has adopted through conviction, I believe he should stand by it, and not change it even if a respected colleague advises him that he may do so. Unless, of course, he is convinced by his colleague's arguments, and changes his mind on the issue. He does not need to consult anyone. However, what if he takes the reverse decision, namely that what he is thinking about and feels inclined to do, is acceptable? I believe humility should lead him to take a second opinion from a colleague, and to change his mind if the colleague advises him to.

I think both humility and professionalism dictate that a colleague's view should prevail over that of the mediator who consulted him, if the colleague proposes a higher standard than the mediator had contemplated. That is, if the choice is between doing what the mediator wants to do (e.g. take a former client to bed) and what he is told by a colleague he is obliged to do, he should always follow the higher advice.

These, then, are the principles by which I try to live as a mediator. And, I hope, in my personal life too. Because I think my behaviour outside the mediation room has been affected, for the better, by my work. If so, I suppose I will have to acknowledge a relationship with Lord George Hell in Beerbohm's story.

I would like to see a mediator body adopt a code that set out ethical principles, and then went on to lay down universally valid rules for mediation practice, each one of which derived, logically and unchallengeably, from the principles. It has yet to happen. As I said earlier, I have looked at a number of sets of rules, and they all seemed either to be arbitrary, in the sense of not flowing from accepted principles or to be designed to make the body that adopted them look good and pure, rather than to help the practitioner in his daily work.

233

Some mediators believe that the profession should not be governed by fixed rules, such as those I have outlined above, but that we should have a set of guidelines. These would be concepts that mediators would be expected to observe, but would not be binding. They would be a bit like what, when I was a young Catholic, were called "counsels of perfection": they represented the "best way", one was encouraged to follow them, but it was not considered to be sinful not to. I do not like this idea. One reason lies within my own history. I have developed a distrust of "thought control" through being exposed to it in my youth. This has left me with a strong sense of guilt, and an equally strong hostility towards people who create guilt feelings in others without need or justification, and use those feelings to control them. I admit this is subjective, and not a valid argument. The first of my reasoned objections is that it seems to me (again, this is influenced by my background) that a course of action must be right or wrong. It is wrong if it offends an accepted principle. If it does not offend a principle, and we do not see a need to evolve a new principle, universally applicable, to deal with it, then it must be permissible.

I dislike counsels of perfection in the same way as I bristle at the word "inappropriate", which I denounced in Chapter Two. If you accuse me of going against non-specific guidelines or doing something inappropriate, I cannot defend myself. I do not know how to act in future so as to avoid being accused again. I cannot even decide whether the right thing to do is to try to defend myself or amend myself.

Secondly, I value diversity of approach. Mediation is an evolving profession, and I think it will evolve in a healthy way, and its practitioners will be helped to develop skill, if different mediator take different approaches, each of which can be justified on moral grounds, and if we share our ideas.

Finally, diversity gives clients choice. And choice for clients is "empowering".

CHAPTER THIRTEEN

ETHICS IN ACTION

Let's look at how some of the principles we talked about in the previous chapter apply in specific situations, and start with the way a mediator called Joseph might handle the separation of Mr and Mrs Potiphar.

Changing relationships

In the last chapter I described one of my clients accusing the other of having an affair with a therapist who worked with them on problems in their marriage. This was an accusation against the other spouse, but also against the therapist. What if the accusation had been made about a mediator? Let's apply the technique of partialising we talked about earlier, and break this into two questions: if a mediator has an opportunity to fall into the role of lover to a client, is he bound to resist it? secondly, if he should resist while working with the couple, is he still bound to when the professional relationship is over?

Different principles seem to apply to each question. The second principle I suggested in the previous chapter, neutrality, is surely infringed if a mediator is the lover of either party. Could anyone argue otherwise?

What if the mediation process is over? I think different principles apply. The first relevant one I see is availability. (I do not mean sexual availability.) Is it clear that there is no prospect of the couple wanting to return to their mediator? I have worked with very few couples about whom I could say that. If a couple have children in common, there is always a possibility that a conflict may emerge years down the road, and they may need to return to mediation. If they thought their original mediator did a good job at least one of them will want to return to him.

If the mediator has become the wife's lover since they ended mediation, what does he do? Is he entitled to act? Can he be impartial as between his lover and her husband? If not, is he not bound to refuse to act? If he refuses to act, is he bound to tell the husband the reason he is disqualified? What if under the relevant law an adulterous wife loses the right of support? Does the mediator then have a duty to the wife to keep her secret, and a duty to the husband to reveal it?

Isn't the conclusion pretty plain? A mediator is obliged not to have any relationship with either party if there is any possibility, however remote, that the couple may want to return to him. If he feels strongly attracted to one of his ex-clients, he is entitled to pursue a relationship with her only if he has explained to *both parties* that it will disqualify him from being their mediator in the future, and got the assent of both.

Even if the mediator has the assent of both, I think he needs to consider professionalism. He cannot be exposed to just criticism if both parties have agreed to what he has in mind, but he should consider whether it may cause people who do not know the full facts to raise their eyebrows, and put the profession of mediation in a bad light.

I recognise that this will be difficult, and may even seem absurd, if a mediator is in the grip of a white-hot passion for an ex-client who reciprocates. But life is never easy, and by deciding to become mediators, we do not make it easier for ourselves – only, we hope, for our clients.

Shared secret

Let's look at another problem. A wife tells her mediator in the absence of the husband that unknown to him another man is the biological father of her youngest child. (The danger of receiving that kind of confidence may be one good reason to avoid caucussing, but it could happen if she phoned the mediator between sessions.) What should the mediator do? Continue with the process in which the husband was making provision for a child that might not be his legal responsibility? Or insist on full disclosure?

Do the principles help us? I think empowerment – a corollary of respect – applies. I said in the previous chapter that if people are to negotiate and make decisions, they must have whatever information they need so that their decisions will be based on adequate information. It can hardly be disputed that the information the mediator now has, and that the husband does not, is information he needs, so that his decisions will be based on adequate information. It must follow that the mediator must not continue to act as mediator unless the husband is told the truth.

So much is clear. At least, it seems so to me. But what does a mediator do in practice, in that situation? Perhaps, something like:

> *Mediator:* "If you do not tell Henry that Peter is not his child, I can no longer work with you."
> *Wife:* "I can't do that. It would kill him. Peter and he have always been very close. Henry has heart problems. When I say it would kill him, I mean it, literally. I think we have to make the best of it, for his sake."

237

Mediator: "I can understand how this might be the best answer, from some points of view, but I am governed by rules in what I am allowed to do, and forbidden to do. If I were to go on working with you, I would be colluding with you in hiding from Henry information that he is entitled to have, and that I am not entitled to withhold from him, since I have it. I would be pretending to be a mediator, while really conspiring with you to hide the truth from him."

Wife: "Are you saying I have to tell him?"

Mediator (on his guard): "That is not my decision. It is yours. The question I have to decide is: can I work with you and Henry while he does not know that he is not Peter's father? I have thought about it, and answered it: no. It is for you to decide now what you should do. I think you have two choices. You can tell Henry, and we can go on working together – though I assume he may need some time out to come to terms with the news. Or you can decide not to tell him.

"If you do, I will not break your confidence. But I will not collude with you in misleading him by working with the pair of you. You may be able to find someone else."

Wife: "If we are going to stop working with you, how will you explain that to Henry?"

Mediator ("on his guard" is now too feeble a description): "I don't think *I* have to explain to Henry. I think *you* have to.

Pause. A pause for people to absorb what has been said can be very helpful. In this case it may be ended by the client putting the phone down, or leaving the room. If she does neither:

Mediator: "Again, you have choices. You can tell him whatever you choose. If you decide to lie, that is up to you. What I will not do is lie to him myself, or collude

238

with you in lying to him. You can tell him that we had a conversation, as a result of which you decided to fire me as your mediator. You can tell him that, at your request, I promised not to disclose what was said in it. If you take that line, and if Henry asks me for an explanation, I will tell him I can't discuss it with him, having promised you not to. But, as mediator to both of you I owe to him the same duty that I owe to you: not to lie or mislead. And I won't."

That approach may seem to some people harsh and self-righteous. Sorry. Doing what we believe is right does sometimes make us look harsh, or self-righteous, or both. Nobody likes looking like that. But if as a mediator I have to choose between doing what I think is right, and behaving in a way that other people will find acceptable or attractive, I hope I won't hesitate.

Request for report

Another ethical problem that came my way concerned a couple who had difficulty about sharing in "parenting". They left me without an agreement, brought their parenting issues to court, and a psychologist was appointed to assess the children and make recommendations to the court. The psychologist, a very respected practitioner, wrote to me saying that he had been appointed, might want to discuss the couple with me, and enclosed a note, signed by both, authorising me to discuss them with him.

What should I do? The first principle I thought of was humility. I am a member of AFM, the mediator body I have mentioned elsewhere, so I consulted them and got these comments:

"The psychiatrist is likely to be asking you to make a judgement about the children and/or the parents' parenting ability, which would put you in the position of becoming an evaluator, and therefore no longer neutral. Although this is certainly not an ethical breach, or even expressly prohibited by AFM's Standards of Practice . . . this question does go to the definition of the integrity of mediation . . . we, as mediators, may have a duty to the integrity of mediation, in addition to our duty to our clients."

You will, I'm sure, notice that these comments relate to some of the principles I have outlined in the last chapter, including impartiality, empowerment, confidentiality and professionalism.

I also consulted a colleague in Dublin, from whom I got helpful advice to similar effect. The result was that, having taken advice and reflected on it, I decided it would be wrong for me to talk to the psychologist because it would mean stepping outside my role as mediator. I was helped by the advice and felt more comfortable refusing because I was supported by my colleagues, but I made the decision on ethical grounds, thought it was right, and believe I would have acted in the same way even if I had received contrary advice.

Was that the right decision? There is no way of telling. Even if I knew the outcome of the court hearing, and felt it was a good result for the children, I don't think I could say I had done the right thing, any more than I would have to say that I had done the wrong thing if I felt the court had decided badly. Having made a decision on grounds of principle I do not abandon my principles because an unprincipled decision might have led to a happier outcome, in one instance. Only if living by my principles consistently produces unhappiness for my clients will I re-examine the principles.

Were not the clients entitled to say: "Michael, you are, or were, our mediator. We now want you to pass on the benefit of what you learnt about us to the person we have chosen as

240

our child psychologist, in order that the decisions the judge will make about our children on his advice may be as well-informed as possible."? I think so. Was I not equally entitled to say "no"?

The AFM debate on "screening"

Here is an example that does not come from mediation, but from a dialogue among mediators within AFM about "screening". A group of experienced mediators, all recognised and respected within the profession, became concerned about a problem with ethical dimensions, in mediation. Their worry was that an intimidating, perhaps violent spouse – let's not pussy-foot, and simply say "husband" – might impose his will on a cowed, terrified, wife, and the couple might pass through the mediation process. They would emerge with what looked like a genuine bargain but in truth was not, because he imposed his will on her. These mediators proposed that, in order to avoid any risk of this happening, AFM should direct all its practitioner members to screen all clients before starting to work with them, to ensure that we were not being used in this way, and did not become unconscious colluders in an unacceptable process. They argued that the only way to screen effectively was to meet each party separately before starting to work with the couple, and that AFM's policy should declare this to be the duty of every member.

I was one of a group who opposed this view, because I was not convinced that what was proposed was the best approach to the problem. I did not believe screening in individual meetings was the only way to detect intimidation. Indeed, I think it may not be the most effective way of doing so. An intimidated wife may be prepared for a meeting with her prospective mediator by an intimidating husband, and

241

may not disclose the facts – at least, not voluntarily. In my view, it is easier for an outsider to detect intimidation if he observes how the two people – let us call them "bully" and "victim", with inverted commas to show this is an accusation, not a verdict – interact. He can see how the "victim" reacts – or fails to react – to what the "bully" says, and how he reacts to any possible thwarting of his wishes. I also had a concern that if clients were tested for intimidation before starting the process, and passed the test some mediators might be less alert to the symptoms of intimidation later, if they manifested during their work with the couple, rather as a doctor who has carried out tests on a patient for a disease which has not shown up may be less likely to speculate later about whether the disease may be present. If the test is imperfect the disease may not be diagnosed.

So long as the debate was framed as: "Is this the right way to handle this issue?", there was no prospect of agreement, because each group was firm in its view. And each was firm. I was firm against being forced to do what I thought wrong and of doubtful value, and the people who proposed obligatory screening were firm in the interests of a group we would all want to protect, namely abused wives.

When the issue was reframed, it was resolved. The reframe was: "If there are two differing view-points on this, both held with conviction and supported by reasoned arguments, is it right for either group to impose its view on the other?" When the issue was re-stated as one of diversity versus uniformity, universally imposed irrespective of conviction, it was no longer an issue. Both groups continue to hold their views and act on them, and each group respects the views of the other, and values the diversity.

Indeed, I think we all emerged from that discussion with renewed respect for each other. "They" learnt to accept "our" view-point, without losing respect for "us". And "we" came

242

to look on them with increased respect, as people who aspired to the best possible standards of practice, but did not seek to impose their views on people who had a rationally sustainable reason to disagree with them.

The principles I see illustrated in this dispute are: respect, with its corollary empowerment; professionalism; and humility.

The thank-you present

The thank-you present does not come my way often, but it can present problems when it does. Some time ago, I ended up spending more time with a couple than I normally would, because they returned to me at various stages in their disengagement process. At our last meeting, they wrapped everything up in a way that pleased both of them, and left. I had an appointment elsewhere, and left too, immediately after them. When I came back, I found they had returned, dropped in a gift for me from both of them with a very warm thank-you note, and left again.

What should I do? Keep it? Return it? Would keeping it affect my neutrality?

The question I asked myself was: what effect will what I do have on my ability to serve these people if they come back to me? In this instance, my answer was: "I will not be less able to serve them if I keep their gift. If I refuse it, they will not respect me more. They will feel hurt, rejected, and perhaps offended."

So I kept it. I do not say that this would always be the right thing to do. Indeed, I think a mediator's instinct should be to return any thank-you prezzies he receives. But I think it was right, in this instance with this couple, bearing in mind that it was a gift from both.

What should I have done if it had been a gift from one

party only? Say, (fantasising) something that I really liked and wanted, but was too stingy to buy for myself, or something I wanted and hadn't been able to find, like an out-of-print book. A little note from the husband: "Dear Michael, A small gift to thank you for all you did for Jean and me. Sincerely, Robert"? There is only one possible answer: thanks, but no, thanks. If I am grateful and pleased, I will find it hard not to favour the giver if they have to return. Or I may be so anxious not to, that I will be unfair to him.

The key question is: how will Jean feel, if they come back to me, and she discovers Robert has given me a gift, and I have accepted it?

I came across one interesting variation on the thank-you prezzie issue some years ago. One party gave me something that was no use to me, but also was no use to anyone else by the time I received it. Let's say a bottle of expensive liquor, of a kind I do not drink, and the person who gave it to me broke the seal when he presented it. What to do?

I have tested this issue in mediation training, both in Ireland and in the US. In the US, the trainees said, pretty well unanimously: "You must return it. It would be wrong to keep it." Almost all my Irish trainees have said: "If it was no use to you, your keeping it should not put you in a position of feeling grateful and therefore biased. It would be no use to the person who gave it to you, so if you returned it all you would achieve would be to hurt and offend him. And, perhaps, make it harder for him to come back to you. The right thing would be to say thank you, and keep it. But not to use it."

I do not adjudicate between the US and Irish views. I am a mediator, not a judge.

The mediator's charge to his clients

There are practical issues with ethical dimensions about a mediator's charge to his clients. One is the basis of the charge, and whether it should be based only on hours worked. In true mediator style let's ask a few questions, as the best way to get answers. If a mediator accepts a flat fee, irrespective of hours, may he find himself trapped in a mediation process where there is no prospect of agreement? Would this serve the clients' interests? I suggest the answers to these questions will indicate that a mediator should not charge a flat fee for his services, unrelated to the hours he puts into delivering them.

What about being paid by results? It is not unknown for a client – usually a husband – to offer a bonus if they reach an agreement, and justify it by saying: "I want you to have an incentive to help us to agree." That might sound okay on the face of it. When I was a lawyer, some clients wanted to pay me by results, in whole or in part, so that I would have an incentive to do my best for them. I sometimes agreed a fee on that basis.

However, there is a big difference. Clients for my legal services wanted me to be committed to working to gain for them what they wanted. My job as a mediator is to ensure that my clients are "enlightened" – that they identify and evaluate their options, and the consequences of each, and that they are not inhibited in deciding whether to reach an agreement, or, if they do, what it should be. Once I have achieved those, they decide what their bargain will be, if they make one. If I have a financial interest in their reaching an agreement, I may be tempted to pressurise them towards one, so that I will be paid my bonus, and ignore the fact that one of them is not happy with the bargain. Or I may be so aware of the financial incentive, and so passionately in love with my self-image as a righteous person, or so afraid of having to acknowledge that I am unrighteous, that I may discourage a bargain, in order to shelter myself from a suspicion that I pushed them towards one through greed. Either way, even on a practical basis, not looking to ethics, the bonus will not deliver for them what they want.

My view is that a mediator should charge by the hour for his time. There may be a temptation to prolong the process in order to maximise income from each couple, but I see no way of avoiding that. I suspect that a mediator will not do this for long. He will become known, clients and recommendations will cease, and so will his practice. Any ethical problems caused by his charging for time will derive not from a flaw in the system, but from a defect in the mediator's personality.

Let me say something else about charging. I see mediation as work that should be done only by someone professionally trained, and dedicated to excellence in his work. Such a person should be paid, like any other professional. And like any other, he should be paid by his clients, unless they are so poor as to be unable to pay. In which case I think he should normally be paid for his work by a state or other agency which sees his work as having a social value.

Another question about charging, again with an ethical content, is who pays? If I am paid by one party only, is there a danger that I may be thought by either or both to be on his (more often that not) payroll, and no longer neutral? If both husband and wife are at work and have incomes, I ask them to share my fee, in proportions they agree. I find they always agree a basis for sharing. (If it represents the first agreement they have made in a long time – as it often does – it may remind them that agreement between them is not impossible.)

Usually, if only one of them – most often the husband, but sometimes the wife – has an income, we agree that the one who has an income will pay me. This may be an opportunity to introduce a helpful concept:

> *Mediator:* "I propose to charge you £40 per hour. Does that seem fair to you both?"

After collecting their assent, he goes on:

> "We have been working for two hours, so I am due

£80. Since Peter is paid for his work and Margaret is not, I suggest he should pay the entire."

Peter: "That doesn't seem fair to me. I am the only earner, but more than half of what I earn goes to Margaret and the children. I don't disagree with the amount, but I think I should pay part of it out of what I have left over, and Margaret should contribute out of what she gets from me."

Mediator: "Margaret: what do you think?"

Margaret: "I can't get by on what Peter pays me. I am in debt already. I can't afford to contribute!"

Mediator: "Do you think the amount is fair?"

Margaret: "I'm not arguing about that."

Mediator: "You may both have to see me in the same way as you see the phone bill, or buying food. You need them and you have to pay for them. It seems you need me too, and you have to pay for me. You may decide to go to another mediator, who will charge you less, or nothing, but if you want to stay with me, £40 per hour is what it costs. "In one sense, it doesn't much matter who pays me. You plan to agree income-sharing arrangements for the future, and it is clear that Peter will continue to provide financially for the support of Margaret, Fiona and young Peter. Whatever pocket the money you pay me comes from, there will be less to go around. What I suggest is that one of you – and perhaps, Peter, it should be you – pays me for this session and, if you like, we can put on the agenda for the next session the question of how you will share in what you pay me at the end of that session."

I am reminding them that spouses who have children cannot effectively separate their finances until their children become self-supporting, because the children have needs that both parents have to meet. Some parents not merely don't recognise this at first, but will never recognise it. Few such

247

parents have asked me to be their mediator and, if they do get into my room, it is useful to have them identify themselves. If they decide not to continue with the process I am not sorry, because mediation is not going to work for them.

Since I have started to talk about a mediator charging and collecting fees, let me just say a few more things on that subject. My rules for myself are:

- name an hourly rate that neither under-values my service nor tries to squeeze out the last penny.
- be paid at the end of each session. Resist an offer to pay the lot at the end of the process.
- do not charge on any basis other than an hourly rate.

If people have not got the cash, or have not brought their cheque book to a first session, I am happy to say: "pay me on the double at the second session." Someone once asked me, grinning: "What happens if I don't bring the cheque book to the second session?" and I returned his grin with the answer: "There won't be a third!"

Standard forms

Another ethical issue arose at a seminar I attended, not organised by AFM. A featured speaker said he had evolved a "standard form" over a period of years, which he kept on computer and adopted when he came to record his clients' bargain. Someone asked if this was an ethically acceptable practice?

This is a more subtle issue than others we have looked at. It is not enough to have a vague sense that to go into mediation with a standard form in the back of our minds somehow feels wrong. If I say it is wrong to use a standard form, it must be because to do so would infringe a principle. If it infringes no principle that we can identify, then either it is not wrong, or we need to add to our list of principles. Does it infringe a principle? If so, which?

I think it infringes the concept of empowerment, which comes from the principle of respect. It is a mediator's duty, as I see it, to go to each mediation session, with each set of clients, with no preconceived ideas on what the outcome may be. The clients should be free to reach an agreement if that is what they think is right for them, or to recognise that, for one reason or another, they are not going to agree. This has been expressed by saying that up to the moment he starts to record his clients' an agreement a mediator's mind should be a blank sheet of paper, on which the clients write their bargain. If I have in mind (even in the back of it) a form of words, I have made an assumption that no mediator should make, namely that my clients are going to reach an agreement. If a mediator knows he has a standard form which he expects to use in recording an agreement his clients may make, the mind that holds that awareness is no longer a blank sheet.

It is a bit like what I said in Chapter Seven about my time as a part-time music critic and not composing my review during the concert. If I did, I couldn't do properly what was my job at that time listening. Also, I would make an assumption that nothing was going to change.

The principle of professionalism may also be offended, because mediators claim to offer our clients something tailored specifically to their needs, and better than something mass-produced. If we use a standard form, we offer our clients something that pretends to be constructed specifically for them, but is not. If we pass off a mass-produced product as tailor-made we are being dishonest, in breach of our duty of integrity.

Although I reject the Procrustean Standard form, and advise clients to reject any mediator who uses it, I think it is legitimate and sensible for mediators to do other things that may seem similar. First is to use a checklist of points that often crop up in mediation work, and second is to keep a record of all the notes we have prepared of what our clients have agreed. When we are working on putting on paper what Joe and Angie have agreed, we may think: "That is much like what Fergus and Marie agreed last month. Let me look at the how I recorded their bargain and see if it contains anything that might suit Angie and Joe."

"For the benefit of those of you who have forgotten your Greek", as Mervyn Griffith-Jones famously said: Procrustes in Greek legend was a bandit who offered travellers a bed for the night. The problem – for them, not for him – was that if they were too short for the bed he stretched them on a rack until they fitted it, and if they were too big he chopped bits off them, until they were small enough. Few survived their stay with him.

Incomplete disclosure

Another ethical issue arises in our work if one party is suspected of not making complete disclosure of relevant information. Suspicion of incomplete disclosure can be a problem in only two ways: the mediator may be happy with the level of disclosure, but the other party may not, or the mediator may think one party is withholding relevant information, but the party seeking the information may be satisfied with what he or she is told. If neither the mediator nor the other party accepts the first one's good faith, there will be no ethical problem, because the process will end.

I think if one person – say, the husband – gives the wife enough information about his wealth for her to feel willing to make a decision about how to divide it, then the mediator has no right to interfere. Equally, if the wife feels her husband is not telling her about all his wealth, and the mediator accepts what he says at face value, he has no right to substitute his judgement for hers. Of course, if she feels her husband is holding out on her, the mediation process will end, whatever the mediator thinks.

If a wife accepts from her husband a level of disclosure that the mediator feels is inadequate, is he bound to write a record of their agreement, based on the husband's questionable disclosure and his wife's acceptance of it? If so, may he inject into his written record something of his own scepticism? My answers to those questions are, respectively, yes and no. I must record my clients' bargain, but if I suspect it is based on inadequate disclosure, I feel entitled to protect a client who may be too trusting. And I want to protect myself, and the reputation of the profession of mediation, because lawyers, judges and people who may be inclined to use mediation will not be impressed with the mediation process if dishonest spouses abuse it, and the trust of their partners, and get away with it. With these objectives in mind, I may include in my draft note of understanding wording like:

> "During the mediation process, Fred and Kathy have made
> full disclosure to each other of the assets they own and the
> incomes they each have. The details of Fred's assets and
> income are set out in the Appendix to this Note, on
> page 10, and the details of Kathy's are on page 11."

I have found that, faced with a draft Note of Understanding in this form, some Freds, or Kathys, or both, have "remembered" things they had previously "forgotten". And the inverted commas may not be entirely fair, in all cases.

I have not yet had the experience of including a list of disclosed incomes and assets and being asked by either party to remove it from the draft note. Perhaps people who have not been completely frank have been too frightened of asking me to delete the list, because the request would look like an admission of bad faith. What do ethical considerations and common sense say I should do if I were asked to cut that material out? Like any other hypothetical question, the answer may be that you can't know what you would do in a given situation because each situation is unique. Even if the hard facts are the same, the mediator's relationship with the parties and the parties' relationship with each other are unique. Within the ethical constraints I work to, my response will be whatever I feel may be most effective at that moment to help my clients to reach a bargain that is both genuine and acceptable. A likely first reaction might be to play innocent, and ask "why do you want to delete it?" And that would be a question – like so many that a mediator asks – the answer to which is intended to be heard by the other party, at least as much as by the mediator. If they both asked me to delete material recording their disclosures, I would do so, but I would keep a careful note, both of the original content of the document and of the changes. I think, too, that if they both joined in a request to me to delete that kind of material, I would look closely at the wife to see if she showed signs of being intimidated by her husband, because joining with him in such a request would be so much against her interests as to make me wonder why she was doing it.

Painting a party into an ethical corner

What should a mediator do if it looks likely that an ethical conflict is going to arise and he may have to say: "Do it my way, or say goodbye"? I see two points here, one of principle, and the other of practice. The first is that a mediator should not abandon or modify his ethical principles. The second, practical one is that a mediator should if possible avoid what I call "painting a party into an ethical corner". That is, he should try to use his control over the process so as not to allow the issue to develop into an impasse, or let a situation develop where he will either have to terminate or force one client to back down, and lose face.

How does a mediator help his client to back down without losing face? The answer is timing. The time to warn a client away from a cul-de-sac is before he starts down it, so that he will not have to walk back the way he came, and re-emerge on to the main street to the jeers of the populace. If a mediator sees a conflict looming on the horizon between one party's wishes and the mediator's ethical code, the time to issue a warning is when the conflict is still hypothetical, not actual. Remember the mediator controls the process. We can use that control to deliver a message and then shift topics to give the parties an opportunity to digest what has been said.

Recording sessions?

Another question with ethical content has arisen in discussions I have had with other mediators, about recording sessions with clients, using either tape or video. I can see the benefits. Imagine being able to play the tape over, note what you had done that produced good results, what you had done that did not, and what opportunities you had missed. What a learning tool! How helpful, too, for people who are in the process of training as mediators, to be able to play over the tape of a session with a mentor, and discuss in detail all that had happened – and all that had not!

Wouldn't it, in the words of the song, be loverly? I look at it, salivating a little, but recognising that the concept is like a nice juicy steak to a hungry vegetarian. It might be pleasant, but the code forbids it, and he knows he would be sorry later. Look at it from the point of view of the clients, because this is how a conscientious mediator looks at every issue. The first session is crucial, so the assumption has to be that you would start by recording the opening session, and continue to record each until they finished. Do I tape their conversation without telling them? Of course not: that would be a betrayal of their trust in me. What happens if I ask their permission? I think there are a few possibilities. The least likely is that one of them will say no. At the beginning of the process, when they are both full of trepidation and anxiety, they will both be reluctant to get up their new mediator's nose by saying no, when he says: "Is it okay with you if I tape this meeting?" Besides, he is the expert, so who are they to refuse?

In other words, by making a request which they may feel they cannot refuse, I have started my relationship with them by abusing my power.

Next, it is a moral certainty that the session will play out differently if we all know we are on tape. Knowing I am being recorded will affect me, especially if I have recorded sessions with clients previously, played them back, and squirmed with embarrassment at what I had said. Or if I have to give the tapes to my mentor. Most likely, I will be determined not to say anything that might make me sound foolish when I play back. So where has my spontaneity gone? I think it is somewhere in the guts of the tape-recorder, but I am sure it is not where it should be, in the chair I sit in, available to my clients.

What about my clients, and their spontaneity? Of course, I have explained to them that the mediation process is "off the record" and "without prejudice", and they have agreed that nothing said in it will be quoted outside the room. They probably half-believe that, but will have doubts. Then they hear me asking to tape them – which, for them, is the same thing as telling them I am going to. Instead of giving them a clear, simple message: "We are off the record, and we are all free to speak our minds in this room", I have given them contradictory messages: "We are off the record, but every word you utter will be recorded."

If my aim is to relax my clients and get them to talk freely, taping their conversations is out. I have heard some people say that after ten minutes people forget the tape, and talk perfectly freely. I reply: "How can you be sure? How can you know that, at some point in the process, one of them may want to say something that he knows won't sound very pleasant, and may decide not to say it because it would be recorded? How can you know that they will not have a fear in the backs of their minds, that if they don't reach agreement and wind up in court, the judge will, somehow or other, get to listen to the tape? Do you really believe that people in high anxiety, whose lives are spinning out of their control, believe without reservation that the mediator they have met today for the first time is completely trustworthy, and their tapes are sacrosanct? And, even if you are right and I am wrong, and they will forget the tape after the first ten minutes, what about the first ten? They may be the most important time we spend together, and I don't think I should risk ruining it."

I think the principles involved here, which to me forbid recording a session, include respect and its corollary empowerment – in the sense that I should not ask for a consent that my clients are entitled to refuse, if they may feel inhibited about refusing. Taping without consent would of course breach integrity and confidentiality.

Some colleagues take a different view on recording sessions. Humility requires me to respect their decision, and integrity dictates that I should cling to my own.

Confidentiality

A mediator agrees with his clients that nothing said in the mediation process may be disclosed in court, if they wind up in the legal process. Let's assume the husband insists that this requires complete secrecy on everything that may happen during their sessions together, and the mediator and the wife agree. The husband then says he is a drug addict, and that he was recently prosecuted for driving a car under the influence of drugs and at high speed, and got off on a technicality. He

255

says neither his life style nor his driving style has changed, and he has narrowly avoided accidents more than once.

The wife says she is not willing to have her children exposed to being driven by their father, as he may put their lives in danger. The process breaks down, and the wife decides to protect her children by seeking a court order controlling his contact with them. She asks the mediator to support her evidence. He reminds her that they agreed to be off the record. She says that if he refuses he will be colluding with her husband in denying his addiction, and his dangerous behaviour, and allowing him to expose their children to serious danger. When she sees the mediator wavering she adds that if the husband kills one of their children the mediator will carry responsibility, because he knows the husband is out of anyone's control, including his own.

What does the mediator do here? On the one hand, he has promised secrecy. On the other, the lives of young children may be at risk if the husband is as uncontrolled as he seems to be. Is a promise made to an addict, whose life is completely out of control, binding?

If a mediator faces a conflict like this, between duties, not between a duty and a preference, I believe he should take all the advice he can get. But he should not delegate decision-making to anyone else. The responsibility is his, and it would infringe the concept of integrity for him to try to pass it on. In this dilemma, as in any other, his rule should be: if in doubt, follow the highest standard.

The problem of the addicted father who is a danger to his children, and whether the mediator should blow the whistle on him, is not one I have ever had to decide. I believe I know how I should deal with it, if I had to. I do not infringe the principle of humility by saying my way is the only right one. Everyone who has read this book is as well placed as I am to decide what they would do, whether they apply or reject the principles I have discussed in these two chapters.

256

CHAPTER FOURTEEN

CHOOSING A MEDIATOR

Inevitably, some of you will find yourselves locked in a conflict, work-place, commercial, neighbourhood, or marital. You may think of using mediation to resolve it, and may want advice about choosing a mediator.

Before I say anything else, let me make it clear that I did not write this book, or this chapter, with a view to promoting my own practice as a mediator. By the time you read this, I will either have retired altogether, or at least reached the point in my working life where I am no longer taking on new clients. So I can give you disinterested advice about your choice.

Recommendations

You can start by talking to friends. One of them may have been through the same process, or know someone who has, and may recommend the mediator he or she went to. This is a good start, if it happens.

But you are less likely to hear someone talking well of their mediator than of most other professionals, like lawyers or doctors, for two reasons. First, people who have gone through the mediation process want to forget about everything connected with that time in their lives, including the mediator who helped them through it. The second reason lies in the nature of our work. We aim to help our clients to develop their own independent negotiating and problem-solving skills, so as to make ourselves redundant in their lives. If our clients leave the process with an agreement, we want them to feel they have negotiated it themselves, without needing much help. If they leave with a confidence and self-reliance born of their success they have a good chance of being able to negotiate new arrangements when they need to. So a mediator hopes to fade out of the process and not be missed. It follows that word-of-mouth may be less useful as a guide in selecting a mediator than it might be for a doctor, a lawyer or a dentist.

Window-shopping

You are entitled to "window-shop" – play the field, talk to a few mediators, and select the one you feel will serve you best. You will get a list from Yellow Pages, or the Law Society or local association of lawyers, from a lawyer you know, or from a government department. Or there may be a reputable professional mediator body that can give you a list of its accredited practitioners in your neighbourhood. I recommend you to do this even if you have a strong recommendation from a friend, or from an ex-client of the mediator you have in mind. The choice you make in selecting your mediator may influence the decisions you make in the mediation process, and in marital mediation those decisions may have a major impact on the rest of your life, and your children's and grandchildren's lives. So take your time, and be as sure as you can be that your choice is good. Look on the bright side. Won't you feel better starting the process if you have been recommended to someone, and have window-shopped, and found the person who was recommended is the one you would have chosen, anyway?

It is important for you that you should at least be disposed to have confidence in your mediator, when you first walk into his room. This is also important for him, if he is going to give you a good service. If he does not recognise that fact, and is not willing to allow you to window-shop and spend time talking to you before you make an appointment with him, you will be better off with someone else. In saying this I assume the mediator does not charge window-shoppers for time spent describing what he offers. If a mediator wants you to pay for time he spends talking to you and answering your questions about his service, I advise you to cross his name off your list of "possibles", and try your next choice.

Next, when you come to choose someone to act as your mediator, the sense you develop of the person you are speaking to is more important than any of the questions you may ask – which I will discuss in a minute. If he makes an initial good impression on you, and seems to be clear-minded, gentle and understanding, fine. If he doesn't strike you as possessing those qualities, or if his personality grates on you over the phone, forget about him.

What if the recommendation you get is not for an individual mediator, but for an agency where a number of different people work? If you phone an agency, it is unlikely that you will find yourself talking to the mediator you will work with. You may talk to a receptionist, not to any of the team of mediators in the agency. If an individual who works there has been specifically recommended to you, I see no reason why you shouldn't ask for him or her by name. If you are told it is not agency policy to designate an individual, you have to decide whether to make an appointment to see someone there – you may be lucky, and get your choice – or to go elsewhere.

Take your time

Whoever you talk to, if you feel you are being pushed into making an appointment on the spot, that is a good indicator that you will not build confidence in that person or organisation, and should look elsewhere.

Remember: this is a choice you don't have to make on the spot. You can talk to the receptionist, or whoever it is, until you feel you have a good understanding of what they offer, and a sense of how they work, and the atmosphere of the place, and you can then say you'll be in touch later. That is your right. If you hear a complaint from any mediator or telephonist or receptionist in a mediators' office about your exercising your right to make a choice and to inform yourself before you do, you may fairly take that as a message that this is not the place for you.

Incidentally, while it may discourage you to be told you can not speak on the phone beforehand to the person who will work with you, I don't think you should necessarily see it as a great drawback. If an agency employs a professional receptionist, he or she will probably give you an adequate picture, not just of how the organisation operates, but of its atmosphere and ethos. Moreover, if you can't get to triangulate your mediator before your first meeting, neither will your soon-to-be-ex-partner.

Questions

As part of your window-shopping, there are questions you can reasonably ask that will help you to gain a sense of how you would feel if you were working with that person, and relying on his judgement, his imagination, and his ability to understand and sympathise with you, your spouse, and your children.

Whether you are talking to an individual who may become your mediator or to the spokesperson for his organisation, a sensible first question is whether the person who will work with you has taken training as a mediator. Being a mediator is, in one way, a frame of mind which cannot be learnt. But it involves taking training, mastering a range of techniques, and developing skills. If the first person on your list has not taken training, I recommend you to cross his name off your list and contact the next person. Even if he has a plausible explanation of why he has not been trained, the fact that he is untrained means that the service you will get from him is likely to be less professional than you would get from a trained mediator.

The next questions are: who trained you? what recognition or accreditation did your trainer have? And this leads on, almost automatically, to question three: what accreditation does your prospective mediator have? If the trainer or the mediator, or both, have accreditation, the reply you get to these questions will simply identify the accrediting organisation. It is going to be very hard for you, not knowing the scene, to assess whether accreditation from that organisation is worth anything. I think accreditation from the American Academy of Family Mediators is worth having; someone who has that qualification has taken a training that was probably reasonably adequate, has worked with an accredited consultant, and his or her competence has been assessed, impartially, by a competent mediator/assessor. I think the same is true of another American organisation, SPIDR, (Society of Professionals in Dispute Resolution) and of some UK organisations, National Family Mediation, Family Mediators Association and Family Mediation Scotland. These three UK bodies have together formed an accrediting body called UK College of Family Mediators. From what I have seen as an outsider, all of them seem to have decent standards in training and in accrediting mediators. I assume the same is true of other bodies in other countries, but there is no other I know enough about to recommend.

I do not suggest you regard accreditation by any of these mediator bodies as final. No system of accreditation is so effective that it is guaranteed to identify and reject, without fail, people who should not be accredited. No matter how well constructed the net may be, some people will slip through it who ought not to, and others who should be accredited based on their ability will fail. I have seen examples of both. Moreover, the fact that someone is a competent mediator does not mean he or she will necessarily suit you, or your spouse, or whoever is the other party to the dispute. A brief chat, even if only on the phone, will give you a better sense of whether a prospective mediator will suit you.

I suggest you ask whoever you talk to to send you literature describing the service they offer. If they tell you they don't produce anything on paper describing what they do and how, I suggest you cross their name off your list. If you collect literature from a number of different people or organisations, I suggest you compare them, and that you ignore their gloss, or lack of gloss, and concentrate on content. Does it answer your questions? Does it give you a sense of how the process will work? Has the writer put himself into your shoes, and imagined the kind of questions you would want to ask, and the sort of reassurances you would hope for? If so, there is a prospect that he – or a member of the team – will be sympathetic and imaginative in his work with you.

A point about the literature that may seem contradictory to the last one: does the written material suggest the focus will be more on working towards an agreement than on sympathising with your unhappiness? If the answer to that question is yes, I would regard this positively. You do not pay a mediator to offer you a shoulder to cry on, but to help you to negotiate a bargain and get on with your life.

I suggest you ask a few further questions, including: "Do you charge fees?" Someone who lives in Ireland, where the state-funded service is free, is leading with his chin in making this next statement, but I will make it anyway. Any mediator or agency tells you the value it puts on its service when it tells you its policy on charging. If it offers a free service, it tells you it values it service at what you will pay for it, that is, nothing, and invites you to accept its self-evaluation.

There is another problem in my experience about a free service. First as a lawyer, and then as a mediator, I have aimed to charge my clients for my work on a basis that was fair to them and showed me respect. I find mutual respect grows from a relationship based on services conscientiously rendered and fairly rewarded, and is displaced if one party shows himself not to be entitled to the respect of the other. The reverse is true of relationships where professional-type services are provided without payment. And, not far from the surface of the mind of each party will often be: "A client is not entitled to complain about the service if he does not pay for it."

Of course, it is right that people who need mediation and cannot afford to pay for it should not be deprived of what they need, for that reason. How mediation should be provided for people who cannot pay their mediator at an economic rate and, if mediators are to work for people who cannot afford to pay them, by whom and how much they should be paid, are political decisions. I do not plan to pursue them in this book, but I do want to mention some convictions I have developed before and during my work as a mediator – perhaps grafted onto political views I had before I started that work. First, mediation, like justice and non-elective surgery, is a service that is effectively denied if those who need it do not receive it with reasonable promptness when they need it. Secondly, it seems to me as a citizen unacceptable if people who need the service and cannot afford to pay for it receive a less professional service than those who can pay for it. Thirdly, mediators are not well enough paid in any country I know of to justify arguing that they should subvent clients who cannot pay for it, by charging an uneconomic rate.

I distrust even more an organisation that does not charge a fixed fee, but asks for "donations". I see that approach as more degrading for both personnel and clients. It resembles too closely the Killarney jarvey's line about the charge for hiring him: "I'll leave it to Your Honour." This means: "I want to be paid for my work, but I won't put a value on it so as not to frighten people off, and in the hope that I will collect more than I might have the nerve to ask for, from people who are afraid of being thought mean." If people won't assess the value of their time and skill, my assumption is that it is worth nothing.

A next question, and an important one, might be: "What access will I have to legal advice during the process if I come to you for mediation?" I have been told that some mediators and mediation organisations require their clients to agree not to consult lawyers during the process, and others discourage contact with lawyers. I understand why mediators might prefer not to have lawyers in the background while they are helping their clients to negotiate a bargain, but to me it seems the reverse of "empowering", and if I were a client I would not trust a mediator who wanted to isolate me from my adviser.

The next question I suggest you might ask is: "On what basis do you assess your fees?" I explained my views on this in Chapter Thirteen. If they charge on anything other than an hourly basis, their ethical standards are suspect.

The next questions might be:"Do you subscribe to a professional ethical code? If so, what one?" If the answer is "no" again, I would cross the name off my list. If they identify one of the bodies I have mentioned above, I would regard that as an acceptable answer.

Next is, "will you use a standard form in preparing your record of what my partner and I agree?" I have given you my view on standard forms, too, in Chapter Thirteen. "No" is acceptable, but the ideal answer is: "I keep a record of what people I have worked with in the past have agreed, and how I have recorded their bargain. I draw on that record if I think it will help me to record other people's bargain in a way that may suit them. If you use me as your mediator, and if you reach an agreement, your bargain will be unique to you, and I will not repeat the language I have used to record other people's bargains unless I have first satisfied myself that I cannot find words that I think would be more suitable, and more acceptable to you, to record yours." Such an answer would tell you that the mediator you are talking to has experience, that he will be reasonably sensitive in his work with you, and that he will be responsible, and responsive, in trying to meet your needs.

You might also ask, "what is your policy about supervision or consultancy? Do you – or does your organisation – use a supervisor or consultant? Do you and other mediators who work with you, have an early warning system in place to protect you and your clients from a decline in standards?" I don't think I need to describe what answers to these questions would be acceptable and what would not.

The last question I suggest you ask is: "What is your policy (or the policy of the agency) about making notes of what happens during the process?" You should not have to express this question in detail, but if you do, the information I suggest you need is: do you (or do the mediators in this agency) write up detailed notes of what has happened during a session? how much time is normally spent in writing up notes? are notes seen by a consultant or supervisor? do you have a system in place to ensure that they will not be seen by anyone else?

Selecting a mediator, talking, listening, asking questions and reading literature, need not be, and should not be, a solo performance. If you need a mediator, it is because you have a conflict with somebody else, and that person also needs to start the process, if not feeling confidence in the mediator, at least with a predisposition to trust him. I think it is important that the person who does the leg-work should pass on the results to the other, and that the other person should let his or her fingers do a little walking too.

Finally, don't think of your choice as being final. You have both chosen a mediator – even if one of you has exercised a choice by default, or has delegated the decision-making to the other – and you have gone to your chosen mediator in the hope that he or she will help you to reach an agreement. If, after the first session, you review what took place during it and decide you don't relate well to your first choice of mediator, change your minds, and go elsewhere. What you are talking about in marital mediation is the rest of your lives, and what are the mediator's feelings, or his vanity, in comparison?

CHAPTER FIFTEEN

BECOMING A MEDIATOR

This chapter is going to be about exactly what the title says. Different "clubs" have different standards, and change their standards from time to time, and I will not list the criteria different mediator bodies apply in processing applications for recognition. I will talk about a change of mind-set that takes place as someone evolves towards being a mediator.

When first I heard talk about being mature, I was impressed by the idea, and felt I would like to become mature – whatever that might mean. I was sure it would be better than being what I was. The concept has been raised with me in numerous conversations by different people since then, I have never got to understand exactly what being mature meant, but gathered that, whatever maturity might involve, I did not have it. I was also advised by my first girlfriend, shortly before she became my first ex-girlfriend, to "grow up". I was impressed by this advice at the time, but didn't quite succeed in following it. Like so much advice I have received since, I would now regard it with suspicion, and am relieved that I failed to carry it into effect.

Much the same is true of mediation. In the same way that we never, quite, become mature or grow up (whatever either of these may mean) I do not think that we ever, quite, become mediators. We may spend less of the time, and to a less extreme extent, being non-mediators, but we do not become mediators, through and through, all of the time. If we convince – rather than fool – enough of the people, enough of the time, we are doing pretty well.

I used to see different stages in "becoming a mediator", but now think of it as an organic process, not measured in stages. We grow as a tree does, and the only valid reason for measuring its height is to assess whether we can responsibly offer our services to the public as conflict-managers.

Probably a number of people reading this book already manage other people's conflicts. Anyone who rears children is a conflict-manager. Anyone who has worked in an organisation of more than two people is likely to have found at some stage that two or more of her colleagues had a row and tried to involve her. If she was asked to take sides, and did not do so, she almost inevitably became involved in their conflict in a way that tried to resolve it. That is, she assumed a mediator role. Much the same would be true of anyone who tried to break up a row on the street, in a bar or in a voluntary body. If a conflict is going on between other people, our choices are to join it, to ignore it, or to try to resolve it. If we take the third choice, we become mediators. Someone who sees a row going on, and says: "Come on folks! Break it up!" has taken the first step away from being a potential mediator towards being an actual one. Or someone who looks after children, and who, instead of shouting: "You two shut up!" says: "What's the problem?"

So, when we have taken the first step, what next? Maybe to read a bit about conflict-resolution, and I thought people who do not work as mediators, but are interested in the idea, might like to have something accessible to read.

Tackling problems that come up between family members, friends and colleagues, and trying to help them to resolve their conflicts, plus some reading, talking to other people in the field, and – most important – thinking about what happens, what works, and why, may be enough for people who do not want to specialise in conflict-management, or spend their lives working as mediators. For anyone interested in pursuing conflict-management further, the next step has to be some form of training. Mediation is skilled work. It is a performance art, and cannot be learnt from books. The only way to develop skill in doing it is by doing it. We acquire skill by practice, first with a trainer, and later with the help of a mentor. It is not a matter of abstract study, but of developing ability. I think the parallel is with learning to play a musical instrument, not with taking a degree in music. And remember a well-trained musician can sight-read – perform a piece of music on the spot, without prior study.

Before you decide to look for training, please listen to warning words. First, you have little prospect, in Ireland or any other country I know, of being paid a living wage for doing this work. The only people I know who make any kind of a living as mediators are the small number lucky enough to have a job where they are paid a salary to work in conflict-resolution, and the even smaller number who supplement their income from mediation by teaching mediation skills. Secondly, taking a training and starting to work as a mediator is only the first step in a long journey. To paraphrase Plunket Greene (Chapter Seven) training is a matter of months, internalising a matter of years. The road to being a good mediator is long, the work is difficult – and it gets no easier. A mediator spends his working life trying to get to the top of a mountain that has no top.

Looking for a trainer

It was easy for me to describe in Chapter Fourteen what you might look for in a mediator, because I have stopped taking on new clients, and can give disinterested advice. When I come to describe how mediation training is delivered, and what you might seek in a trainer, it becomes harder, because I still offer training to people who want to work as mediators. So, when I discuss how to make your choice of trainer, some readers may think my message is "choose me!" I decided not to allow this possibility to stop me offering advice about training. I evolved my way of mediating, and, later, my way of training, because each seemed to me to represent the best way I could serve the people I worked for, whether clients or trainees. It seemed likely that people who felt drawn to mediation work and who read this book might expect it to offer some advice about training. I decided my duty to those people was to give the best advice I could. That advice is based on the views and convictions that influence my approach to training, and inevitably my message is, "if you want mediation training, choose as your trainer someone who approaches the work in the way I think is best".

In Chapter Fourteen I recommend anyone who needs a mediator to shop around, before selecting one, and to regard the first session, at least, as an experiment. Signing on for a training involves a large commitment in time and money, and you cannot reasonably sign on for a training and then drop out if you don't like the trainer, or the methods he uses. All the more reason, then, why you should shop around carefully for a trainer.

Anyone who offers training to people who aspire to be mediators should have a written description of what he offers. If I were back at the stage of looking for training, and talked to a trainer who did not produce a written description of his training, I would cross his name off my list. Written information should give you a picture of what you may be signing up for, but you should have no hesitation in supplementing it by asking questions. The process will be mutual. You will get a better sense of the training, and of the person who presents it, and he will get a better sense of who you are, whether he wants to offer you training, and, if so, who else should be in the group to make it cohesive.

Number in training group

Now for a piece of controversial advice which a number of my colleagues may not support. I suggest you ask the trainer how many people are in a group for training, and if he tells you more than ten I suggest you thank him politely and look elsewhere. A number of mediator friends – people I like and respect – offer training in groups of twenty or more. They work in tandem with another trainer, or invite an experienced colleague to join them in observing role-play, so that, they argue, the ratio of trainees to trainers does not exceed ten to one. I know people who have come through similar training and have developed into excellent mediators.

Even so, when I started to offer training, I felt I could not deliver a training as good as I wanted it to be, with so large a number. I feel this is not just an inadequacy in me, and a really good training can only be delivered in a small group. Having colleagues help in observing role-play and critiquing what happened during it ensures that each trainee gets individual attention but I think the training process is too complex for a large number. First, the trainer should not just keep an eye on everybody in the group, but should develop a one-to-one relationship with them all. Next, every member of a group needs to recognise what they start with and what they need to acquire, in order to develop the ability to do the work. Then they should get what they need from the entire group, including the trainer. The process works really well if everybody recognises not only their own needs, but everyone else's too, and aims to see them all met. It becomes a process of mutual education. The trainer may give more than he gains, and some members of the group may have less to

271

impart within the group than others, but we all give as well as gain. And learning to give at the same time as you gain is part of the process – not so much of working as a mediator, but of developing into one.

If, say, twenty people are involved, it is possible to ensure that each is individually observed in role-play, but it is not possible to bring about the exchange of ideas and gifts that I now see as an essential first step in the process of developing into a mediator. The stronger personalities, or the more vocal, will contribute their questions and comments, but it is not possible for the person running a group of twenty to ensure that everybody is heard, or to maintain one-to-one contact with each of them. Indeed, I remember one co-trainee with me who hardly opened his mouth. He may have learnt from our trainer, but he offered nothing to the other trainees, and so far as I could assess, took nothing from us.

I now offer a training stretching over sixty hours, to a group not exceeding eight, and if more than eight want to join a training, I do not increase numbers and invite a colleague to join me. Instead, I offer a second training. The training I took from John Haynes at the beginning of my mediation career ran over less than sixty hours, and I was one of twenty people. John is a man of exceptional gifts, and transcended what I now see as a weakness in his training. I could not. In retrospect, I feel the initial training I got from John would have been even better if it had been longer, and had been offered to a smaller group.

If you are window-shopping for mediation training I suggest you quiz each prospective trainer in depth. Questions to ask include: the length of the training, the number of trainees, the gender mix, whether the training is accredited by any professional body, and, if so, which; what written material it includes, whether it involves role-play, and if so, how much, and how it operates; and what "after-sales service" the trainer offers.

Written materials

I mentioned written materials in that list. I have two reasons
for including a substantial training manual in my training. If
my trainees know that everything discussed in the training is
recorded in the manual, they will not feel the need to take
copious notes. This means that their minds are liberated to
develop understanding (which is different from knowledge)
and attitude, to absorb skills and techniques, and learn to use
them. Secondly, they may want the written material as a sort
of life-belt – for them and for their clients – when they start
to work as mediators. Since it is meant to be a lifebelt, my
training manual includes a check-list of issues that may need
to be covered in a marital mediation, but for reasons
discussed in Chapter Thirteen it does not offer specimen
forms of note of agreement. In my view a training that does
not include a substantial manual cannot be adequate.

Role-play

If a training does not include role-play, cross it off your list.
Training needs to include a lot of role-play, for the same
reasons that a medical student has to spend time cutting up a
dead body, before being turned loose on a live one.
("Reasons", not "reason" is intentional. It is worth thinking
about.)

Qualifications for taking training

How can I describe mediation training as a long process,
while the training I offer runs for only sixty hours? Let me
explain. Before people take my training they must go through
what – though I don't necessarily think of it that way – is a

selection process. I assess their personality, not using any specific tests, but "seat of my pants," establish their backgrounds and then decide if they have qualifications to take the training.

"Qualifications" for this purpose does not mean academic qualifications. The skills that make a good mediator are not developed in academia. Academic degrees are irrelevant if they are not accompanied by intuition, capacity for empathy, intellectual clarity, self-discipline, and ability to communicate clearly and amicably, orally and in writing. If people have an academic degree, I assume they can communicate on paper, and have shown their examiners some intellectual gifts. A degree suggests they probably have either self-discipline or above average intellect, but not that their intuition or empathy have been tested or developed.

I have been asked for training by people who have just qualified in a relevant discipline, such as law or psychology, and have consistently replied that they should come back to me in a year or two if they are still interested. I say that because, if they still want mediation training a few years later, they will then not merely be qualified, but will have developed skills in practising their profession. I particularly welcome people with experience as marriage counsellors, social workers and lawyers, because they have all had a chance to develop relevant skills by everyday dealing with fellow human beings in distress.

I have welcomed to a training course people who had little or no academic qualifications but had reared a family. The experience of raising children will introduce a mother (it is rarer for a father to have had the same exposure) to conflict-resolution, and encourage or require her to develop skill at conflict-management. And, if she wants to persist in conflict-management having reached a stage in her life where she has more time and needs conflict-management skills in the home less often, she shows dedication too. Interestingly, any time I have felt after a training that one member of a group did not contribute as much, or as effectively, as I had expected, they have been people who on paper had the "right" qualifications, never someone I chose based on my "seat of the pants" judgement and their life experience.

After-sales service – a mentor

A responsible trainer will tell you that the course he or she offers is only the beginning of a long road. If one of the people you talk to tells you that completing his training will equip you to set up as a mediator, I suggest you should thank him warmly in a quiet voice (mediators are polite, and do not raise their voices), and go elsewhere. Someone who promises to teach you to fly solo is more likely to teach you to crash. And, if you crash, the people you are transporting will go down with you.

You will need companions throughout the journey, but most of all at the beginning. Everybody I have worked with who has decided to go on to work as a mediator has understood the need to have a mentor in the background. Indeed, I would not accept into training anyone who planned to work unsupported as a mediator as soon as he had completed training. A mentor will support the aspirant mediator intensively through his work with his first clients and then, over a period of time, in a way that moves gradually from a master-pupil relationship to a relationship of equality, as the trainee begins to find his own way and to develop an individual voice.

No matter how many hours you have spent in role-play during training, starting with your first clients is un-nerving, though less so for you than for them. Do not feel that you are treating them unfairly by taking them on though you have no experience. It is true that if you did not work with them, they would probably find someone more experienced, though not necessarily better than you, to help them. But that person is mortal, and if novices (which I hope seems an acceptable word to describe people starting in their careers as mediators) allow scruples about their ability to deter them, and do not begin now to equip themselves to work as mediators, there will be no mediators left when the present generation dies out. Few people who work in mediation expect to continue in that line of work for the rest of their lives, and those who do are probably the least suited to doing so. The work is hard and draining if it is done well. So if you get to know someone who seems to be at the top of the profession today, he or she will probably have moved out of it within the next five or ten years. Mediation is a profession that needs continuing replacements.

However, while I encourage anyone who has taken a good basic training and shown ability during it, to start consolidating what he has learnt by putting it into practice, I also think we – mediators, trainers and trainees – have a responsibility to the clients, "the people with whom we have the privilege of working" in Michael Lang's words (see Introduction). We must use them as the people through whom we gain experience, but we should make sure that they get the best service we can give them, and that they do not suffer through working with an inexperienced mediator.

If the novice mediator works in the area of marital separation, he or she has an even greater responsibility. One of the core values of mediation is a belief that if we can help parents to co-operate, their children have a better chance of living happy, productive lives. Mediators who work with separating spouses have a responsibility to the clients' children as great as the responsibility to the clients. If we handle a serious mediation – that is, not one where the clients

276

have gone to mediation as part of their continuing "game", with no intention of separating – badly, and the clients are dissatisfied, and leave, it is unlikely they will go to another mediator. Carrying such a responsibility, we must feel awful when we "blow it" with clients, as we inevitably will.

We have a better prospect of discharging that responsibility with a dedicated senior colleague to support us with our first clients. If the novice mediator works in an agency, where his work is done under close supervision by a line superior, he will probably see his first clients jointly with a senior colleague. This is called co-mediation, and is a good way of work, used by experienced teams as well as by beginner mediators partnering experienced colleagues. A mediator who does not work in an organisation that gives him the opportunity to start his career by co-mediating, probably has to rely on discussion with a senior colleague outside mediation sessions. Different mediator organisations I know of use different names to describe such a person, and the different labels illustrate what I said in Chapter Three about precision in language.

AFM, the American body, uses "consultant", which describes someone who is kept in the background, and I find inadequate. In my work as a lawyer, I have used consultants and been one. In each case the consultant had no right to intervene, or take an initiative. He is, in the literal sense of the word, a referee – someone who becomes active only if a problem is referred to him. I do not think a novice mediator working with his first clients can give them a good service if his sole back-up is someone in the background whom he consults only if he feels the need. If the process started to go badly, an inexperienced mediator might not recognise the problem, or recognise it too late. I think protection of the clients dictates that a novice mediator's work is regularly and consistently examined, whether he thinks it necessary or not, by an experienced colleague.

Another mediator body uses the word "supervisor", which, again, I think is wrong, indeed, worse, because it may mislead. It indicates that someone of seniority takes responsibility for the quality of the novice mediator's work. Clearly this cannot be so unless the novice works under the close supervision of a superior, in an institutional setting. If the novice is a private practitioner, not part of a team in an institutional setting, his work cannot be supervised in the true meaning of that word, and the use of the word "supervisor" is misleading.

I like the word "mentor" to describe the person who supports a novice mediator in finding his feet and developing his gift. Ignoring mythological overtones, its accepted meaning is "a wise and trusted counsellor", but to me it indicates more than that. I see a mentor as an older person, who, by his wisdom and guidance, helps a younger one to grow. A mentor is older than a novice in experience as a mediator, not necessarily in years. This is just the kind of person I would have wished to have when I started to work as a mediator in the 1980s, and the kind of person I would like anyone starting off in the 1990s or the next century to have by his side.

Methods of mentoring

The following are some ways a mentoring process might operate:

1) I think the ideal is an "internship" in a mediation agency or organisation, where the novice mediator, after completing training, works with a team of experienced practitioners, one of whom is designated his mentor. The novice co-mediates only initially and then gradually moves,

through taking a more active role as a co-mediator, to a stage where he can "fly solo". All the people in the organisation support him, and he has a special relationship with his mentor.

2) The next best system might have the newly trained mediator gain his first experience by co-mediating with a mentor, and take on solo clients only when he and his mentor agree he is ready. The problem is the difficulty of arranging co-mediation when novice and mentor or both work separately as solo practitioners – as most mediators do. It is very hard for a mentor to ask new clients to agree to someone else sitting in during his first session with them. As a mediator working privately, I feel that for me to ask new clients to agree to someone else being present would involve me imposing my will on my clients, and I have consistently refused to do so.

The problem of co-mediating in the novice's first cases is even greater. He would have to say to his first clients: "I will be delighted to work with you, and try to help you. But another mediator, senior to me, will have to sit in and we will work with you together." Most clients would have enough sense to reply: "Give me the other mediator's name, and we will make an appointment with him direct. If you aren't competent to work on your own, you are no use to us!" How could a mediator in private practice hope to build his practice on that basis?

3) In theory, the next option would be solo mediation by the newly trained mediator, with each session audio- or video-taped, and discussed with the mentor between sessions until the mentor decides this frequency of mentoring sessions is no longer required to protect either the novice mediator or his clients. I mention this method because the taping of the sessions would make the work of the mentor and mediator easier and more productive, but it is acceptable only in

theory. The drawbacks from the clients' point of view to the taping of sessions described in Chapter Thirteen exclude this option.

4) As three above, but without tape and with detailed case notes. I believe this is probably the only ethical and practical way to help a novice mediator in private practice to gain experience and develop his gift, while protecting the clients' interests. When I work as mentor on this basis, the sequence is like this:

◆ first mediation session between novice mediator and clients;
◆ novice prepares detailed written case notes on that session, sends them to me, and I study them;
◆ we meet for a mentoring session;
◆ second mediation session;
◆ same process.

This is hard work and time-absorbing, for the aspirant mediator as well as for me. But the duties he owes to his clients and their children, and that I owe to him and, through him, to his clients and their children all leave us with few acceptable alternatives, at least for his first cases.

The advice I gave to anyone who needs a mediator or seeks a trainer applies to any mediator who needs a mentor. Talk to a few qualified people and select one in whom you feel confidence, and with whom you feel you could build rapport. Confidence and rapport with your trainer were important, but will be even more important between you and your mentor. You will work with your mentor more closely and for longer than with the person with whom you take basic training. You will also have to rely more on his judgement, both in how to help you to develop your gift and in assessing your progress.

Being a mentor is challenging work. A conscientious mentor asks himself the same questions about each novice but gets radically different answers about each one. Assuming a female mediator, using a male mentor, so as to avoid the he/she formula, his questions will be:

◆ what are the strengths she brings to her work?
◆ what are the weaknesses she brings to her work?
◆ what can I, with the strengths and weaknesses I bring to my work (and that I strive constantly to understand, and, respectively, improve and eliminate) do to help to develop the strengths she brings to her work?
◆ what can I, with the same strengths and weaknesses, do to help to eliminate or compensate for the weaknesses she brings to her work?
◆ what are her special gifts as a mediator?
◆ how do I help her to release and develop those gifts?

I recommend people who have taken their introductory training with one trainer, to ask someone else to act as their mentor. I think it is better for beginners to work with a range of practitioners. They can take from each of them the best of what they have to offer, and reject what they think will not fit in with their own developing way of doing things.

Because – it cannot be said too often – there is no one right way of doing this work. The way I have evolved over the years I have been mediating may be the best way for me. Every year I come home from the AFM annual conference with new ideas about how I will work in future, and I am often given new ideas by people who take training with me, but the essence of how I work is probably pretty well fixed by now. Since I have evolved it over time, it is probably the best way for me, and for the people with whom I have the privilege of working – to repeat Michael Lang's words.

It is not necessarily the best way for others. The style I have evolved, the shape within which I operate, are influenced by my initial training, and by things about me, such as the fact that I am a man, that I was in my fifties when

281

I started to work as a mediator, and that I had worked as a lawyer before that. My way of mediating might not suit someone younger than I am, or a woman, or someone from a different background. That is, it might not enable them to give the best service that they are capable of giving their clients.

I compare mentoring to a musical master class, where an established musical performer works with gifted younger musicians, all with a solidly based technique on their instrument. I have watched master classes, and one, given by an internationally respected violinist, disappointed me greatly. The Master (he would have insisted on the capital M) had set the Bach Fugue in G minor for unaccompanied violin for his students – a piece of music that, over 250 years after it was written, still astounds by its beauty, its technical difficulty and its intellectual power. His teaching included some discussion of technical problems, but consisted mainly of the Master constantly interrupting his students' performance to demonstrate how he played the Fugue. For example, he said: "This is the last entry of the main subject, so you should emphasise it, like this", and played the passage. His approach to playing the Fugue suited him, and certainly could not be called wrong, but it was his approach, and his teaching invited his students to imitate him, and, in effect, to become copies of him.

Some years later, I saw another Master, this time of a different instrument, the double-bass, also a superb player, give master classes. His approach was quite different. First the students played their music through, without interruption. They next discussed it, on a technical and interpretative level. The teacher made comments and suggestions, which they discussed. Next the student played the music again. This time there were interruptions from the Master (I don't think he would ask for the capital, but he deserves it), each pinpointing an area where the performance needed technical improvement, or as a departure point for a dialogue about what the music was about, where it was going, and how the player might follow and explain its progress. Interruptions varied between the extremes of suggesting a different bowing or fingering, and asking whether a different approach might work.

Almost every interjection was in the form of a question. And they were genuine questions, not: "Don't you think it would sound better if you did . . . ?" Some required the student to make a judgement, and led to a debate. Others were not intended to be answered on the spot, but to be pondered. The master rarely gave an indication of what answers he expected. For him, there was no one "right answer". The essence of his work was to encourage his students to continue to ask themselves questions, about how they played, and the work they were studying, and the whole art of music, until they had found how to communicate music more effectively, and a better understanding of what lay at the heart of the work they were studying. Each student would answer these questions for himself, in his own way. In the process, each would not just find a key into the heart of one work, but develop a master-key that would unlock other doors too.

That teacher is my role-model as a mentor.

For any of you who do not like the comparison between a mentor and a master musician, what about seeing him as a gardener? A good gardener rears young plants with care. He understands his plants, and knows when they need to be cossetted and kept warm. He also recognises that they cannot expect to spend their lives in a hothouse, and there are times when for their own sake they need to be exposed to cold, to toughen up. He knows they need to be kept watered, but they may have to get used to drought too if they are to survive. I prefer the master-musician analogy to the gardener, perhaps because music is more important to me than gardening, but perhaps because a gardener is a person, and a plant is not. A student who studies with a master-player, expects to grow, and perhaps become a better player than his teacher. One of a teacher's great joys is to see his students take off.

Another reason I like it is that music players, like mediators, do not serve themselves only, or, if they are of first quality, their audiences. Their first ambition is to serve with humility the music they play, and the geniuses who wrote it.

Case discussion

Like practising musicians, practising mediators need to pursue further education throughout their working lives. Remember Harry Plunket Greene's advice quoted in Chapter Seven that a singer's technique may "get out of control" and he "will do well to submit it to a master whom he can trust."

For mediators, that includes two things. One is that he should have a mentor in the background, and not necessarily the mentor he used when he was a novice. A change may be beneficial. The other is regular case discussion with colleagues. To have value, the case discussion group must consist only of people rigorous in their willingness to criticise each other's work. Its members should be dedicated to improving the quality of their work, and insist on stringent mutual examination and criticism. A group where each member praises the others' work without discrimination will not help any of its members to improve. Worse, if the group does not distinguish between good work and poor work, and is not rigorous in pursuing the best standards, the quality of work done by all its members will decline.

284

What makes a mediator?

What qualities do people need to evolve into good mediators? I think we need to partialise this, and see it in stages. What may seem to be an acceptable level of competence in someone starting out as a mediator will not seem so in someone who has been doing the work for a few years. Shortly after I started out as a mediator, I was asked by the Irish Law Society to lecture law students on mediation, and later, to make a short video for students and practitioners, showing part of a mediation session – not with real clients, but with colleagues role-playing.

Some time later, it seemed to me that I was not as busy as I wanted to be. It turned out to be a temporary lull, but I began to fret about whether my work was up to standard. (Doubts of this kind may make one's life miserable from time to time, but someone who has no such doubts has no prospects of delivering a good service, or of improving the quality of his service.) I was in the Law Society during that time, and watching the video assured me that I was doing competent mediation and, whatever the reason for the fall-off in work might be, it was not low quality work.

Time passed, and with it the temporary dry-up in the flow of work, and I didn't see the video for a year or two. When I did, my head was in my hands. Was that really me? Was I really as clumsy and crude as the video told me? Had people seen it, meanwhile? Could I steal it, or find some way of destroying it? The way I go about my work had improved, or at least had changed, in the interim. I was now working on a different plane, with different standards.

I suspect that if I were to make a new video of myself in action, and show the two, one after the other, a lay person might not notice a great deal of difference. But another mediator would. And I certainly would. And, I hope that if I

285

made such a video this year, I would want to destroy it too in a year or two. The process of becoming a mediator does not stop.

So what do we need to reach stage one, where we can say: "I am a mediator, and have taken the first steps towards becoming a good one." Or, to put it another way, what knowledge, or understanding, or aptitudes should we have gained from a basic training? My list is:

1) Self-discipline;

2) An understanding of conflict, to be able to control it, and not to be intimidated by it;

3) Calm and confidence in dealing with other people's conflict;

4) An ability to apply a limited range of techniques intended to bring agreement out of conflict. We need to use techniques with some skill, and probably the most important skill lies in using a technique without being seen to do so.

5) Enough understanding of the area of conflict to recognise a false note when we hear it. In family mediation, this would include knowing a little about the psychological and economic impact of separation on spouses and their children, tax, law, pensions and life assurance. The danger of becoming too expert in the area of conflict is that the mediator may substitute his expertise – which is irrelevant – for the clients'.

6) An ability to approach our work with both detachment and sympathy. If we do not have sympathy for people caught in the misery of a marital collapse, we will not be able to help them. If our sympathy is not genuine, but comes from the teeth out, its falseness will be detected. If we do not keep a degree of detachment from their problems, we will not be able to contribute towards solving them.

7) An ambition to help people we work with to preserve:
◆ control over their lives, and the lives of their young children;

286

- autonomy in making their decisions;
- their dignity.

8) Self-discipline.

I put self-discipline at the beginning of my list, and at the end. There is no room in the field for people who are not willing to be intensely disciplined in their work. I have spoken often in this book about the area where most mediators need self-discipline – or their clients need from them – recognising our own values, and ensuring the clients' bargain reflects theirs, not ours, if they differ. Apparent lack of curiosity can be a sign of self-discipline. Often when I think about married couples I work with, I wonder about their histories. When my work with them is over, I am still wondering. I don't know the answers because I don't ask the questions, and I don't ask the questions because it isn't my business as a mediator. My job involves ignoring past-related issues, because they encourage my clients to fight to no avail, and distract them from planning for the future. So long as I am still wondering about my clients' past when I finish helping them to organise their futures, I know I am exercising some control over myself. (Of course, I may be failing in self-discipline in other areas, and I will need to identify those failures and eliminate them.)

I mention in Chapter Eleven that if I am disciplined about not asking irrelevant questions, I can be dogged about insisting on getting answers to questions I do ask, because I can be confident my question was legitimate. Similarly, I can be reasonably sure that when I pick up information about the history of a marriage, it was not obtained through prying.

If your basic training has given you all of these, you are ready to start working as a mediator, but not before you have made an arrangement with your chosen mentor. The fact that a responsible mediator is willing to act as your mentor is an endorsement of your ability, and confirms you in your decision.

If you do not carry these from your basic training, there has to be something wrong, either with it or with you.

Bias, conscious and unconscious

I have said more than once in this book that the mediator's own prejudices should not intrude. There are two distinct problems here, that a mediator should recognise. There are convictions, which we believe in, and think are "right", often to the point where we may think less of someone who we find does not share them. Then, there is baggage that we carry with us unconsciously from our own lives, and particularly from childhood.

I believe that the second set – the unacknowledged baggage that we carry from our families of origin – influence the first set, our thought-out convictions, a lot more than many of us recognise. However, the first set is in our conscious minds, and can be dealt with at a conscious level, whereas the second lot are things we are not aware of about ourselves until we go to the trouble of educating ourselves, so, for the purpose of a mediator's work and of this book it may be sensible to treat them as distinct. We need to be aware of both kinds of "values" that we carry into the room where we do our work, and try to ensure that they do not influence its outcome.

Here are some of my consciously-held values:

I believe in an unwritten, unspoken contract between parents and children. I believe that people who bring children into the world, whether intentionally or not, are morally bound to care for them and support them until they reach an age at which they can support themselves – or should be able to.

I do not think parents have further obligations. If we give our children further support after they are grown-up, we do so by choice, not obligation. ("Love" is another name for this.)

I think if parents have discharged this duty to their children, the children may have specific, limited reciprocal obligations. I think these are normally limited to supporting their parents in old age, if they are then unable to support themselves and need help. (Many do so by choice, not duty. "Love" is another name for this too.)

The time when aged parents are most likely to need support is when their grandchildren are at their most expensive, so I think prospective grandparents have a duty to their children to try to avoid being a burden in later life. (This was illustrated by a letter I read in an American magazine recently, from a man who said his parents had made inadequate provision for their retirement, so he had to support them in their retirement home, and this cost him so much, on top of educating his children, that he and his wife were not able to provide for his own retirement, as a self-employed person. He expected that he and his wife would be financial burdens to their children, just as his parents had been to them.)

I do not think a decision by parents to separate affects this obligation to their children.

I think if people have children, and decide that one of the parents – usually the mother – will change careers and devote herself to rearing the children, this creates mutual obligations for both parents, which surface only if they later separate. The father is bound to supplement his ex-wife's efforts to support herself, if she is permanently disadvantaged economically by their earlier decision that she should become a full-time child rearer. If the way of life the mother adopts creates closer bonds between her and her children than those between the children and their father, she is bound not to abuse that greater closeness.

I do not think spouses in an unhappy marriage have any obligation, to children of any age, to "stay together for the sake of the children". If their lives together are miserable, they have a right to part. I also believe this will often be better for their children than staying together, because I think parents, among other things, educate their children for their own lives as adults, and that this is done largely by example. I doubt if many children get a good education for life from parents locked in a relationship that causes them misery.

I believe separating parents of young children have a duty to co-operate in bringing those children up.

I do not believe that duty normally requires parents to sacrifice the rest of their lives for the next half dozen years of their children's lives.

I am not entitled to impose my values on my clients, or substitute my beliefs for theirs. My clients need me to be aware of my own values, in order that I can leave them outside the door of the room where I work.

It gets harder when we look at the stuff we carry around unconsciously. In order to exclude our prejudices we must first identify them, and label them. It is all too easy to become hooked by something that comes from our own past, and to wind up no longer working as a mediator, because our own "stuff" has taken over. This happened to me recently. Luckily, on this occasion, it was not in a mediation session, but during a workshop I gave to trainee therapists. I decided to show them how mediation might work, by giving a "fishbowl" demonstration. ("Goldfish, in the privacy of bowls, do it": Cole Porter.) I asked two of the group to role-play separating spouses, coming to me as mediator, while the rest of the group observed, through the "bowl".

The problem presented to me was that the husband had left home over a month ago, and had had very little contact with their children since he moved out. This is quite a common issue in marital mediation, but the twist was that while he said emphatically that he wanted to see them, and planned to, he was evasive about timing. (As St Augustine famously was about chastity.) He was working very long hours to meet the extra expenses that the separation created, was too tired to see his children at the weekends, or when the day's work was over, and so forth. I asked him when he thought he would have these problems under control, and be able to spend time with the kids. He said probably in about three months. It seemed to me he was abandoning his children. Now, for reasons I do not feel I need to go into, this tapped into my own feelings, going back to my childhood. So, as soon as I got the feeling that one parent had abandoned his six-year-old daughter, I identified with the child, ignoring the differences in gender, to the point where I was unable to offer even a remotely acceptable example of mediation. My own "stuff" had got in the way.

In order to protect our clients against this sort of thing wrecking the process, I believe we need to conduct a voyage of exploration and discovery into ourselves. As we do, we may have to accept that some of what we thought were convictions are really prejudices.

Such a journey is never easy, and it can be very painful. But, if you want to be a mediator, it is one you cannot avoid taking.

And it is not a journey that we can take just once, buy a single ticket, and decide when we have arrived. Any adult's hang-ups are unlimited in number. If I get to understand at some level issues I carry from my childhood and how they affect me, my immediate reflexes come under control. There

291

will be further stages, about the same issues at a deeper level, or about something else. Getting to understand and grapple with our hang-ups is part of becoming a mediator.

I include a preliminary "internal exploration" for me, and each trainee, in each mediation training I offer. When I describe my childhood, and ask trainees to help me to identify some of the hang-ups I carry into my mediation work, each group always comes up with something new, that neither I nor any previous group have thought of. The list of potential hang-ups I carry may be the same, but the list of those I identify and am ready to deal with is growing all the time.

And I have no doubt that as soon as I put a label on one, two things start to happen. First, the labelled bag starts to disguise itself so that it can appear again, without my spotting it. Second is that, just in case its disguise isn't good enough, another unlabelled hang-up will join it. Because we are all like Ibsen's Peer Gynt and his onion: when we get through one layer, we find another, and when we get through it, we find a third, and so on. Maybe there is a heart, a centre. Maybe not. There are an awful lot of layers.

Good luck!

When you have taken training, made an arrangement with a mentor, and started with your first clients, you will have taken the first steps towards being, first a mediator, next a professional mediator, and ultimately an excellent one. Good luck!

The process it is not like climbing a mountain, where you know when you have reached the top, because you can't see anything higher. Nor is it like going on a journey from one city to another, where either you are still travelling or you have arrived. It is more like a long walk with no fixed destination. All you can say with certainty is that, after a while, the landscape seems a bit different, and you don't think you are going around in a circle.